D1300171

RASTAFARI

RASTAFARI

From Outcasts to
Culture Bearers

ENNIS BARRINGTON EDMONDS

OXFORD

UNIVERSITY PRESS

2003

OXFORD
UNIVERSITY PRESS

Oxford   New York
Auckland   Bangkok   Buenos Aires   Cape Town   Chennai
Dar es Salaam   Delhi   Hong Kong   Istanbul   Karachi   Kolkata
Kuala Lumpur   Madrid   Melbourne   Mexico City   Mumbai
Nairobi   São Paulo   Shanghai   Taipei   Tokyo   Toronto

Copyright © 2003 by Ennis Barrington Edmonds

Published by Oxford University Press, Inc.
198 Madison Avenue, New York, New York 10016

www.oup.com

Oxford is a registered trademark of Oxford University Press

Library of Congress Cataloging-in-Publication Data
Edmonds, Ennis Barrington.
Rastafari : from outcasts to culture bearers / Ennis Barrington Edmonds.
   p.   cm.
Includes bibliographical references and index.
ISBN 0-19-513376-5
1. Rastafari movement.   2. Jamaica—Religious life and customs.   I. Title.
BL2532.R37 E36   2002
299'.676—dc21   2002074897

/NJG: 185

9 8 7 6 5 4 3

Printed in the United States of America
on acid-free paper

To Donnaree, my wife, and Donnisa, my daughter,
the two persons around whom my life revolves;
and to the ancestors whose struggles have enabled us
to survive and thrive

Foreword

One of the most useful things about Ennis Edmonds's *Rastafari: From Out-casts to Culture Bearers* is that it correctly traces the connection between the emergence of Rastafarianism and the history of resistance and black consciousness that has been part of the Jamaican experience for years. The truth is that there has always been a committed Jamaican counter-culture that celebrates and sees redemption in Africa and rejects the European values that have oppressed a society. But prior to the advent of popular culture and especially the music recording business in the late twentieth century, its apparatus of cultural formation was controlled fully by the elite who, to a large extent, ran the educational apparatus and the economic system. But much of the country was beginning to question in earnest the structure of colonial society by the early 1930s. The emergence of Rasta during that period corresponds with so much that was happening around the world. Rastas could tell that social unrest in Jamaica was going to lead to a movement away from colonial rule and, having heard Marcus Garvey speak of the importance of Africa to black people in the New World, found in his remarkable success as a leader of thousands in the United States quite an amazing thing. Those who would presage the arrival of Rastafarianism also witnessed and read about the dramatic struggle of Emperor Haile Selassie to remove the Italians from his homeland of Ethiopia, which became the first African nation to effectively oust, by force, a colonial power. These were monumental times, and these men, fully steeped in the apocalyptic visions of the world, saw something important in all of these happenings.

I grew up in Jamaica at a time when Rastas were still regarded as useless, lazy, half-insane, ganja-smoking illiterates who were of no value to society. Teachers, students, office workers, and anyone of social importance could not grow locks, and families would go into mourning when their sons would start sprouting them. I heard the term "black heart man" used again and again as a means of expressing fear or ridicule of the Rastafarian. And this was in the early 1970s—after Bob Marley's emergence as an internaɔnal star, after Selassie's arrival in Jamaica, and after so much had been ɾritten about the importance of Rastafarianism. The problem was that ʟasta was counter to the strong Christian structure that dominated and continues to dominate Jamaican life and was seen first as heretical and misguided before its powerful social and political ideas were fully appreciated. Most important, however, was the Rastafarian insistence that Africa was the promised land and that Jamaicans should look to Africa for their model of value rather than to Europe, which was seen as foolish and a painful reminder of slavery and oppression. Rasta was an offense to those who wanted to deny the African part of their heritage. And the truth is also that in Jamaica at that time the privileging of lighter-skinned people was standard practice. Rastas were confronting so many of these long-held notions and so were bound to face a great deal of resistance.

What Edmonds manages to do here is offer us a way to appreciate the importance of Rastafarianism as a religious phenomenon that is consistent with much of what happens when religious groups and movements grow and develop. Indeed, there is a remarkable logic to the development of Rasta that defies the notion that it is a movement of the insane and the misguided. Given the way in which Rastafarianism has arrived in the world, it is useful when someone is able to help us understand its origins and propose how we can then comprehend how it functions in the world today. Again and again, I encounter students who are interested in reggae music and the music of Bob Marley, but they remain deeply puzzled by Rastafarianism because of its seemingly peculiar tenets of faith. Some of the oddities that would seem to suggest that Rastafarianism is an absurd religion include:

1. Rastafarianism has been around for only about seventy years. Yet in that time it has gained inexplicable fame around the world, boasting converts from all races and nationalities.
2. Adherents of the faith appear to be relatively small in number. One study suggests that less than one percent of Jamaicans describe themselves as Rastafarians. Yet the average non-Jamaican assumes that Rastafarianism is the national religion of Jamaica.
3. Rastas believe that Selassie is the returned messiah, that he is Jah, or God. They believed this fully prior to his passing in 1975 and after. Many believe that Selassie was a dictator and a cruel leader. That he is regarded as God incarnate seems patently absurd.
4. It is not clear whether Selassie believed himself to be a God.
5. For Rastas, marijuana, which is illegal in Jamaica, is a sacrament for worship.
6. Rastas regard western society as part of Babylon—a system and a place that is the enemy of the blacks of the world.

7. There is still no organized set of doctrines and teachings that constitute Rastafarianism, and no organized Rastafarian church, temple, or worship space exists.

8. There are numerous sects and groupings of Rastafarians, each holding to its own belief system and structure.

9. Rastafarianism is a deeply patriarchal religion that remains completely behoven to the Bible.

10. For the Rasta, the land mass of Africa, one of the poorest continents on earth, is the promised land.

11. Finally, Rastas seem to harbor a great deal of anger against white people, and yet the religion is accepted and popular among some white people.

Most non-Rastafarians tend to be puzzled by the movement. And yet there is little question that it has come to define Jamaican culture in ways that few people can understand. The value of examining the history of Rastafarianism and placing it in the larger context of social, political, and religious resistance to colonial hegemony cannot be underestimated.

What we discover in this book is that there is nothing absurd or far-fetched or insane about Rastafarianism. Its formation is part of the genius of an anticolonial intelligence married to a strong nationalist sensibility. What is clear is that Rastafarianism is one of the most complex and insightful reactions to colonialism and the oppression of blacks that has emerged in the last hundred years.

Rastafari: From Outcasts to Culture Bearers helps us to make sense of Rastafarianism's strange oddities that have puzzled many. Most important, the book helps us to understand this religion as one that patterns the emergence of religions in so many other cultures. There is an immense social and cultural logic to the emergence of Rastafarianism, even as it is, like all other religions, shaped by mystery and pure faith. This work helps us to understand the complex and sometimes elusive truth of how religions grow and sustain themselves, but Edmonds realizes that models that have been used to explain other religious phenomenon don't always apply comfortably to the peculiar developments of Rastafarianism. For instance, very few modern religions have assumed such a significant place in the mainstream of popular culture through the use of music. Marley is not seen as a religious figure; rather he is seen as a rock star, a pop hero, an icon. And yet his faith is at the core of his music. Rastafarians have dubbed Marley the psalmist and prophet of the movement. This is a crucial part of the wonderful complexity of the Rastafarian movement.

Jamaica owes a great debt to the men who formed the Rastafarian movement in the 1930s. Rastafarianism has served as a lightning rod of discussion about race, identity, and the history of oppression that has been part of the Jamaican society for centuries. If Jamaicans have rejected in part the denial of their African heritage, Rastafarianism is the reason. If Jamaican churches have come to reexamine the extent of their relevance to the real experience of the poor, black members of their congregations, they owe a great debt to Rastafarianism for reminding them of the cultural history of race in religion. If Jamaicans have evolved a language that is willing to see in itself a quality of resistance and creativity that challenges the control of the colonial structure, it owes much of this to the music of the Rastafarians and to the way that it has transformed the way Jamaicans view themselves in the world. These are all some of the ideas that Edmonds helps us to appreciate in this book.

Kwame Dawes
University of South Carolina

Acknowledgments

As the raising of a child depends on the efforts of many in the community, so the writing of a book depends on the input and support of many people in the life of the author. For this reason, I wish to express my appreciation and gratitude to all who have contributed to my intellectual growth and the undertaking of this project. First, I acknowledge those teachers who, over the years, have been my role models, mentors, and inspiration: Dulcie Roach from Hopewell Primary School, St. Elizabeth, Jamaica; Elaine Bortner and Philip Hirai from Jamaica Wesleyan Bible College, Savanna-la-mar, Jamaica; and Roger Ringerberg, Jamaica Theological Seminary, Kingston, Jamaica. Second, thanks to my professors and advisors at Drew University, Karen Brown, Jonathan Reader, and Roger Shinn, whose advice and insights have helped to shape the focus and hone the arguments of this book. Third, the research for this book was facilitated by Barry Chevannes, who directed me to resources and provided critique of my approach; Samuel Vassel, who was not only my intellectual sounding board but also the most avid supporter throughout the entire project; and Charlene Adams, my research assistant in 2001, who read the manuscript and suggested many editorial changes. Finally, thanks to my wife, Donnaree, for her support and inspiration, especially when I despaired about ever bringing this book to fruition.

Contents

RASTAFARI

Introduction

Since its emergence among the poor in Jamaica in the early 1930s, the Rastafarian movement has progressed from being an obscure group of protesting outcasts in the ghettos of West Kingston to being a movement firmly entrenched in Jamaican society.[1] From Jamaica, the movement has spread around the world, especially among oppressed people of African origin.[2] Beyond people of African descent, Rastafari has been embraced by persons from numerous other ethnic groups around the world, especially by those who perceive themselves as suffering some form of oppression and marginalization. Furthermore, the Rastafarian movement has made itself felt across the globe through the influence it has exerted on popular music and fashion (clothing, hairstyles, personal accessories, and so on). Against this background, this study seeks to investigate how the movement has made the transition from obscurity to popularity; how Rastas, much maligned, persecuted, and repressed because of their perceived threat to Jamaican society, have gained a place at the table of acceptability; and how, starting out as denigrated outcasts, they have over the last forty years of the twentieth century become the dominant force in the evolution of popular culture in Jamaica.

In this book, I will analyze the factors responsible for the entrenchment of Rastafari in Jamaican society. My use of *entrenchment*[3] is synonymous with *routinization*,[4] a term used by Max Weber to signify the process by which an emergent charismatic movement institutionalizes itself and secures a permanent existence.[5] Both terms will be used to refer to the process whereby a nascent movement becomes established and embedded in the social and cultural fabric of a society.

Weber maintains that for any movement to continue to exist beyond the initial period of the charismatic eruption that brought it into being, it must be routinized. Although the Rastafarian movement has been in existence since the early 1930s, scholars have been rather hesitant in affirming its routinization. Leonard Barrett, the first widely recognized authority on the movement, contends that there is "ambivalent routinization."[6] How-

3

ever, he neither indicates what necessitates the use of the term *ambivalent* nor explains what it signifies. Jack Anthony Johnson-Hill, by viewing the essence of Rastafari as an experience of liminality—that is, a threshold experience of leaving "Babylon" but not yet arriving in the "promised land"—has eliminated the possibility of routinization.[7] Neville G. Callam argues that the movement has gained a kind of "functional" routinization, partly through its ability to adapt itself to "contextual exigencies" and partly because of the accommodating strategies used by the established order to defuse the Rastafarian threat to its stability.[8] Callam starts in the right direction but ends his discussion by interpreting the Rastafarian movement in terms of Troeltsch's church-sect typology, and thus he concludes that the Rastafarian emphases on individualism, sojourning, and repatriation militate against the emergence of formal organizational structures and, by implication, genuine routinization.[9]

These scholars have failed to affirm the routinization of Rastafari primarily because they have uncritically accepted the idea that the development of formal organizational structures (whether rational-legal or traditional) is the only indicator of the routinization of new movements. In contrast, this interpretive study unequivocally asserts the routinization of the movement. Of course the use of Weber's theory of routinization is somewhat problematic, because Rastafari lacks the institutional structures that Weber posits as the evidence of routinization. However, I am affirming that, even without these structures, Rastafari has carved out a niche for itself and has become embedded in the social and cultural fabric of Jamaican society; it thus ought to be considered entrenched or routinized.

My thesis is that the entrenchment of Rastafari in Jamaica is made evident by three factors: (1) the internal development of the movement, (2) the gradual rapprochement between the movement and the wider society, and (3) the impact of Rastafari on the evolution of Jamaica's indigenous popular culture. The internal development includes the emergence of a network of "houses" and "mansions" as the collective units of the movement,[10] of a world view or ideology encoded in a variety of symbols, and of collective ritual activities, which initiate and confirm individuals in the principles of Rastafari. With regard to the rapprochement between Rastafari and the rest of the society, the attitudes of the wider society toward Rastas have gone through several phases, from outright repression, to efforts of accommodation, to the cooptation of Rasta symbols and music by political campaigns of the 1970s, to the "coronation" of Bob Marley as a culture hero in the late 1970s, and finally to the culture tourism of the 1980s and 1990s. Rastas' influence on Jamaica's indigenous culture is quite pervasive, especially in popular parlance, the visual arts, tourist art, and the performing arts. However, their most celebrated contribution is to the development of reggae music, which Jamaicans regard as their cultural contribution to the world. Later I will return to these issues and will demonstrate how they contribute to the routinization of Rastafari in Jamaica.

The nature of this book dictates a heavy reliance on documentary analysis. My focus is interpretation not ethnography. Therefore, I have not sought to generate primary data on the movement but to analyze and re-analyze the growing body of scholarly and popular literature on the movement, including sociological and anthropological studies, biographies, monographs, dissertations, published and unpublished essays, and periodical articles. Archival sources, such as newspaper reports, policy statements, pamphlets, and organization manuals have also provided useful information.

Chapter 1 reviews and refines Weber's theory of charisma and routinization, using insights from a number of social movement scholars. Though this book focuses on routinization, it is necessary to locate routinization and its twin concept, charisma, in the wider context of Weber's view of social change.[11]

In chapter 2, I identify the economic, political, and cultural deprivation of the poor in Jamaica as the sociohistorical context that precipitated the emergence of the Rastafarian movement. I demonstrate that the African and Afro-Christian religions, Ethiopianism, and Garveyism are the sources that shaped the Rastafarian ideology, its posture of resistance, and some of its practices and beliefs. I also trace the career of Leonard Howell, the charismatic personality who exerted the most influence on the movement in its formative stages.

Chapter 3 looks at the Rastafarian view of Babylon and the Rastafarian development of a distinct culture as a response to life on the underside of a society shaped by the history of plantation slavery and organized around European-derived values and institutions. The chapter points out that the Rastafarian response to the oppression and alienation of the Jamaican situation is in essence an atten.pt to create a cultural alternative based on the re-appropriation of an African identity. I include this chapter for two reasons. First, it highlights what I consider the essence of Rastafari: the rejection of Babylon and the re-appropriation of Africa. More important for this study, it contrasts the Rastafarian rejection of Jamaica as Babylon with the fact that the movement has become entrenched in that very society.

Chapters 4, 5, and 6 present the evidence for the entrenchment of the Rastafarian movement in Jamaican society. In these chapters, I spell out the factors I have identified as responsible for the routinization of Rastafari, namely, the development of a distinct Rastafarian ethos uniting all

Rastas, the gradual rapprochement between Rastas and the rest of the society, and the impact of Rastafarian creativity on cultural formation in Jamaica.

Chapter 7 summarizes my findings, makes some observations on their implications for the theory of charisma and routinization, and discusses the future of the Rastafarian movement.

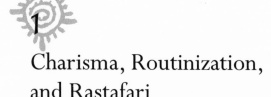

Charisma, Routinization,
and Rastafari

In this chapter, I analyze and critique Weber's theory of charisma and routinization in order to develop a revised version of this theory, which will be particularly applicable to an analysis of the entrenchment of Rastafari in Jamaican society. I begin by placing the theory of charisma and routinization in the wider context of Weber's work and proceed to discuss and critique Weber's treatment of charisma and routinization. In this critique, I draw on insights from social movement theorists while focusing on issues that have particular relevance to the phenomenon of Rastafari. Finally, I conclude by outlining my revisions to Weber's theory in order to render it more applicable to the phenomenon I am analyzing.

Charisma and Routinization
in the Context of Weber's Work

Weber's theory of charisma and routinization must be placed within the broader context of his work. At the most general level, the theory of charisma and routinization is related to Weber's concern with the role of ideas as social forces, that influence the social actions of individuals and groups. At an intermediate level, his theory of charisma and routinization forms part of the theory of social change implicit in his work. At the most immediate level, it is one element in his theory of legitimate domination. Therefore, I will discuss how charisma and routinization relate to ideas as social forces, to rationalization, and to legitimate domination, before outlining Weber's theory of charisma and routinization.

Charisma and Ideas as Social Forces

As in much of Weber's work, his theory of charisma and its routinization is in conversation with Karl Marx. While Marx sees all of social life, and hence all social change, as emanating from and shaped by the economic

7

substructure of the society, Weber contends that ideas and the human actors who conceive and countenance them are often independent variables shaping cultural and social change. As sociologist Lewis Coser observes, "He [Weber] attempted to show that the relations between systems of ideas and social structures were multiform and varied and that causal connections went in both directions, rather than from infrastructure to superstructure alone."[1] In *The Protestant Ethic and the Spirit of Capitalism,* Weber makes this point quite explicitly.[2] He demonstrates that a group of people armed with a set of ideas and ideals went about organizing their lives according to those ideas and ideals. As a result, they ended up changing the nature of the capitalist economic endeavor by injecting it with an eminently calculating spirit. This calculating spirit has become the distinctive feature of Western capitalism and Western societies in general. *The Protestant Ethic and the Spirit of Capitalism* is part of a series of cross-cultural studies, which specifically investigate the relationships between religious ideas and economic life in the West, ancient Israel, India, and China.[3] Weber's argument throughout is that the character of each religious system affected its approach to rational economic activities.

While the conversation with Marx is rather explicit in *The Protestant Ethic and the Spirit of Capitalism,* the conversation is only implicit in Weber's discussion of charisma and its routinization. What is obvious, however, is that the charismatic leader is a person who emerges with essentially new ideas and who, by propagating those ideas, is able to reorient people's approach to the problems they face or the things they consider significant. If the charismatic leader succeeds in gaining a following, and if the charismatic community succeeds in routinizing, then the emergent forces, originally linked to charisma, are likely to have long-term consequences for the direction of cultural and social formation. Seen in the light of Weber's overall concern with ideas as social forces, his theory of charisma and routinization is yet another argument for the role of ideas as effective instruments of social change.[4]

Charisma and Rationalization

Although Weber's work has no specific or systematic treatment of the subject of social change, there is an implicit theory of social change in his treatment of rationalization and charisma. Rationalization, or rationality, is the master concept that runs as a unifying theme through all of Weber's work. As Talcott Parsons observes in the introduction to *The Sociology of Religion,* rationalization is the process through which cultures create their religious cosmologies and address the problem of meaning.[5] Accordingly, Weber is supremely concerned with how human beings, as purposeful social actors, create, maintain, and change their cosmologies as well as their concrete situations. The centrality of rationalization in Weber's sociology reflects his fundamental assumption that human beings are purposeful social actors. That is, their actions are driven by certain motives or motivations and are geared toward certain ends, whether ideal or material.[6] Hence, Weber's generic meaning of *rational* (rationalization, rationality) must be understood in terms of the purposes that the actors have in mind. For example, the actions of rain dancers are rational to the extent that the participants believe that their dancing is the efficient means of producing rain. Although their belief may not correspond with the facts as we understand them from a modern, scientific point of view, their actions are rational in as much as they are geared toward certain goals. Therefore, Weber argues that even in the most primitive situation, "religiously and magically motivated behavior is relatively rational," in that the behavior is purposively geared to the addressing of existential needs, especially economic survival and the problem of meaning.[7]

In modern Western societies, however, rationalization or rationality has become embedded in bureaucracy, which seeks to employ "the most technically efficient strategy for attaining goals."[8] In *The Protestant Ethic and the Spirit of Capitalism*, Weber explores the distinctive characteristic of rationalization in the West and argues that it has its roots in Puritan Protestant theology and practices. He seeks to demonstrate that capitalism in the West is characterized by rational calculation, which matches means with ends. This rationalization grew out of the Calvinist-Puritan ethos in which believers systematized their behavior in order to bring glory to God and to prove their election by Him through success in a worldly vocation. These believers saw material success as a sign of their election and proof that they were glorifying God in their calling. Therefore, they set about their worldly business in a systematic manner, using the most efficient means to achieve success as indexed by the accumulation of material resources.[9] Although largely detached from its religious roots, this calculating spirit has become entrenched in the West and finds its purest manifestation in bureaucracy, which is a type of organization based on rationally developed and clearly expressed rules, characterized by clearly defined hierarchical relationships and specific responsibilities, and geared toward the attainment of specific goals by the most efficient means available.

Whether in societies of ancient antiquity or in modern Western societies, as human knowledge increases, rationalization adjusts and matches means to the desired ends, effecting a process of social change generated by rationalization that is gradual and incremental.[10] For example, as scientific knowledge increases in industrial societies, there is a gradual increase in technological innovations and an attendant increase in the efficiency with which problems are solved and goods and services are produced.

The other force generating social change in Weber's scheme is charisma. Borrowing the concept of charisma from the New Testament, where it simply means "gift of grace," or the possession of divine powers, Weber gives it a much wider sociological application.[11] For him, charisma refers to an extraordinary quality, often claimed and considered to be of divine or supernatural origin, which enables some social actors to secure the devotion and commitment of others to the causes they espouse.[12] An individual possessing this quality, prototypically the prophet, "takes the responsibility for announcing a *break* in the established normative order"[13] and calls people to a commitment to a new world view, a new standard of behavior, or the undertaking of certain new endeavors.[14] The person declaring this break and calling for this new commitment legitimates such action by claiming to stand in special relationship to the divine and to have received special gifts or revelations.[15]

Because of charisma's radical departure from the normative order, Weber regards it as "the great revolutionary force."[16] Being bound neither by past traditions nor by the present legal or rational structures of society, charisma is indeed revolutionary. The bearer of charisma "preaches, creates and demands *new* obligations—most typically, by virtue of revelation, oracle, inspiration, or by his own will, which are recognized by the members of the religious, military, or party group because it [*sic*] comes from such a source."[17] Charismatic personalities are therefore innovators and agents of social change, not by making some technical adjustments or further systematizations of the prevailing ideas, but by espousing new ideas, making new demands, and creating new visions for potential followers.

That rationalization and charisma should embody Weber's view of social change is somewhat paradoxical and may lead to the accusation that Weber is somewhat contradictory. The source of the alleged contradiction lies in the fact that Weber claims that charisma is irrational and antirational, the opposite of rationalization or rationality.[18] However, Weber is well aware of the potential contradiction and points out in what sense each is revolutionary. The revolutionary force of rationalization, he says, "works from *without*: by altering the situation of life and hence its problems, finally in this way changing men's attitudes toward them; or it intellectualizes the individual."[19] Weber continues in another context:

As we have seen, bureaucratic rationalization, too, often has been a major revolutionary force with regard to tradition. But it revolutionizes with *technical means*, in principle, as does every economic reorganization, "from without": It *first* changes the material and social order, and *through* them the people, by changing the conditions of adaptation, and perhaps the opportunities for adaptation, through a rational determination of means and ends.[20]

On the other hand, charisma produces change by effecting "subjective or *internal* reorientation," which may then produce "a radical alteration of the central attitudes and directions of actions with a completely new orientation of all attitudes toward the different problems of the world."[21] Thus, charisma and rationalization do not really conflict. On the contrary, Weber's treatment suggests that ongoing change is only possible as the processes of rationalization and charismatic eruption operate in dynamic tension. Thoroughgoing rationalization, which Weber believes has become characteristic of Western society, will solidify into an iron cage, which robs people of their intuition, creativity, and freedom;[22] and charismatic eruption, without routinization (a rationalizing process), will be an eminently transitory phenomenon having no lasting effect on social change.[23] Therefore, according to Weber, the evolution of cultural and social systems turns on two foci: gradual adjustments of the means that people use to achieve the ends they desire and the sudden eruption of essentially new forces embodied in and expressed by individuals who claim special gifts or special revelation.

Charisma and Legitimate Domination

The other context in which Weber's treatment of charisma belongs is his sociology of domination. Weber defines *domination* as the likelihood that the commands given by a person, or groups of persons, will be obeyed by those to whom the commands are given.[24] Having noticed that the domination of some by others is a universal phenomenon, Weber raises the question of what disposes some people to obey others. In answering this question, he notes that people obey others for different reasons. Some people's acceptance of the authority of others is simply a matter of custom, habit, or self-interest. They obey because that is what they have always done or because they derive some economic, political, or ideal benefits from submitting to the authority of others.[25] Others obey because those in power have an administrative apparatus that threatens noncompliance with some form of punishment, including the withholding of resources and privileges or the use of physical force.[26] Weber argues that no system of domination is satisfied to have compliance based only on habit, self-interest, or threat of punishment. "Every system," he says, "attempts to establish and cultivate the belief in its legitimacy."[27] Wherever this attempt succeeds, compliance is a result of a belief that those commanding obedience have a legitimate basis to do so. Weber calls this *legitimate domination,* or authority, and he identifies three types of such domination: traditional, based on accumulated customs; rational-legal, based on standards arrived at by accepted procedures; and charismatic, based on personal appeal.

Traditional domination is believed to be legitimate because it is based on the acceptance of the cumulative beliefs and customs that have accrued and precedents that have been established in a particular culture. Patriarchal households and patrimonial estates provide the best examples of social systems where the exercise of authority invokes this type of legitimacy.[28] Domination or the exercise of authority may also be justified because it is based on accepted rules and procedures, which have been legally constituted and instituted and which stipulate that certain persons holding certain positions have the right to exercise authority over others. This type of domination is called rational-legal authority, and finds its highest expression in the bureaucracies of the Western world.[29] The third type of domination eschews both legal and traditional norms and procedures and finds legitimacy in the belief that those demanding compliance with their commands are endowed with extraordinary qualities and exceptional powers (qualities and powers not accessible to ordinary persons), which predestine them to lead others.[30] This is charismatic authority, and it is characteristic of leaders who do not attain their positions on the bases of age-old traditions or by procedures rationally arrived at and legally instituted, but on the basis of their claims to special powers, inspiration, or revelations.

In periods of relative stability, the transfer of power from one individual to another takes place according to normative procedures, whether they have been arrived at traditionally or rationally. However, societal stress, institutional crises, and social conflicts may lead to the weakening, if not the demise, of traditional and rational-legal authority and to the emergence of charismatic leadership. Conversely, because of the unstable nature of charisma, it tends to remain the basis of authority only for brief periods, after which it is replaced by traditional or rational-legal structures.

The Meaning of Charisma and Routinization

Having established the relationship of charisma and routinization to Weber's broader concerns, I will proceed to outline Weber's theory of charisma and routinization in more detail. According to Weber, in its purest form, charisma is a certain quality of an individual personality by virtue of which he is considered extraordinary and treated as endowed with supernatural, superhuman, or at least specifically exceptional powers and qualities.[31]

What is obvious is that, while legal and traditional authorities are based on established norms, which give leaders the right to demand certain courses of action from their followers, the authority of charismatic leaders is based solely on the force of their personalities and on their ability to attract a following and to evoke loyalty. Speaking of the manner in which prophets become leaders, Weber says, "They do not receive their mission from any human agency, but seize it, as it were."[32] Weber claims that charisma, in its purest and most potent form, "transforms all values and breaks all traditional and rational norms,"[33] and it "overturns all [established] notions of sanctity" and propriety.[34] In other words, since authority is vested in the individual whose right to rule is legitimated by charisma, the norms of the external or established order do not hold sway over such an individual. Followers or potential followers are likewise called to march to a different drumbeat—the one sounded by the charismatic leader.

The genius of charismatic leaders is their ability to embody and articulate a certain mission with which others identify and to which they commit themselves.[35] The identification of groups of people with the message of charismatic personages is necessary for the formation of charismatic communities. Otherwise, those claiming charismatic qualities will remain isolated individuals and are likely to be regarded as eccentric.

Because charismatic leadership is dependent on its recognition by followers, leaders are frequently called upon to validate their possession of charisma by the demonstration of "magical powers, revelations, heroism or other extraordinary gifts."[36] To maintain recognition of their charismatic qualities, charismatic leaders must continue to furnish proofs and achieve successes that are of some benefit (psychological, political, or economic) to their followers. Otherwise, their ability to command awe and devotion will wane and eventually disappear.[37]

This leads to the question of the milieu and conditions that are likely to generate a charismatic eruption. Weber makes only brief references to the sociohistorical conditions favoring the emergence of charismatic leadership, and in each case, he characterizes those conditions as extraordinary. He notes, "All *extra*ordinary needs, i.e., those which *transcend* the sphere of everyday economic routines, have always been satisfied in an entirely heterogenous manner: on a *charismatic* basis."[38] From this, he extrapolates that charismatic leaders are persons outside the routine power structure, who emerge as "'natural' leaders in moments of distress—whether psychic, physical, economic, ethical, religious, or political."[39] In another reference he asserts that charisma "arises out of the anxiety and enthusiasm of an extraordinary situation."[40] In yet another reference, Weber postulates, "The charisma of the hero or the magician is immediately activated whenever an extraordinary event occurs: a major hunting expedition, a drought or some other danger precipitated by the wrath of the demons and especially a military threat."[41]

These references reveal Weber's image of charismatic figures as those leaders who are able to summon the will of their followers to deal with societal exigencies not amenable to the solutions proposed by the normative order. These leaders emerge "during times of crisis, when traditional ways of doing things seem inappropriate, outmoded and inadequate to the problems confronting people."[42] Therefore, in its essence, charismatic authority is innovative because it calls would-be followers to new ideological orientations and practices and seeks to effect changes in the social order.

For Weber, the charismatic eruption is by its nature unstable and temporary. Charisma, in its purest form, only exists at the moment of its initial emergence. In Weber's words, "It cannot remain stable, but becomes either traditionalized or rationalized or a combination of both."[43] So Weber argues that, for the charismatic eruption to have perpetual existence, it has to become transformed and routinized in line with the material and ideal interests of the charismatic community.[44]

While material or ideal interests are the internal or social-psychological motivations for the routinization of the charismatic community, there are objective factors pressing the demand for routinization. Weber identifies these factors as the problem of succession at the passing of the original charismatic leader, the problem of economic support (the pressure to secure a more regularized and rational source of financial support than free-will gifts), and the problem of administration (the need to establish formal procedures for recruiting new members and to foster relationships and exercise authority by some means other than personal appeal).[45]

There are three distinct emphases in Weber's discussion of the routinization of charisma. The first involves the formation and perpetuation of a group, society, or movement based on the initial charismatic impetus. The second is concerned with how authority is gained and legitimated in the movement after the passing of the charismatic personage. The third deals with how the ideas or message born in the charismatic eruption may become embedded in the social fabric of the society. Weber explains the first two in some detail, but merely hints at the third.

In Weber's first emphasis, routinization refers to the process by which a charismatic eruption becomes a social or religious movement and gains a state of permanence and a recognizable place in the life of the society.[46] A routinized movement is therefore one that has gained regular and predictable modes of existence, rather than an existence that is dependent on the personal dictates of a charismatic leader. At this point, Weber's discussion of routinization is primarily devoted to the institutionalization of the initial charismatic experience. He emphasizes the fact that the community that gathered around a charismatic leader is later transformed into a state, church, sect, academy, school, party, newspaper, or periodical.[47] This means that the informal personal relationships, that usually characterize a charismatic community are transformed into an organizational hierarchy in which there are formal rules that govern relationships and the exercise of authority. Also, this typically means that the charismatic message, which is usually freely uttered by the charismatic leader under the claim of inspiration or revelation, becomes solidified into "dogma, doctrine, theory, reglement, law or petrified tradition."[48]

Weber's second emphasis is on how successive leaders are chosen and how their authority is legitimated. With the passing of charismatic leaders, the members of the movements founded on the leaders' personal appeal must decide who are going to become the new leaders and how they are going to be chosen. According to Weber, this may be decided in one of several ways: (1) by appointment on the basis of established criteria of charismatic qualities, (2) by appointment through the use of oracles, (3) by designation of a successor by the original charismatic leader, (4) by appointment by the administrative staff or election by the community, (5) by succession according to heredity, or (6) by achievement of the qualifications of leadership through ordination or education.[49] The end result is that the authority of successive leaders is legitimated, not by virtue of their extraordinary gifts or special relationships to God, but by some secondary agents, either their predecessors or those they wish to lead, or by some established procedures. Though second- and third-generation leaders have the right to exercise authority—and some have almost total authority over their followers—their authority is not based on pure charisma but on "depersonalized charisma."[50] That is, the right to exercise authority over others does not inhere in the special qualities of these leaders or in their calling by God, but in the position they occupy in a traditional or rational organization.[51] Depersonalized charisma can take at least three forms. It may become transferable, as in "lineage charisma," where leadership resides in a family and is transferred from one member to another according to established traditions. It may be acquired, usually through education or training. Or it may become attached to an office, which one comes to occupy through appointment or ordination.

Weber's third emphasis is often missed by his interpreters. This empha-

sis involves essential elements of the charismatic ethos becoming incorporated into the social fabric of the society. Weber argues that all or some
elements of the charismatic ethos may penetrate existing structures and
become "fused with them in the most diverse forms, so that it [trans-
formed charisma] becomes a mere component of a concrete historical
structure. In this case it is often transformed beyond recognition, and
identifiable only on an analytical level."[52] In this case, charisma does not
become transformed into an organized institution, but the ideas, concerns, and practices of the charismatic community become diffused in or
assimilated by the wider society, thereby exerting influence on the society
in a manner similar to how the Protestant ethic became a pervasive and
vital element of Western capitalism. This aspect of routinization remains
undeveloped in Weber's discussion, but it is of particular importance to
this study.

A Critique of Weber's Theory

Weber's theory of charisma and routinization has been subjected to much
criticism, especially from subsequent social movement theorists. In this
section, I maintain that while these criticisms identify weaknesses in
Weber's theory, they do not constitute an invalidation of the theory as a
whole. My focus is on several issues: the social location of the charismatic
leader, the sociohistorical preconditions favoring charismatic eruption,
the elements (or sources) that converge to give form to the charismatic
message, and the nature and substance of the routinization process.

The Social Location of Charismatic Leaders

Some scholars have taken Weber to task for characterizing charismatic
leaders as emerging from and operating outside of the routine structures
of their societies. Theodore Long, for instance, argues that charismatic
eruption can take place within relatively ordinary situations and that the
charismatic personality can arise from within the establishment or the
routine structures of the society.[53] Peter Berger also challenges the notion
that the charismatic personality has to be from outside the power structure, arguing that the Old Testament prophets were professionals within
the cultic institutions of Israel.[54]

Although there is some validity to these criticisms, they are not as
weighty as they first appear. First, not all so-called prophets represent
Weber's ideal-typical charismatic personality. Berger himself makes reference to Weber's distinction between prophets who are religious func-

tionaries within the cultus and prophets who are driven by a sense of divine mission. [55] Weber, therefore, recognizes that some so-called prophets routinely function as diviners, healers, and counselors. Such were many of the court prophets of Israel. But the prophets who are the ideal-typical bearers of charisma do not function according to preestablished codes. Their activities are determined by their sense of mission, which is given to them not by the cultus but by divine revelation. In the Old Testament, therefore, Amos, who disclaimed any link to the religious institutions of Israel, represents the genuine charismatic type, not the diviners connected to the cultus nor the court prophets who were the king's political and military counselors. [56]

Second, Weber is aware that someone within routine structures may indeed become the bearer of charisma and initiate charismatic activities within those structures or become antagonistic to those structures. Writing about political party bureaucracies, he states:

> In normal times such a bureaucratic apparatus, more or less consistently developed, controls the party's course, including the vitally important nomination of candidates. However, in times of great public excitement, charismatic leaders may emerge even in solidly bureaucratized parties, as was demonstrated by Roosevelt's campaign in 1912. If there is a "hero," he will endeavor to break the technician's hold over the party by imposing plebiscitary designation and possibly by changing the whole machinery of nomination. Such an eruption of charisma, of course, always faces the resistance of the normally predominant pros, especially the bosses who control and finance the party and maintain routine operations. [57]

Therefore, a court prophet can conceivably become a genuine charismatic prophet upon receiving new revelations or upon having an encounter with the divine. Isaiah is an example of such a case. Prior to his visionary encounter with God (Isa. 6), he was apparently a counselor at the king's court. Thereafter, he became Yahweh's mouthpiece and crusaded against the decadence of his society.

Notwithstanding the possibility of the emergence of charismatic activities within routine structures, by their very nature routine structures are less fertile ground for such activities and are, therefore, less amenable to the emergence of charismatic influences. The sector of society that benefits the least from the routine structures, especially during periods of stress and social unrest, tends to be the most fruitful ground for charismatic eruptions. Weber's studies, as well as the history of charismatic religious and political activities, show that the charismatic leaders who have effected the most enduring changes have usually been marginal to and operated outside of the normative institutions of their societies and the status quos of their times (for example, Jesus, Mohammed, Gandhi, Buddha, Martin Luther King, Jr., and Elijah Muhammad).

Sociohistorical Conditions and the Eruption of Charisma

Weber provides substantial treatment of the meaning of charisma, the personal qualities of the bearer of charisma, and the character of the charismatic community. However, beyond stating that the conditions are extraordinary, he uncharacteristically provides no analytic treatment of the objective factors favoring the emergence of charismatic movements. Subsequent social movement theorists have sought to provide more definitive answers to the question of why social movements emerge. The scholarly efforts to date may be subsumed under four theories: relative deprivation, mass society, structural strain, and resource mobilization.

Much has been written about these theories, and an extensive analysis of each is not possible in this context.[58] Therefore, I present here only what each theory considers to be the critical factors that facilitate the rise of social movements. According to relative deprivation theory, the primary impetus for the rise of social movements is discontent, which emanates from the perception by a group of people that they have been barred from the resources they deserve.[59] For mass society theory, the threats of insignificance and anonymity that people feel in complex societies drive them to form social movements as the means of establishing identity and belongingness.[60] Structural strain theory sees a convergence of several objective conditions as responsible for the emergence of social movements: (1) structural conduciveness, that is, highly differentiated institutions, significant conflict of interests, and significant social problems, (2) the experience of "strain" by a group (or groups) of people as a result of economic, political, ecological, or demographic factors, (3) the emergence of generalized beliefs, which explain the causes, consequences and solutions to the strain being experienced, (4) certain precipitating factors, or events that set off collective action, (5) mobilization for action, that is, activities aimed at securing support and following, and (6) the absence of stifling social control.[61] Claiming that discontent and strain are inherent in all societies, the resource mobilization theory contends that the critical factor affecting the emergence of social movements is the availability of the resources, human and material, necessary to sustain the new movement.[62]

I will not review the individual strengths and weaknesses of these theories in this context, but I will make three broad observations about how these theories relate to Weber's view of the emergence of charisma. First, these theories, with the exception of the structural strain theory, run the risk of reductionism. By seeking to identify the one factor critical to the origin of social movements, they fall into the trap of monocausality. Because of the complex nature of social phenomena, the isolation of a single causal factor for a particular social movement is difficult, if not impossible. It is therefore even more difficult to identify one factor as decisive in the emergence of all social movements. The origins of social movements are likely to be explained more adequately by theories that recognize that several factors usually converge to give rise to new movements and that in one instance a particular set of factors may be more decisive, while in another instance, a different set of factors may be more critical. This leads to my second observation.

Some theories focus on social-psychological factors as decisive and causative in the emergence of social movements (relative deprivation and mass society), while others focus more on social-structural factors (resource mobilization and structural strain). However, they all recognize that both social-structural and social-psychological factors are involved in the emergence of social movements.[63] For example, James C. Davies, who is a proponent of the theory that movements for revolutionary change originate in the discontent that people feel, points out that the feeling of discontent is often generated by fluctuations in individuals' economic or political fortunes, or by the fact that their possessions and positions do not match those of their reference groups.[64] Mass society theorists admit that it is the complexities of modern society that generate in people the feeling of insignificance, which drives them to create organizations as shields against the loss of personal identity. Structural strain theoreticians, while proposing a convergence of several "objective" factors, recognize that some factors are structural (structural conduciveness) and others are social-psychological (generalized perception of the causes, consequences, and potential solutions of the particular strain in the society). The resource mobilization theory argues for the availability of material and human resources as the critical elements in the rise of successful social movements. However, it is almost self-evident that resources by themselves do not produce a movement. These resources must be utilized by human actors with psychological motivations.

The recognition of both social-psychological and social-structural factors in the emergence of social movements to some degree reaffirms Weber's basic thesis. He contends that a charismatic movement typically arises in "unusual, especially political or economic situations, or from extraordinary psychic, particularly religious states, or from both together. It arises from collective excitement produced by extraordinary events and from surrender to heroism of any kind."[65] Although Weber does not elaborate on these brief remarks, they clearly reveal his awareness that both social-structural and social-psychological factors contribute to the emergence of charismatic movements. Thus I conclude that these theories, instead of refuting Weber's conclusions concerning the origins of charismatic movements, only make distinct a number of factors already implied by Weber.

Third, these theories seek to make pronouncements concerning all types of social movements. Thus, they are concerned with a wide range of phenomena of which charismatic movements form a subcategory. This is particularly true of the discussion of social movements in Western industrial societies. A significant number of these movements are pressure groups with a limited number of objectives vis-à-vis the established authority.[66] In other words, the objective of these groups is to get the government (or other established authorities) to address their particular concerns. They do not declare the established social order illegitimate and seek to replace it with their own ideal, and therefore, they are not charismatic movements in the sense that Weber indicated. Furthermore, from their inception, they are organized in a manner that Weber would call rational-legal. Because of the latitude of these theories, their conclusions are only applicable to charismatic social movements at the most general level. They do not address the origin or character of charismatic movements with any specificity.

Having made these observations, I would like to suggest that Ann Ruth Willner's theoretical construction of the preconditions necessary for the emergence of charismatic political activities is more compelling, because it makes up for the shortcomings of these theories. It sets out to elaborate and to make more precise Weber's rather ambiguous statements concerning the conditions necessary for the emergence of charismatic leaders. It does this while refusing to fall into reductionism. Moreover, it combines social-structural (political and economic), social-psychological, and personal factors in the explanation of the rise of charismatic movements.

Drawing on a diversity of charismatic political movements (Gandhi's in India, Sukarno's in Indonesia, and Nkrumah's in Ghana), Willner describes the conditions in which the charismatic phenomenon is likely to appear as "some convergence of social and psychological needs of people and of the situations of institutional failure in which they find themselves."[67] Three sets of conditions usually converge to constitute what Willner calls the "frustration-eruption formula" necessary for the emergence of charismatic leadership. The first set of conditions is latent, which refer to a state of imbalance and instability in the social order, which may manifest itself in intergroup conflicts and in the marginalization of certain groups in the society. The second set is precipitant situations, which refer to events or crises that are likely to intensify instability, conflicts, and marginalization. The third set is perceptual reactions, which have to do with the cognitive and emotional manner in which people perceive and experience the latent conditions and the precipitant siuations.[68]

Willner is quick to point out, however, that these objective conditions and the perceptions that people bring to them do not by themselves lead inevitably to the generation of charismatic leadership as Weber seems to indicate in his statement "The charisma of the hero or the magician is immediately activated whenever an extraordinary event occurs."[69] She notes that extreme deprivation and situations of alienation may exist for a long time without the emergence of a charismatic leader, even when there are many aspirants for leadership positions.[70] The extraordinary (to use Weber's term) situation or "situation of acute social crisis" must converge with the emergence of charismatic personalities who are able to creatively embody and articulate the grievances, feelings, and expectations of those for whom they will become leaders.[71] Willner argues that the charismatic personalities may be instrumental in creating the conditions necessary for their own emergence as charismatic leaders. They often define the situation and raise to consciousness the dire realities of alienation and deprivation. For example, she argues that many Indians, Indonesians, and Ghanians were not aware of how dismal their situations were until Gandhi, Sukarno, and Nkrumah, respectively, articulated the social, political, and economic contradictions under which they lived.[72]

Other scholars concur with Willner on this point. Curlew O. Thomas and Barbara Boston-Thomas demonstrate that for a long time blacks in the United States faced "widespread psychological insecurity," extensive political and economic deprivation, and institutional failure to deal with the society's underlying racism. However, it was only as these conditions were combined with the charismatic leadership of W. D. Fard and Elijah Muhammad that the Nation of Islam emerged in the 1930s.[73] Similarly, Robert Alun Jones and Robert M. Anservitz argue that the rise of Saint-Simonism in France in the 1820s was due to the convergence between the social dislocation of the French Jews after the Bourbon Restoration (1815) and the charismatic appeal and message of Saint-Simon.[74]

Therefore, the eruption of the distinctly charismatic phenomenon most typically occurs when and where there is a convergence of a societal crisis with charismatic leadership. The societal crisis may be precipitated by social, political, or economic deprivation, public disorder, or feelings of alienation and discontent. The charismatic leader's blend of personal style and message must appropriately embody and express the deeply felt needs of those caught in the throes of tension-filled sociohistorical circumstances. Furthermore, the would-be charismatic leader must be able to articulate an attractive alternative vision that purports to remedy the existing crisis.[75]

Sources of the Charismatic Message

Weber's treatment of charisma leaves one with the impression that the substance—the ideological content and the social posture—of the charismatic eruption emerges ex nihilo. In characterizing Weber's view of charisma, Jones and Anservitz say that "charisma thus represents the sudden eruption of quite *new forces*, often linked to quite new ideas."[76] Weber's emphasis on the newness of these forces and ideas is probably an attempt to escape Marx's reductionism, which contends that all ideas are products or reflections of the economic substructure. Weber wishes to establish that ideas (especially religious ideas) do have a life of their own and cannot always be explained in reference to the economic substructures.

However, though there is always a certain novelty to the charismatic message, further examination will reveal that elements of this message are often distilled from ideas that have had currency in some elements of the society. Several scholars writing from within the Weberian tradition fill out Weber's theory on this point. Anthony Wallace discusses the role of charismatic leaders in the "mazeway reformulation," which is characteristic of revitalization movements, and comes to this conclusion:

> Whether the movement is religious or secular, the reformulation of the mazeway generally seems to depend on a restructuring of elements and subsystems which have already attained currency in society and may even be in use, and which are known to the person who is to become prophet or leader.[77]

In analyzing the charismatic message of Saint-Simon, Jones and Anservitz come to a similar conclusion. They point out that Saint-Simon's "New Christianity," drew heavily on two sources: the Christian notion that all persons should love one another and the "Jewish hope for the coming of a Messianic Era."[78] In fact, Saint-Simonism indicates that the appeal of the charismatic message is derived not only from the fact that it addresses the existential circumstances of a certain cross section of the society, but also from its ability to give fresh expression to ideas already extant in this sector of society. More specifically, Saint-Simonism was attractive to the French Jews not only because it promised them freedom from discrimination, but also because it gave expression to their already existing belief in industrial and commercial activities as the means to higher status and to their belief in the coming of a messianic era.[79]

In the same vein, Ann Ruth Willner and Dorothy Willner indicate that part of the appeal of charismatic leaders comes from their ability to associate themselves with the traditions of a certain group of people:

Specific to the charismatic leader, according to our theory, is the role of myths in validating his authority. His appeal, therefore, can best be understood by reference to the body of myths in a given culture that his strategy taps and manipulates, and the actions and values associated with and sanctioned by these myths. In brief, the charismatic leader is charismatic, because, in the breakdown of other means of legitimizing authority, he is able to evoke and associate with himself the sacred symbols of the culture.[80]

Richard H. Dekmejian and Margaret J. Wyszomirski express a similar point of view: "The revolutionary nature of the message does not preclude the selective incorporation of certain of the prevailing values and symbols. In this sense there is continuity between old and new: the leader selectively invokes history, myths and past heroes to reinforce the sanctity of his mission."[81]

Whether they are embodied in symbols, myths, folklore, history, or even a certain attitude toward the society, extant ideas often become sources from which the charismatic personalities distill their message. As we will see in the case of Rastafari, these sources are to be found in the traditions and attitudes of mind that oppressed Jamaicans developed over centuries of exploitation and deprivation. The ability of Rastafari to survive without a centralized organization, therefore, is best explained by the fact that it draws on ideas and attitudes that were long prevalent among the lower classes in Jamaica. Thus, without formal organizational structures and rationalized strategies, Rastafari has been able to tap into the predisposition of many in the society.

Routinization of Charisma

Weber's treatment of routinization presents a charismatic movement with two options: institutionalization or demise. In other words, the charismatic movement must take on a formal institutional structure, whether rational or traditional, and must accommodate itself to the routines of life in the society, or it will face extinction. Mayer N. Zald and Roberta Ash argue that Weber's limitation of the alternatives to either demise or institutionalization is constrictive and becomes a kind of "iron law."[82] They point out that in addition to or in place of institutionalization and accommodation, there are various other transformations that are possible. These include "coalitions with other organizations, organizational disappearances, factional splits, increased rather than decreased radicalism, and the like."[83] The kind of transformation that is experienced, according to Zald and Ash, depends on several factors: the character of the movement (inclusive or exclusive), its ability to sustain a support base, its ability to maintain and achieve its goals, its ability to develop stable leadership, and the changing conditions and sentiments within the society at large.[84]

Strictly speaking, Zald and Ash are dealing specifically with social movement organizations (SMOs) and not with social movements per se. Social movement organizations are not coterminous with social movements. SMOs are usually created within social movements and are usually in the forefront in espousing the ideas and pursuing the goals of the social movements. However, social movements generally embrace many adherents who have no organizational links to the SMOs.[85] In consequence, the insights of Zald and Ash are specifically applicable to the fate of SMOs, the very existence of which Weber and others view as indicative of the beginning of the routinization process.[86] However, some of Zald and Ash's insights are modifications of Weber's view of routinization. Particularly relevant is their postulation that the fate of a social movement depends to some extent on the vicissitudes of its relationship with the wider society, and that the character of the movement affects its chances of survival and the nature of its organizational structure. I concur with Zald and Ash on this point, but would add that the fate of a new movement, and particularly a charismatic movement, is also linked to the ability of its ideas and practices to became absorbed into the mainstream of the life of the society in which it emerges and operates.

For Weber, the factors influencing the routinization of charismatic movements are the problems of succession, support (economic), and organization. While these problems constitute the internal factors contributing to routinization, Weber fails to acknowledge that there are also external factors. Also critical for the survival or demise of a new movement are the vicissitudes of its relationship with the wider society, particularly the manner in which the guardians of the status quo respond to the movement and the quality and intensity of the public sentiments that the movement elicits. That Weber pays no attention to these factors in discussing the routinization of charisma is rather surprising. Since charisma represents an eruption of "new" forces that directly or indirectly challenge the legitimacy of the established order, some form of reaction or response from the established order is to expected. The nature of the reaction, as well as the ability of the new movement to deal with it, will to a large extent determine the survivability of the movement.[87] Hence, to the problems of succession, support, and organization must be added the problem of dealing with the response or reaction of the wider society.

As one of the indices of routinization, Weber identifies the development or adoption of hierarchical/bureaucratic structures. However, the Rastafarian movement demonstrates that these structures are not the only means available. The preference shown by Weberian scholars to look for rational, bureaucratic institutions as the index for routinization probably belies their uncritical acceptance of the modernization paradigm—secular rationalization—which purports to explain social change in the modern world. But as Paget Henry points outs, while the modernization paradigm may be used to explain social and cultural changes in modern industrial societies, many changes in societies peripheral to the industrial world occur through the manipulation of symbolic structures.[88] I will add to Henry's observation that movements for social change in these societies are often not united by a bureaucratic structure or centralized organization, but by what I call a shared ideological-symbolic-ritual ethos. The research of Barry Chevannes concerning the relationship between Afro-Christian religions and Rastafari bears out this point. He finds that the unifying element in Rastafari, as in the Afro-Christian traditions, is not a centralized organization but "a fairly uniform system of beliefs," shared symbols, and symbolic actions.[89]

Furthermore, instead of becoming institutionalized as a rational-legal bureaucracy or traditional organization, as Weber's theory emphasizes, a charismatic movement may become a diffused social/cultural force. Jones and Anservitz, in their study of Saint-Simonism in nineteenth-century France, conclude that while Saint-Simonism failed to achieve continuity as an identifiable social movement, Saint-Simonist ideas of progress through scientific and industrial innovations became the impetus for many early French industrialists. Such ventures as the building of the Suez Canal, the building of the French railway, and the creation of financial institutions were all undertaken under the influence of ideas postulated by Saint-Simon.[90] The point is that the ideas of a charismatic personality became a significant force in the social/cultural development of modern French society.

Theodore Long points to the effect of charismatic movements on what he calls "culture formation." Long illustrates this by drawing on Weber's study of prophecy in ancient Israel. He calls attention to the fact that while the prophetic movement did not result in a permanent religious/social organization, the ideas of the prophets became formative in the development of Israelite/Jewish culture in the post-exilic era:

> The pre-exilic prophets had created the resource for culture-building in their call to maintain the covenant with God. Though it had fallen mostly on deaf ears before, that proclamation planted the cultural seed that was cultivated in captivity and grew to sustain a nation which otherwise would not have been. Only after the prophets are gone do the effects of their prophecy become manifest in the ". . . subjective or inter-

nal alteration of the central system of attitudes and directions of action
with a completely new orientation of all attitudes toward the different
problems and structures of the world."[91]

Long goes on to point out that charismatic activities may not lead to the
creation of a new movement; rather the long-term outcome of these activities "may center on culture as much or more than on social organization," and the outcome "will depend on historical and situational factors
operating at the time, as well as the emergent trajectory of and response
to the prophetic effort itself."[92]

The impact of the charismatic ethos and ideas as cultural forces falls
within the ambit of Weber's theory. As already mentioned, one of his
overriding theoretical concerns is how ideas have a life of their own and
how they may influence social and cultural changes. The reason he does
not pursue this possibility in his discussion of routinization in this context,
I believe, is due to the fact that he is focusing on the legitimation of authority. Therefore, his treatment of routinization is understandably focused on what happens in the authority structure of the new movement
to change the mode of legitimation from charismatic to traditional or
rational-legal, and not on how the movement affects the society as a
whole. However, the idea of routinization as cultural formation is of particular importance for the study of Rastafari. While there are questions
concerning whether or not Rastafari constitutes a cohesive movement,
there is no denying that for the last forty years of the twentieth century
Rastafari was the most dominant force influencing the development of
popular culture in Jamaica.

Conclusion

One of Weber's enduring contributions to the study of sociology is his development and use of ideal types as tools to be employed in the quest for
the interpretive understanding of social phenomena. Charisma and routinization are two types that have significant heuristic value. Despite the
various criticisms of Weber's theory, charisma as a concept does identify a
type of authority that is distinct from rational-legal and traditional authorities. Furthermore, routinization is an appropriate conceptualization
of the process by which new movements assure their perpetuity and become entrenched in society.

I must point out that Weber does not conceive ideal types as static entities, which never change once they are constructed. With the growth in
knowledge and understanding of the facts, ideal types may be modified,

corrected, elaborated, or abandoned. In the case of Weber's theory of charisma and routinization, the various criticisms reveal that it is a tool that needs to be sharpened or improved, not abandoned. Berger's categorization of his own criticisms of Weber is quite applicable to the criticisms raised earlier: "They do not invalidate the ideal-typical construction of charismatic authority as against traditional and legal-rational authority. More importantly, these modifications in no way weaken Weber's sociological elaboration of the process of routinization of charisma."[93] I am therefore embracing Weber's concepts of charisma and routinization, while proposing several revisions in his overall theory.

First, the fundamental assumption that seems to inform Weber's theory is that leaders and leadership are the most significant variables producing social change. Therefore, his theory of charisma and routinization focuses primarily on leaders and leadership in the creation and maintenance of new social movements. I contend that leaders are but one variable in the complex social and historical contexts that produce charismatic movements. As Willner's research on charismatic leadership demonstrates, the rise of charismatic movements is linked to a combination of social and historical factors, including latent conditions (social stress, instability, rivalry, and conflict), perceptual reactions (emotional and cognitive responses) to those conditions, precipitant situations (which heighten stress and instability and trigger collective action), and persuasive leadership (which embodies the people's feelings, invokes their traditions, and addresses their aspirations).

Second, leaders and the institutions they forge constitute only one of the factors that may facilitate the entrenchment and perpetuity of these movements. The routinization of a new movement is not bound exclusively or necessarily to the development of hierarchical leadership and administrative structures. In addition to leadership/administrative structures, routinization is affected by how the rank and file of the movement relates to the ideas, symbols, and rituals that constitute the ethos of the movement. Furthermore, the new movement exists within the context of a wider society, which may facilitate or hinder its development. Therefore, any theory of routinization must take into consideration the dynamics of the movement's relationship with the wider society, especially its relationship with the guardians of the establishment. In the same vein, the ability of the new movement to engage and shape the culture within which it exists is a key factor determining whether the movement will establish itself permanently in the society. As Long and Jones and Anservitz indicate, the entrenchment of a charismatic movement may not be in the institutions it creates and perpetuates, but in its influence on culture formation.

This leads to my third modification of Weber's theory. In Weber's theory, the end product of routinization is either an organization with a rational-legal leadership structure or one with a traditional structure. As my analysis of the Rastafarian movement will show, a movement may develop a reticulate or weblike structure without recourse to a centralized or hierarchical organization.

With the above modifications in mind, I now turn to my analysis of the emergence and entrenchment of Rastafari in Jamaica.

Dread Uprising

The Emergence of Rastafari

In the previous chapter, I maintained that Weber's theory of charisma is in need of some modifications. I indicated that the theory should give more precision to the combination of sociohistorical factors that are likely to facilitate the rise of charismatic leaders. I also contended that the charismatic message, though new in some respects, draws from and synthesizes ideas that already have currency in some element of the society. With these modifications, Weber's theory of charisma is a relevant tool for the analysis of the emergence of Rastafari. Here I want to set out the sociohistorical context in which the movement emerged, the sources from which it drew, and the charismatic personality most responsible for its emergence.

Sociohistorical Context

Both Max Weber and Ann Ruth Willner place the charismatic eruption within the social context of stress or distress. This is particularly true of the Rastafarian movement. The latent conditions out of which the Rastafarian movement emerged were the economic deprivation, political disfranchisement, and cultural alienation that prevailed among Afro-Jamaicans in the 1920s and 1930s. The precipitant situations were aggravation of the hardship faced by the poor as a result of tax increases in an economy ravaged by the worldwide depression (1920s and 1930s) and the rekindling of the hope of liberation occasioned by the crowning of Haile Selassie as emperor of Ethiopia in 1930. The perception of life in Jamaica as a "Babylonian," or exile experience, and of Haile Selassie as the messiah/liberator of the African people constituted the perceptual reaction. Thus the Rastafarian movement emerged among the poor (both urban and rural) in Jamaica in the early 1930s as a response to both the social realities in Jamaica and the crowning of Haile Selassie in Ethiopia.

Economic deprivation occurred in the context of the colonial plantation system. Of course during slavery the masses had no control over their economic output. They were property used at their masters' will to maximize their profits. While emancipation (1834–1838) changed the status of former slaves, it did not substantially improve their economic conditions, and both the British and the local colonial authorities sought to keep the plantations system intact after emancipation. Land policies sought to keep the former slaves attached to the plantations by placing certain restrictions on land ownership. Immigration policies led to the importation of indentured workers from India and Africa in order to depress the wages that the former slaves could demand. Nonetheless, many former slaves gained access to land with the aid of the nonconformist churches (Baptist, Moravian, and Methodist) or by squatting on marginal and government lands. On these lands, the former slaves developed into the Jamaican peasantry in the decades following emancipation.

The late nineteenth century saw a revival of the plantation system through the infusion of British and American capital. The revival of agribusiness led to the concentration of land in the hands of a few, as government-owned lands were reclaimed from squatters and sold to business interests. Lands formerly considered marginal for agricultural use were now utilized to produce bananas and coffee. As a result, the peasantry that had emerged after emancipation became increasingly landless and "agroproletariat,"[1] having to sell their labor for the meager wages offered by big estates (mostly sugar and banana farms). Furthermore, the expulsion of squatters from government lands in the rural areas led to an urban explosion as many moved to the city in search of work. As usual, urbanization was accompanied by massive levels of unemployment and sprawling slums. As already mentioned, tax increases and the depression of the 1920s and 1930s greatly aggravated this already pauperizing situation.[2]

In addition to their economic marginalization, the masses of the poor were all but excluded from the political process. At the time of the emergence of Rastafari, Jamaica was under Crown Colony rule, a form of direct rule by Britain, which had been imposed after the 1865 Morant Bay Rebellion. Prior to 1865, the country was ruled by an assembly whose members were elected by and from the land-owning class. Even the local ruling class willingly gave up its relative autonomy for fear that emerging "colored" (persons of mixed race, usually from black and white miscegeneration) and black middle classes would become enfranchised and would dominate the political process. The peasant rebellion in Morant Bay generated even greater fear of the black majority.

Under the Crown Colony statutes, executive and legislative powers were vested in the governor, who was appointed by the British Crown, and in the Crown Council, the majority of whose members were appointed by the governor. Additional members were elected from the local land-owning class. The political system was therefore responsible to the British government and not to the people it governed. Thus the government was not sensitive nor responsive to the needs of the people, and the people had no legal means of influencing the political system. Universal adult suffrage was not granted in Jamaica until 1944. This came as a result of the agitation for political representation and self-government, which began in the late nineteenth century and escalated in the 1930s.[3]

The cultural alienation that existed (and still continues at some levels) in Jamaican society is best illustrated by the tension between what Rex Nettleford calls "the melody of Europe, and the rhythm of Africa."[4] According to Nettleford, although the Jamaican populace is mostly of African descent and tends to act according to the rhythms (modes of being and acting) of their African heritage, the people find themselves in a situation where African cultural mores and expressions are defined as crude and uncultured, and European values and mores are defined as civilized and desirable. What is patent in this cultural situation is the imposition of the European ideology of white supremacy upon Afro-Jamaicans. University of the West Indies social scientist Aggrey Brown refers to this situation as "cultural invasion." He writes, "The invaders penetrate the cultural context of another group in disrespect of the latter's potentialities; they impose their own view of the world upon those they invade and inhibit the creativity of the invaded by curbing their expression."[5]

Leahcim Semaj, an adherent of Rastafari and a social scientist, refers to the imposition of European values on the black masses in Jamaica as "cultural imperialism." Cultural imperialism occurs when one group imposes its definition of reality, via "theories, concepts and ideas—metaphysics, epistemology, ethics and even aesthetics—on another."[6] According to Semaj, cultural imperialism in Jamaica was even more effective than physical and economic oppression. While these overt forms of oppression met constant resistance, there was widespread acceptance of the ideas that associate whiteness with beauty, goodness, and God and that associate blackness with ugliness, evil, and the devil. Even the black intelligentsia, Semaj points out, accepted European cultural values and found themselves aping European aesthetics in music, the visual and performing arts, and grooming. The end result was an endemic lack of self-knowledge and healthy self-identity among Afro-Jamaicans.[7] Thus the context in which Rastafari emerged and to which it responded was the denigration of African cultural heritage, values, and forms and the imposition of cultural values, associated with Great Britain.

These economic, political, and cultural conditions culminated in a period of unrest in the 1920s and 1930s and drew three clear-cut reactions from the Jamaican populace. The first reaction highlighted mainly the interests of the working class, culminated in the strikes and mass demonstrations of 1938, and crystallized into the trade union movement. The second reaction reflected the desire of the middle class to control the political institutions of the country, found expression in the agitation for universal adult suffrage and internal self-government, and culminated in the political independence of Jamaica in 1962. The third reaction brought to the fore the frustration and disillusionment of the unemployed and underemployed. Grounded in the history of folk resistance to the imposition of European values on the black masses, this reaction articulated a profound rejection of Jamaica as the place to achieve human fulfillment, while embracing the lure of Africa as the paradisiacal homeland. Rastafari is the embodiment of this third reaction.

Historical Roots

According to Willner, the event precipitating the emergence of charismatic activities involves a crisis that heightens the tensions already rife in the society. She seems to think that the event that acts as a catalyst for the charismatic eruption is usually negative. However, although the hardships of the 1920s and 1930s were indeed part of the precipitant situations, the crowning of Ras Tafari (his original name) as Haile Selassie, emperor of Ethiopia, was the main catalytic event that called the Rastafarian movement into existence. To understand why the crowning of Haile Selassie took on such significance, we have to recognize that Rastafari has its historical roots within the liberative struggles of the African diaspora, and that those who founded the movement regarded Selassie as the one who would bring these struggles to fruition. In Jamaica, this tradition of struggle is best exemplified by the radicalism of African and Afro-Christian faiths, by the ideology of Ethiopianism, and by Garveyism, all of which fed the Rastafarian movement and shaped its essential posture as well as many elements of its beliefs.

African and Afro-Christian faiths have a consistent tradition of what musician Bob Marley calls "resisting against the system."[8] At the ideational/spiritual level, this resistance was evident in their maintenance of an African-oriented world view, one that defined the social realities in ways other than those provided by their European masters. In this respect, African religion with its myths, values, and rituals formed the basis for identity and meaning in an otherwise alienating situation. But beyond giving the slaves and former slaves a sense of identity, their African religion provided them with an ideological platform from which to launch their resistance against their white masters. For example, from the point of view of the slaves in Jamaica, slavery was an evil that had its origin in the sorcery of the white masters. Thus "myalism," which has its roots in African religions, became an instrument for counteracting the sorcery of the slave masters.[9] Myalism is often confused with or subsumed under "obeah" because it is an art of dealing with the spirit world. However, in the strictest sense, myal is really the opposite of obeah. While obeah is the art of putting hexes on people, usually with an evil intent, myalism is the art of removing hexes or making people immune to them. The slaves believed that slavery was some kind of hex that their masters had placed on them. By their myal art, they sought to break that hex.

Even when Africans converted to Christianity, the elements of Christianity to which they showed the greatest affinity were those that reinforced their Afrocentric world view, informed their struggle for liberation, and promised them eventual freedom from and redress of the evil perpetrated against them by the colonial system. Thus we find in Afro-Christian religions a preoccupation with baptism, belief in spirits (angels, demons, and the spirits of the dead), messianic eschatology, and biblical apocalypticism.[10]

At the sociopolitical level, African and Afro-Christian religions were the milieu in which uprisings against slavery and colonialism were fomented. The religious beliefs of the slaves often inspired violent insurgence. For example, myalism seems to have been at the heart of the Tacky Rebellion (1760), one of the most violent slave insurrections in Jamaica's plantation history. It was carried out by slaves who believed that the potions they received from Tacky, their leader, had made them immune to the white men's weapons.[11] The 1831 rebellion, aimed at destroying the plantation owners and securing freedom for the slaves, was inspired and orchestrated by Sam Sharpe, who was a "daddy,"[12] or priest, in the slave religion and at the same time a deacon in the Baptist church. In addition, Paul Bogle, another deacon in the Baptist church, incited and led the Morant Bay Rebellion of 1865. The nexus between religion and resistance continued with Alexander Bedward, who lived in the late nineteeth and early twentieth centuries, and who was one of the most colorful figures in this Afro-Christian tradition. He labeled the white oppressors as evil and called for people of African descent to rise up and crush this evil. Because of his agitation against the Jamaican establishment in the early twentieth century, he was arrested and jailed for treason.

Though Rastafari rejects certain elements of African and Afro-Christian religions, Rastafarian Afrocentricity, messianism, predilection for biblical apocalypticism, and militancy are all influenced by the tradition of resistance in the African and Afro-Christian religions. Furthermore, Rastas frequently invoke the examples of Sharpe and Bogle in their struggle against European domination.

The most cursory reading of the literature on Rastafari or the most passing personal acquaintance with the movement will reveal that Ethiopia looms large in its philosophy. But Rastafari did not create its Ethiopianism ex nihilo. Rastafari's Ethiopianism has been shaped by ideas that existed in the African diaspora for at least two hundred years prior to the advent of Rastafari. Historically, Ethiopianism conflates *Ethiopia* with Africa (using the appellation *Ethiopia* to mean Africa in general).[13] This identification is supported by a 1542 map taken from the *Geographia* of Claudius and edited by Sebastian Muenster. On this map, the word AETHIOPIA is inscribed across the land mass we now know as Africa. Hamharich is the name given to the area that is roughly equivalent to present-day Ethiopia.[14]

Ethiopianism in the African diaspora has long celebrated the greatness of Ethiopia/Africa. Ethiopia, with its long history and religious tradition, came to represent the pride of Africa and Africans everywhere.[15] Thus H. Easton and J. C. Pennington in their writings extolled and celebrated the greatness of ancient Ethiopia.[16] Behind the back-to-Africa movements of the nineteenth century and behind the emergence of black churches with a conscious emphasis on Ethiopia/Africa in the eighteenth and nineteenth centuries was this tradition of extolling the greatness of Ethiopia/Africa.[17] Edward Wilmot Blyden, an early Pan-Africanist and a fervent proponent of "back to Africa," claimed that in the glories of the African past Ethiopia represented the zenith of learning and civilization.[18] This tradition was of course fed by the Sheba legend, which traced Ethiopia's religion and monarchy to Menelik, who is believed to have been born to Solomon and the queen of Sheba.[19]

In addition to the identification of Ethiopia with Africa and the celebration of the greatness of Ethiopia, Ethiopianism espoused a vision of African liberation and a future Ethiopian empire.[20] In this respect, Psalm 68:31, "Princes shall come out of Egypt; Ethiopia shall soon stretch out her hands unto God," was interpreted as a prophecy of African redemption. Casely Hayford, author of *Ethiopia Unbounded*, held out hope of an "African racial redemption." Furthermore, Hayford referred to Edward Wilmot Blyden, who repatriated to Liberia and became a distinguished professor and statesman, as "God descended upon the earth to teach the Ethiopians anew the way of life."[21]

Explicit Ethiopianism in Jamaica had its beginning in the eighteenth century with George Liele, a former slave from the United States who introduced the Baptist faith to Jamaica.[22] Liele's sermons, which highlighted the African and Ethiopian elements in the Bible, usually began with the call, "Arise ye sons of Ethiopia."[23] Liele and his colleague, Moses Baker, attracted a large following and established what is known as the Native Baptist church. The arrival of British Baptist missionaries was an attempt to dispel the "confusion" of the Native Baptists concerning the essence of Christianity.[24] Obviously, what disturbed the British Baptist missionaries was the unabashed emphasis on Ethiopia and Africa and on salvation as sociopolitical liberation. Despite the efforts of the missionaries, Ethiopianism flourished, and before long some Jamaicans began claiming to be Ethiopians, some even tracing their lineage to Ethiopian royalty.[25] By the early twentieth century, there was a groundswell of preoccupation with Ethiopia among Jamaicans of African descent.[26] The significance of George Liele and the Native Baptist movement is that they blended Afrocentricity, biblical messianism, and apocalypticism with Ethiopianism to create a liberative vision among Jamaicans of African descent.

In Marcus Garvey and the international grassroots movement he founded, all of the elements of Ethiopianism converged. For Garvey, Ethiopia is either interchangeable with or representative of Africa. Nowhere is this more evident than in the anthem of the Universal Negro Improvement Association (UNIA), which is entitled, "Ethiopia, Thou Land of Our Fathers."[27] To counter the ideology of white racism, Garvey pointed to the history of the great civilizations in Africa. He recalled a time when "Egypt, Ethiopia and Timbuctoo towered in their civilization, towered above Europe, towered above Asia. When Europe was inhabited by a race of cannibals, a race of savages, naked men, heathens and pagans, Africa was peopled with a race of cultured black men."[28]

Garvey's aim was the creation of a new "Africa for the Africans—this is, that the Negro people of the world should concentrate upon the object of building for themselves a great nation in Africa."[29] This project of rebuilding Africa was foretold, Garvey believed, in the words of the psalmist: "Princes shall come out of Egypt; Ethiopia shall soon stretch out her hands unto God."[30] Garvey's own longing was for the day when the people of the African diaspora could "lay down our burden and rest our weary backs and feet by the banks of the Niger and sing our songs and chant our hymns to the God of Ethiopia."[31]

As Dale Bisnauth points out, the early leaders of the Rastafarian movement, by their acquaintance with Pan-Africanist movements in general and Garveyism in particular, must have been cognizant of the ideas of Ethiopianism.[32] Arguing that Ethiopianism permeated all movements for liberation of the African diaspora, Robert Hill concludes, "The origin of Rastafari is bound up . . . with the identification which blacks have consistently made with Ethiopia by virtue of its Biblical symbolism."[33]

That Rastafari has its roots in the Afrocentric movements that preceded

it is underscored by the fact that the nascent movement drew its leadership and following mostly from former Garveyites or from those who
were in some way influenced by Garveyism. The Rastas regard Garvey as
a prophet and cite his supposed prediction regarding the crowning of a
king in Africa as proof of Haile Selassie's divinity.[34] That the crowning of
Selassie drove the first confessors of Selassie's divinity to their Bibles further underscores Rastafari's links with its predecessors. The purpose for
searching the Bible was to see if they could find any evidence that Selassie
was the fulfillment of a prophecy concerning their liberation. As it turned
out, the title taken by Haile Selassie at his coronation seems almost calculated to encourage them to find proof of his messianic identity. Part of his
title was "Ras Tafari, son of Ras Makonem of Harar, King of Ethiopia,
Haile Selassie,[35] King of Kings, Lord of Lords, Conquering Lion of the
Tribe of Judah."[36] Several biblical texts (Rev. 5:2–5; 19:16; and 1 Tim.
4:13–14 are examples) about the "king of kings, lord of lords" and the
"lion of the tribe of Judah" proved to those steeped in biblicism and
"proof texting" that Haile Selassie was indeed the messiah prophesied in
the Bible and hoped for in the African diaspora.

Against this background of messianic eschatology, biblical apocalypticism, and the tradition of Ethiopianism, it becomes quite understandable
why the crowning of Emperor Haile Selassie took on the significance it
did among a certain group of Jamaicans. The genius of the early exponents of Rastafari was their ability to combine Ethiopianism with biblical
apocalypticism and messianic eschatology to identify Selassie as the messiah, who would effect the liberation of Africans everywhere and recreate
the glorious African/Ethiopian past. Dale Bisnauth's observation is to the
point: "The Rastafarians used their spiritual genius to translate the dreams
of Garvey and the Pan-Africanists into the messianic and millenarian
terms of the Bible."[37]

Charismatic Personality

Establishing the charismatic personalities behind the emergence of the
Rastafarian movement is complicated by the fact that little is known of
most of the early exponents. The situation is further complicated by the
fact that from the beginning the movement was never united under the
leadership of a single person or group of persons who were acting in concert. Several people, seemingly without previous contact with each other,
began to proclaim Selassie as the divine messianic liberator of the African
race between 1930 and 1933.[38] The only explanations for such a convergence of ideas are the common sources that they share in the Afro-

Christian and Ethiopianist traditions and the prevailing, heightened sense of Africa and African liberation brought about by the Garvey movement. The most famous of these exponents include Leonard Howell, Joseph Nathaniel Hibbert, Henry Archibald Dunkley, and Robert Hinds.[39]

Though all of these men seemed to have come to the conviction of Selassie's divinity independently, Howell appears to have been the first to introduce the idea to the public. He soon catapulted himself to a place of prominence by the effectiveness of his preaching in attracting followers and by his penchant for drawing the attention of the civil authorities. From the records that we have of him and his activities, Howell clearly cast himself in the role of a charismatic messenger of God (Selassie) and even claimed to be divine himself. His followers clearly perceived him to be an extraordinary leader, who deserved their loyalty.

Before profiling Howell as a charismatic leader, I would like to outline his activities briefly, since he was the most significant personality in the first thirty years of the Rastafarian movement. From 1933 to 1940 Howell expounded the doctrines of Rastafari between Kingston and St. Thomas. Robert Hill describes Howell during this time as the "catalytic agent in igniting the radical millenarian consciousness that based itself on the doctrine of the divine kingship of Ethiopia's Ras Tafari."[40] During this time, Howell, through the use of "powerful propaganda and personal charisma," secured a following much larger than any other exponent of Rastafari.[41] Howell's message, especially in St. Thomas, was revolutionary in its import. To his followers, he advocated hatred of and violence against the white ruling class as revenge for their years of oppressing black people. He declared the African race superior to the white race. He admonished his followers to withdraw allegiance from the British Crown, to be loyal only to Haile Selassie, the supreme being and the only true ruler of the African race, and to prepare for repatriation to their African homeland.[42] To buttress his doctrine of repatriation, in December 1933, he sold picture postcards of Emperor Haile Selassie, which were supposed to be passports to Ethiopia.[43] The colonial authorities, recognizing the inflammatory nature and revolutionary potential of Howell's message, arrested and convicted him on a charge of sedition. He was sentenced to a two-year prison term.

After his release from prison, Howell formed the Ethiopian Salvation Society, supposedly a branch of a society of the same name in the United States. He purchased "Pinnacle"—an abandoned colonial estate in Sligoville, St. Catherine—on behalf of the society. In 1940 he established a Rastafarian commune at Pinnacle with a group of his followers, variously estimated to number between five hundred and two thousand.[44] The commune supported itself by growing local food crops and growing and trading ganja (marijuana).

Howell exercised autocratic leadership over this commune and kept it isolated from the rest of Jamaican society. Although his purpose seems to have been to escape the gaze and pressure of the establishment, he soon drew its attention because of repeated reports that Rastas were harassing the peasant farmers who lived in the environs of Pinnacle. In 1941, the police raided the commune and arrested and charged a number of its members with perpetrating violence against their neighbors and with producing and selling ganja. Howell, who at first eluded the police by allegedly miraculous means, was eventually arrested on a charge of assault and sent to jail for another two years.[45]

Howell returned to the commune in 1943, and from then to 1954, he administered the commune with even stricter security, the main components of which were his "belocksed" guardsmen and a breed of vicious watchdogs. The approaches to the commune were manned by these guardsmen and dogs, and the presence of strangers was signaled by the sounding of gongs.[46] Because of the alleged persistence of the harassment and intimidation of the people in the neighborhood by members of the commune and because of the colonial government's paranoia concerning the commune becoming a guerrilla training camp, the police again raided Pinnacle in 1954. This time, they demolished the buildings in the commune and scattered its members, a significant number of whom ended up in the slums of Kingston.[47] Howell was again arrested, but this time he was acquitted on appeal. However, this event marked the end of his tenure as the "leading light" in the Rastafarian movement.[48] In 1960 he was interned in a mental hospital, and after his release, he lived in relative obscurity until his death in 1981.[49]

During his period of prominence, Howell exhibited many of the characteristics that Weber associates with the charismatic persona. He was at the forefront of a movement that rejected the legitimacy of the Jamaican colonial system and called for allegiance to a new authority, namely, Haile Selassie. In this way, Howell became a prophetic voice, articulating the new doctrine of Selassie's divinity, declaring the certain downfall of the colonial establishment, and inspiring hope of repatriation to Ethiopia/ Africa.[50] In his prophetic role, Howell directly projected himself as the emissary of Emperor Haile Selassie, the divine king and the latest manifestation of God on earth.[51] According to an account by one of his early followers, Howell portrayed himself as the Christ, sent from his father, Haile Selassie. The same follower quoted Howell as saying:

I am the Ambassador of Ethiopia, Addis Ababa is the capital, it's where I am from. My father sent me to promulgate his work. Don't be afraid, I am here and shall be with you forever. . . . I am the same Jesus Christ that was crucified. I was buried but not dead, the breath of life is mine. I am the giver of life through my father.[52]

Howell also presented himself as—and was believed by his followers to be—a man of extraordinary or divine endowments, including healing and prophetic powers.[53] Even those who knew him before his assumption of the role of ambassador of Selassie held similar views of him. An official of the Universal Negro Improvement Association, Z. Munro Scarlett, who was acquainted with Howell when he lived in New York, described him as a mystic, that is, a person who is in touch with or can manipulate the spirit world. Hope L. Howell claimed that his brother Leonard P. Howell was a healer (in the Jamaican myal/balmyard tradition) who helped many people while he was living in New York.[54] One of his early followers, Jephet Wilson, described Howell as a prophet who possessed secret powers and who brought the "light" of Rastafari.[55]

To enhance his image as a specially endowed prophet, Howell assumed a "ritual personality" named Gangunguru Maragh,[56] with *Gangunguru* meaning "teacher of famed wisdom" and *Maragh* meaning "king." At Pinnacle this title was used in its abbreviated form, "Gong."[57] The obvious claim is that Howell was the enlightened one and the bearer of enlightenment to his followers.

True to Weber's portrayal of the charismatic leader, Howell was able to elicit total devotion from his followers. Robert Hill highlights the fact that people were willing to dispose of their possessions and part with families and friends to join him at Pinnacle. At Pinnacle everyone gave unwavering allegiance to the Gong, whose words carried the force of law. They even accorded him ritual devotion, as shown by the appearance of his name in Rastafarian songs. This devotion was so great that he was regarded as Christ reincarnated.[58]

Howell clearly qualifies as a charismatic figure who was able to embody and articulate the feelings and hopes of those who were caught in the throes of social stress and who was able to secure the allegiance of a significant following for more than twenty years. The loss of his status as a charismatic leader may have been brought about by three factors. The first two relate to Weber's idea that the maintenance of charismatic status depends on the ability of the charismatic personality to deliver on his promises. Howell obviously failed to effect the return to Africa, which was part of his message from the beginning and for which he sold picture postcards of Haile Selassie (as supposed passports) as early as 1933. And despite his claim of divine powers, Howell was unable to protect himself and his followers from the wrath of the civil authorities. Repeated raids, arrests, beatings, and imprisonments eventually eroded belief in his extraordinary qualities. The third factor was infighting among the Rastas concerning certain practices, especially spiritual divination (which was apparently practiced by Howell). The most outspoken opposition to divination came from young Rastas who belonged to a group called the House of Youth Black Faith, which emerged in 1949. Those opposed to this practice seemed to have held sway, and dabbling with spirits in any form became taboo in the movement. This, in effect, constituted a rejection of Howell and may help to explain his downfall as the foremost leader in the movement.[59]

Summary

In this chapter, I have pointed to those sociohistorical conditions to which Rastafari is a response. The movement emerged as a response to economic, political, and cultural subjugation, as well as to the perception of Haile Selassie as the messianic liberator longed for in the African diaspora. Here we have an example of the frustration-eruption formula that Willner describes as the necessary precondition for charismatic eruption. In this chapter, I also highlighted the fact that Rastafari draws from sources that have deep roots in black resistance in general and in Jamaica's African and Afro-Christian religions in particular. This illustrates my contention that charismatic messages do not usually emerge ex nihilo from the minds of charismatic leaders. Indeed, they usually have a novel combination of ideas, but they are frequently synthesizing ideas already current in some sector of the society, and this is one of the reasons charismatic leaders are able to secure a following. Their ideas resonate with some people in the society. Rastafarian Afrocentricity was adopted and adapted from ideas long circulated in Jamaica concerning the role of Ethiopia in the history of Africa and in the future of Africans in the diaspora. Finally, I have outlined the career and characteristics of the most distinguished leader of the movement in its nascent stages. Howell clearly matches Weber's image of the prophet who "takes the responsibility for announcing a *break* with the established normative order"[60] and for calling people to espouse a new view of the world, to adopt new values, and to embrace a new lifestyle.

Babylon and Dread Revitalization

Part of the impetus for social change inherent in charisma comes from its antiestablishment nature. As was noted in chapter 1, charisma and the movement it spawns generally refuse to accept the legitimacy of the status quo. In Weber's words, charisma "transforms all values, . . . breaks all traditional and rational norms," and "overturns all notions of sanctity."[1] Anthony Wallace expresses a similar point of view concerning the antiestablishment nature of charisma in his theory of revitalization. He defines a revitalization movement "as a deliberate, organized, conscious effort by members of society to construct a more satisfying culture."[2] The need for revitalization or cultural innovation arises when members of the society as a whole, or subgroups within that society, perceive the normative order as no longer capable of satisfying their needs or as inimical to their well-being.[3]

Both Weber and Wallace, therefore, highlight how the rejection of the status quo and the attempt to create a new social reality are characteristic of charismatic movements. When the interpretation of the significance of Rastafari is approached from this perspective, it becomes quite clear that the movement is a conscious attempt to deal with the historical experience of colonialism and its contemporary legacies. From this perspective, Rastafari represents an attempt of the African soul to free itself from the alienating fetters of colonial domination and exploitation and to recreate itself in the image of Africa.

In the light of the foregoing discussion, this chapter focuses on the Rastas' ideological assault on the culture and institutions that have dominated the people of the African diaspora since the Middle Passage.[4] In this respect, I discuss Rastafari's portrayal of *Babylon*, the term the movement uses to express the conviction that the social, political, and economic institutions that have shaped their historical and day-to-day experiences are evil and must be overcome. This chapter also focuses on the Rastas' attempts to create an alternative culture to overcome their sense of alienation. I will outline elements crucial to the Rastafarian project to construct a new reality, the creation of a distinct Rastafarian culture or way of life as part of an attempt to put distance between Rastas and Babylon.

"Beating Down Babylon": Ideological Delegitimation

Rastafari is first and foremost a response to the Babylonian conditions of the Jamaican society and, by extension, of the whole Western world. The Rastafarian phenomenon was forged in the crucible of oppression that started in plantation slavery and that has persisted in post-emancipation and postcolonial Jamaica. The manner in which some experienced and perceived the realities of the colonial society called forth the response and shaped the perspective of Rastafari. Every belief that has been espoused, from the divinity of Haile Selassie to the precepts of *ital* (organic, natural, vital) living, and every ritual that has developed, from Nyabinghi drumming to the sacramental use of ganja (marijuana), constitute an attempt to escape from or deal with the reality of oppression in Babylon. The centrality of the concept of Babylon to Rastafari cannot be overstated, since it highlights the Rastafarian perception of the context of their suffering and struggle. Escaping, overcoming, or "beating down Babylon" is paramount on the agenda of Rastafari.

Ernest Cashmore, discussing the Rastafarian movement in terms of the social construction of reality theory of Peter Berger and Thomas Luckmann, maintains that the construction of the Rastafarian social reality begins with the delegitimation of the status quo,[5] or the assigning of a negative status to the establishment in which the African diaspora has lived since its deportation from Africa:

> The appeal of the Rastafarian theory lay in the range of effects imputed to a single malevolent cause—Babylon. This was the source of all evil in the world and its destruction would presage the start of what Rastas called "the new age," the entry into Zion.[6]

Cashmore goes on to point out that Rastas interpret the whole history of contact with white people "in terms of a systematic denial of freedom, material and cognitive, and every event in the development of colonialism was a recycle of the same pattern."[7] Thus "the mechanics of colonialism" worked to suppress "the black man's realization of his own gifts and capacities."[8]

Echoing Cashmore, Patrick Taylor describes Rastafari as a "symbolic system which constructs patterns of meaning and brings order to the contradictions of social reality."[9] The social reality that the Rastas see as needing ordering is the colonial history and its legacy, which have denied the Africans in the diaspora their dignity. As part of the effort to construct new "patterns of meaning" to bring coherence to their existence, they have unleashed an ideological assault on the Jamaican and Western establishment by dubbing it "Babylon."

The Background and Signification of Babylon

The term *Babylon* is loaded with biblical significance. It has its origin with Babel, the world's first city, according to Genesis 11. The Bible intimates that egomania and the desire for cultural homogeneity led Babel's leaders to embark on a project to build a tower that would reach up to heaven. According to Rastafarian interpretation, the effort to reach up to heaven was born from a desire to topple God from a position of lordship over the world. Because of this attempt to build a monument to themselves, the inhabitants of Babel were thrown into linguistic confusion and dispersed geographically.

The city-state was later revived and became Babylon of Mesopotamia, a world power that dominated the Near East. On one of its military campaigns, it ransacked Jerusalem, killing many Hebrews and taking many others into captivity. This inaugurated the Babylonian exile of the Jewish people. In Daniel's apocalyptic vision, Babylon appears as the "Great Beast" and as the head of the great statue, which is destroyed by a stone cut out of the mountain.[10] With reference to Babylon of Mesopotamia, the Bible again focuses on the egomania of its leaders, exemplified by Nebuchadnezzar's golden image of himself, which he required all of his subjects to worship. Furthermore, the Bible points to "violence, sexual and moral degeneracy" as characteristic of the Babylonian civilization.[11]

The New Testament invokes the imagery of Babylon to describe the Roman Empire because of its opposition to the early church and its persecution of Christians and Jews. In other words, the writer of Revelation sees in the Roman state the spirit of selfishness and opposition to God and his people that was displayed by the city of Babel and by the ancient Babylonian civilization.[12]

Rastas may differ concerning many of their beliefs, including the divinity of Selassie and repatriation, but all agree on the Babylonian nature of life in the West. The experience of forced captivity in the West paralleled the Babylonian experience of the ancient Hebrews, and the constant subjugation recalled the Roman iron rule over its empire. Hence, Rastas find the spirit of Babylon alive in the twentieth and twenty-first centuries and operative in and through the ideology and institutions of the West in general and of Jamaica in particular. The Rastafarian choice of Babylon as the symbolic designation of the forces that seek to dehumanize them is, in effect, an attempt to neutralize those forces. As already stated, the use of the term *Babylon* constitutes a symbolic delegitimation of those values and institutions that historically have exercised control over the masses of the African diaspora.

According to John Paul Homiak, who researched the role of eldership in the Nyabinghi Order,[13] Babylon is

> a term of varying levels of concreteness and specificity; historically, the predecessors of the Romans and the entire white European colonial world; presently, the entire post-colonial western power structure and its supporting ideology and political apparatus; the oppressive condition of "exile" in the Black diaspora; the cosmic domain presided over by the pope of Rome and his Anglo-European political cohorts; the source of death-dealing and destructive spiritual power.[14]

As indicated by Homiak's definition, the term *Babylon* has several levels of application. The most immediate referent is the gut-wrenching experiences of suffering, hardship, and estrangement faced by the underside of Jamaican society. It is not only the pain of economic hardship, but a sense of not belonging, of cultural alienation. It is a feeling of uprootedness and of being "out of whack" with one's environment. This sense of being in exile recalls and parallels the experience of the forced deportation of the ancient Hebrews under the Babylonian world power. Reggae musician Bob Andy expresses this feeling of exile when he sings, "I've got to go back home; This couldn't be my home."[15] Rastafarian intellectual Dennis Forsythe sums up this aspect of the Babylonian experience:

> The Rastafarian imagery of Babylon is the first-person, gut-level experiences of alienation and frustration under slavery, colonialism and their legacies. It is not an imposed concept, but one that has grown out of the gut feelings and experiences of "souls on ice," and of dismembered beings. Babylon is the psychic image sustained by real life experiences, busted hopes, broken dreams, the blues of broken homes and of disjointed tribes of people trapped by history. It is an image of fire and blood, of being on the edge, in limbo, in the wilderness, in concrete jungles. . . . It is a desolation in which man feels disjointed and out of line with the plans of creation.[16]

Reggae's most famous superstar, Bob Marley, echoes Forsythe's feeling of alienation in even more terse language: "I've been down on the rock so, I seem to wear a permanent screw."[17] Obviously, the contortion of the visage manifests the contortion of an alienated spirit.

At the sociopolitical level, Babylon is primarily used in reference to ideological and structural components of Jamaica's social system, which metes out privileges to some and exploitation to others. In this respect, Babylon is the complex of economic, political, religious, and educational institutions and values that evolved from the colonial experiment. The church and the police get honorable mention. The church is labeled an arm of the Babylon system because of its ideological justification of the status quo and its brainwashing of the populace. The police are considered Babylon's agents, because through their use of force, they maintain the pattern of oppression and inequity in the society.

Rastas understand that Jamaica is but a part of an international colonial/imperialist complex. Hence the designation Babylon is extended to the Anglo-American alliance, which has received the benefits of colonialism and international capitalism.[18] These two power centers, through their domination of international politics and their exploitative relationship with the rest of the world, demonstrate that they are the successors to the ancient Babylonians and Romans. Babylon is, therefore, "the whole complex of institutions which conspire to keep the black man enslaved in the Western world and which attempt to subjugate coloured [sic] people throughout the world."[19]

Globally, Babylon is that worldly state of affairs in which the struggle for power and money takes precedence over the cultivation of human freedom and the concern for human dignity. Rastas include in this state of affairs not only the West, led by the Anglo-American alliance, but also the former Soviet bloc and the politically powerful Catholic church presided over by the pope. Many Rastas believe that the political leaders of the world derive their authority from the pope, and they cite the frequent visits of world leaders to the Vatican as evidence for their position.[20]

At the highest level of generality, Babylon is the forces of evil arrayed against God and the righteous (Selassie, Rastas, and the poor). The forces of evil, however, are not metaphysical entities, but human attitudes and activities that are out of touch with the divine, natural order. Any human activity that is inimical to harmonious human relationships is a reflection of Babylonian values. This includes nuclear proliferation and the overexploitation of natural resources, which threaten human existence and the continued viability of the world's ecosystems. In this context, Babylon is not a specific locality or a specific social system, but any "system of thought and behavior" or any "general cultural pattern in which men find themselves trapped" and out of touch with Jah (God or Haile Selassie) and the reality of Rastafari.[21]

Features of the Babylon System

Since Rastas do not have official theologians or social theorists to codify and systematize their beliefs, there is a lack of systemic treatment of the Rastas' point of view on any subject. This is particularly true of their treatment of Babylon. However, in their limited writings and particularly in their poetry and reggae lyrics, their evocative images address various aspects of Babylonian reality.

HISTORICAL ATROCITY   Rastas can recite almost ad infinitum the historical atrocities of Babylon, from its days as a Middle Eastern world power to its contemporary Euro-American manifestation. As the conqueror of the ancient world, Babylon wreaked havoc on Jerusalem and deported the ancient Hebrews (who the Rastafarians believe to have been black people) to Mesopotamia. The Roman Empire, a later incarnation of Babylon, made incursions into Africa, conquered the African queen Dido, fought Hannibal, and sacked Carthage. Rome, the Beast of Revelation, persecuted Christians and executed Jews. In more recent history, Mussolini, the Roman, invaded Ethiopia with the blessing of the pope.[22] The implication of the Catholic church in the invasion of Ethiopia and its role in the enslavement of Africans in the Americas gives rise to the Rastafarian view of the church as an institution of oppression for black people.

Most painful for Rastas is the Middle Passage and the subsequent suffering in modern Babylon. In "Redemption Song," Bob Marley describes the experience of enslavement as Africans being stolen by pirates and sold to merchant ships, which transported them to America, where they have struggled every day to survive in the crucible of oppression.[23] The manner in which Rastas speak of the Middle Passage and the slave experience reveals that they still bear the psychic scars of those experiences. They seem to reach back across the years to feel the pain and indignity of everything that befell their forebears, and thus, they are able to speak of such experiences in the first person, as though they underwent them personally. In "Slave Driver," Bob Marley gives evidence of such a psychic scar by speaking of his blood running cold at the memory of them slave driver's whip and the squalor and stench of the holds of the slave.[24] Burning Spear, another Rastafarian reggae singer, echoes the same theme in a passion-filled tone, when he asks his audience repeatedly, "Do you remember the days of slavery?"[25]

Babylon's predilection for atrocity remains unabated into the twentieth century, exemplified by the millions killed in two world wars, the Holocaust, Soviet labor camps, the killing fields of Vietnam, the Gulf War, apartheid in South Africa, and "ethnic cleansing" in Africa and the Baltic. What is more, the evil powers of the world continue to increase their capacity for monstrosity, especially in the proliferation of nuclear arms and precision instruments of mass destruction. Bob Marley clearly expresses the Rastafarian foreboding about the twentieth century's predilection for violence. In "Survival," he lashes out against the use of science and technology to perfect instruments of death, to threaten human well-being, and to create and spread fear everywhere.[26]

At a more personal and immediate level, Babylon continues its atrocity in the brutal treatment of those who threaten or are perceived as threatening the system. State oppression of grassroots movements for social and political change is the most egregious form of this barbarity. Rastas have personally experienced this oppression at the hands of police both in Jamaica and abroad. Rastas often refer to the police simply as "Babylon," or describe them as "dressed in uniforms of brutality."[27] As Cashmore observes, "The police more than any other group personified the Rastafarian conception of evil. They were the living proof that Babylon was alive, active and waiting for any opportunity to suppress them; they constitute the empirical referents to the Babylon conspiracy theory."[28] This conception was formed in the crucible of repeated persecution, intimidation, and harassment of Rastas by the Jamaican police. Sometimes, police brutality was in response to the slightest provocation from Rastas, and at other times, it was at the whim or caprice of police officers. The police, as Babylon's frontline agents, are responsible for defending and protecting the system. Along with their brutality, the police and the entire judicial system use trickery and cunning to keep the black masses in their places. As frontliners, the police are mere puppets in the hands of the custodians of the system. Cashmore quotes a young English Rasta as saying, "Them just respond to the needs of Babylon, wearing 'the badge of brutality.'"[29]

ECONOMIC RAPACITY   Exploitation is written large in the economic history of Jamaica. It began with the Spanish colonists and continued with the British, whose plantation economies were fueled by slave labor. Emancipation from slavery did nothing for the economic empowerment of the black masses, who were either still tied to the plantation as cheap laborers or left to eke out a living on the marginal lands not considered fit for plantation use. In the twentieth century, the Jamaican economy was dominated by British and American capital in agriculture, light manufacturing, mining, and tourism. The availability of cheap labor was always at the forefront of making Jamaica attractive for investors.

Rastas' critique of the Jamaican economic system, and capitalism in general, is directed at the fact that it is based on the ethic of profiteering and exploitation. The Rastafarian view is succinctly expressed in two of Marley's most powerful images. One refers to the Jamaican and capitalist economic state of affairs as "Pimper's Paradise."[30] The point is clear. Here is an economic system that justifies the profiting of some at the expense of others. The prostitutes—those who labor in the enterprises of others— sell themselves not so much for their own profit, but for the profit of their pimps, those who control the economic system. The other image is that of a blood-sucking vampire extracting the life forces from its victims.[31] By describing the Babylon system as a vampire, Marley highlights the predatory nature of Babylon's economic system and its deadly effects on the poor. Changing metaphors but addressing the same theme, Marley portrays the guardians of Babylon's economy as greedy landowners who expropriate all the produce of their tenants while treating them with disdain.[32] Again, Marley's message is clear. The economic philosophy and institutions of Babylon sanction the exploitation of the poor and justify the avarice and profiting of the well-to-do.

Rastas argue that exploitation destroys any sense of communality. Economic activities in Babylon become a struggle for the survival of the fittest, a struggle in which people trample one another to get ahead. Bob Marley gently laments over such behavior by likening it to a race in which rats trample each other to get ahead.[33] The competitive and exploitative nature of Babylon's economy has led many Rastas, especially in the early days of the movement, to refuse to work for any Babylonian enterprise, choosing instead to hustle, to work at subsistence farming, or to establish self-help ventures.

MENTAL SLAVERY   According to Rastas, the educational and religious institutions of Babylon specialize in obfuscating the truth and teaching the people "misphilosophy." Thus Rastas are firmly convinced that Babylon's education is contrived to brainwash black people. In the words of one Rasta, "What is taught is untrue, immoral and indoctrination."[34] Bob Marley concurs by calling Babylon's education a brainwashing exercise designed to create ignorance and alienation.[35] The end result of Babylon's education is the "whitewashing" of the African mind, stripping it of its African vibrations (de-Africanization), and inculcating European values, perspectives, and tastes (Europeanization).[36] Walter Rodney claims, "The brainwashing process was so stupendous that it has convinced . . . many black people of their inferiority."[37] For this reason, many early Rastas were reluctant to send their children to school, and when they did, some children were rejected or subjected to abuse on account of their dreadlocks (the distinctive Rastafarian hairstyle consisting of uncombed hair, which is then twisted or matted).[38]

Rastas have taken a posture of resistance against Babylonian education because of its evil intent and its dehumanizing effects. Rastafarian poet, Bongo Jerry pleads for an end to the "double meaning" and "crossword speaking" of the English Language, which lead not only to linguistic confusion but also to cultural alienation.[39] Bob Marley is even more blunt in his expression of resistance to Babylonian education. Declaring that he is resolute in not changing who he is and that the cultural oppression has gone on far too long, he calls on his listeners to stage a rebellion in order to secure and ensure cultural freedom.[40]

The church joins the school in enslaving the people mentally by teaching them to be patriotic and by engaging in philosophical trickery to provide rationalizations for the Babylon system. The church teaches the people to bear their suffering bravely because they have "a pie in the sky when they die," instead of telling them the truth about the forces that conspire to oppress them, thus preparing them to take their liberation into their own hands.[41] This conviction led Marley to declare his feelings about "bombing a church," because of the lying preacher.[42]

When Babylon's educational and religious institutions are not busy enslaving the poor, they are busy training those who, under the guise of middle-class respectability, engage in socially predatory behaviors. Bob Marley speaks of how these institutions teach deception and train "theives and murderers,"[43] Rastas are not impressed with the aura of respectability that seems to surround the educated in Jamaican society. Instead, they are likely to see, under the facade of respectability, con artists who are "slicker" than Anancy, the scheming trickster of Jamaican folklore.

POLITICAL TRICKERY   This leads me to the Rastafarian view of politics, which they refer to as "polytricks" or "politricks":

"Politricks" refers to the Rastafarian perspective on the tricky, deceptive nature of Babylon's political activity. Since Babylonians deal in politricks, they only pretend to be a government which is representative of the people.[44]

This quote captures the essence of the Rastafarian perception of politics. It is not the art of statecraft, but the art of deception, machination, and manipulation. It was from this perspective that a Rasta said, "As far as I am concerned, politics is not the black man's lot, but the white man's plot."[45] Politics, therefore, is but the unending scheming of the powerful to maintain their positions of privilege and to keep the populace in its place. Mikey Smith, a Rastafarian poet, expresses the conviction that politicians engage in deceiving the populace with "lies and secrecy" to fur-

ther their oppression and exploitation of the poor.[46] Bob Marley agrees
with this portrayal of politicians, by describing them as con artists who
use bribery to further their causes.[47]

Since their intention is to deceive, politicians are mired in hypocrisy
describerd by Mikey Smith as "full of complexity an[d] folly formalities like
demockroicy."[48] The politicians must project the image of being public ser-
vants. But in reality, their goal is personal profit and self-aggrandizement.
Thus their civil ceremonies are masquerades—"folly formalities"—and
their claim to govern by democratic principles is a sham, "demockroicy" (a
mockery of the people). Politicians are therefore accomplished con artists
who continually deceive the people while exploiting them.

Beyond being deceptive, Babylon polytricks is divisive. Marley's "Ambush in the Night" describes how the oppressors employ bribery and
the instigation of intercommunity conflicts as elements in their political
strategy.[49] Part of Babylon's strategy of domination is to sow seeds of dis-
cord among the poor and powerless ("divide-and-rule"). By setting them
against one another, Babylon creates a situation where the dominated lack
unity to undertake any collective action to change their situation and to
challenge Babylon's power structure. Rastas have firsthand experience of
this divide-and-rule strategy, because they have seen Jamaican ghetto
youths drafted into political factionalism. Instead of uniting to fight their
common enemy, for meager handouts they fight and gun down one another in the name of allegiance to political parties. That is why most Rastas take a stance of nonparticipation in the political process. Politics in
their estimation is mired in craftiness and corruption, deceit and division.

This analysis of the Rastafarian view of Babylon must be considered
heuristic, because the Rastas see Babylon not so much as an assemblage of
distinct institutions but as a tightly knit system in which each institution
intertwines and interlocks with all of the others. That is why in "Crazy
Baldhead," Bob Marley can address the penal system, the economy, politics, and education—all in conjunction with one another. All of these institutions are contrived and controlled by "those crazy baldheads," people
who are without Rastafarian consciousness and who are agents or instruments of Babylon's schemes.

The Demise of Babylon

Babylon is the "primary symbol for the interpretation and assessment of
the colonial establishment."[50] The import of this symbol lies in the fact
that in one word, Rastas have effectively relegated the Jamaican establishment to the realm of evil, extending to it the same fate that befell ancient
Babylon.[51] But Rastas are not only concerned with analyzing and describ-

ing Babylon, they want to destroy it or at least escape from it. Bob Marley's "Crazy Baldhead" is therefore not a dispassionate analysis of Babylon institutions, but a revolutionary call to "chase those crazy baldheads out of the town."[52] Nor is Marley's "Babylon System" a detached portrayal of its economic system; it is a call to "rebel, rebel, rebel now."[53]

Rastas regard themselves as the agents of Babylon's destruction and reggae music as their primary weapon. Since reggae music is seen as a potent instrument for "chanting down" or "beating down Babylon," reggae musicians and lyricists are regarded as the avant-garde in the struggle against Babylon. As an anti-Babylon musical weapon, reggae has a three-fold significance. First, reggae is the medium through which the people are restored to self-awareness. This is accomplished by telling them the truth about their African roots and African identity, so that they do not have to chase after European trappings and a Western lifestyle in order to achieve a sense of dignity. Second, reggae is the medium through which the people learn the truth about the system under which they live. The reggae lyricists constantly portray the oppressive, deceptive, and divisive nature of Babylon. Third, reggae is the medium through which the poor express their frustrations with and grievances against the political and cultural guardians of Jamaican society and through which they express "their demand for change and the need for a new ordering of society."[54] Rastas and other reggae musicians are the self-appointed voice of the people, the ones who make known their causes to the Babylonian powers. As Linden F. Lewis observes, reggae is the Rastafarian vehicle for "political, cultural, moral and religious purposes and protests."[55] As such, reggae has a particular attraction for blacks, who experience economic exploitation, political marginalization, and racial discrimination in their various societies. Reggae therefore sets the stage for a departure from the Babylonian lifestyle and the eventual demolition of the Babylonian system.

In addition to their belief in the power of reggae to beat down Babylon, Rastas also believe that the demise of Babylon will come about by self-destruction. I Jabulani Tafari puts it pointedly:

Jamaica and the so-called West Indies are part of a white Western Civilization of corruption, which through the soon to be resurrected European-based Roman Empire, represents the iniquitous Mystery, Babylon of antiquity and promotes its decadent devil-devised doctrine to the detriment of deluded mankind and which sinful shitsem [system] will therefore be destroyed in a predestined apocalyptic judgement of volcanic eruptions, earthquakes, lightening bolts, brimstone, molten lava, thunder, plagues, hurricanes, drought, famine, tidal waves, hail and heat waves . . . in short by what could be described as a supernaturally controlled ecological backlash.[56]

Thus the cataclysmic destruction of Babylon will come by its own hands. Its predatory and exploitative relationship with the environment will eventually precipitate an ecological backlash. Furthermore, Babylon's refusal to live naturally and its commitment to artificiality are out of step with the divine principle manifested in nature, and hence it must ultimately self-destruct.

One of the indicators of Babylon's impending doom is that it has no more power over Rastas. Rastas have made the mental and cultural break with Babylon and are in the process of recreating and revitalizing themselves. This is reflected in the Rastafarian phrase "steppin' outa Babylon."

"Steppin' Outa Babylon": Cultural Revitalization

Concomitant with the relegation of Babylon and its ways to the realm of evil is the Rastas' attempt to rescue themselves from the deformities brought on by Babylon. In the process, they have reconstituted their pride, self-confidence, and self-possession, which repudiate the identity forced upon them by their oppressors. It is this "stance of self-possession and assured identity" that has a marked attractiveness to the dispossessed in Jamaica and elsewhere.[57]

Important to an understanding of Rastafari is the recognition that Rastas are aiming at rediscovering their true selves and at creating a cultural identity that synchronizes with their sense of their African past. Nettleford describes this enterprise as a quest in which Rastas are being "liberated from the obscurity of themselves."[58] That is why Leahcim Semaj, a Rastafarian intellectual, identifies the essence of Rastafari as follows:

> In a generic sense a Rastafarian is one who is attempting to restructure identity so that s/he can consciously live from an Africentric [sic] perspective. This covers the physical, mental and spiritual dimensions of life. Rastafari therefore provides a vehicle through which and by which the Africans in the Diaspora can recreate an African identity.[59]

Semaj goes on to point out that the first step in the creation of identity is the creation of a culture, because culture "gives you designs for living and patterns of interpreting reality."[60] Claudia Rogers quotes another Rasta, who concurs with Semaj in describing this attempt at culture building: "We must work at recapturing and rebuilding our African heritage, our culture, for a man without culture is a weak man, he knows not what he does or what he says. But when a man has a culture, he becomes strong and does the right things."[61] The rediscovery of their African heritage and the recreation of what they perceive as their African culture are intended by Rastas as a source of self-knowledge and power to be used in the struggle against Babylon, which seeks to strip Africans of their cultural heritage and sense of self-worth.

This reconstruction of self must be viewed against the background of European assault on African and Afro-Jamaican cultural ways. Barry Chevannes gives an apt description of this background:

> Many of the most important aspects of Jamaican folk culture were the object of ideological denigration. The folk religion, in all its variants, was described by one of Jamaica's leading intellectuals of the 1920s and 1930s as *the mud*, which he contrasted with *the gold*. The mud was that tradition of African superstition and savagery, with its wild drumming, dancing, spirit possession and polytheism, in which the ignorant masses were mired, the gold the tradition of real religion, with its Easter morning pealing of bells, one true God and studied reflection.[62]

British hegemonic culture denigrates not only the Jamaican folk culture, but also Africa and all that is associated with it. As Forsythe reminds us, Africa, to the white colonists, is "the antithesis in terms of which they defined themselves."[63] Forsythe continues, "Africa, in terms of this white-constructed symbolic imagery, was the 'dark' continent inhabited by ape-men, and incapable of creating the 'arts,' sciences and other evidences of authentic civilization."[64] In this context of cultural denigration, Afro-Caribbean people became alienated from their African selves and their cultural heritage and began to evaluate their goodness in terms of their degree of approximation of the European ideal. The result was that Caribbean people of African descent became sandwiched between their maligned African ways, which came naturally, and the European ways, which were held out as the best of human civilization. The tension produced by this conflict gave rise to the question of identity.

In response to Europeanization, the phenomenon of Rastafari represents a turning of the table. Again, Forsythe addresses this issue:

> Rastafarianism is the first mass movement among West Indians preoccupied with the task of looking into themselves and asking the fundamental question, *Who Am I?* or *What Am I?* As such, it reflects the spirit of Garveyism at the roots level, and it is now flourishing in all those areas where black West Indians are concentrated. It is a desperate call for an alternative counterculture more suitable to the needs of black people in these times.[65]

Semaj concurs, arguing that Rastafari seeks to banish the dichotomy of the African body with a European mind, by proposing "attainable and psychologically healthy answers to the question of WHO AM I."[66] He goes on to point out that the Jamaican institutions—church, school, and government—could not provide these answers "because of their subtle and not so subtle philosophical ties to the colonial and imperial powers."[67] Noting that those most likely to be attracted to Rastafari are those with the most tenuous ties to the institutions of Babylon, Semaj observes, "It appears that limited exposure to these institutions have [sic] been a prerequisite to an answer to the question WHO AM I?"[68]

Rastafari challenges the European notion of its own goodness and of African "darkness." It also imbues Africa with desirability and seeks to recapture the essence of Africa in the Rastafarian lifestyle. Rastafari therefore "affirms the African spiritual and cultural presence in the New World"[69] and becomes the mirror through which the African diaspora can see possibilities of self-identity other than those projected by Babylon.

Reappropriation of Africa / Ethiopia

A polarity is at the center of Rastafarian cosmology. It consists of Babylon, Jamaica, and the West on one side, and Zion and Africa/Ethiopia on the other. While Babylon is symbolic of negative forces, Africa/Ethiopia is evocative of positive vibrations—pride, community, charity, and serenity. As much as Rastas seek to escape from or overcome the negative forces of Babylon, they also seek to imbibe the positive vibrations of Zion. The deification of Haile Selassie, the call for repatriation, and the adoption of the Ethiopian national colors are indicative of the reappropriation of Africa/Ethiopia.

As indicated in chapter 2, the crowning of Ras Tafari as Haile Selassie, emperor of Ethiopia, was a key event in the rise of the Rastafarian movement. For a group of people steeped in biblical messianism and versed in Ethiopianism, a doctrine that celebrated the ancient glories of Ethiopia and looked forward to its future rise to eminence, this crowning signified the appearance of the messiah who would restore the glories of Ethiopia (Africa) and liberate all of its children dispersed by the colonial enterprise. Selassie was therefore perceived as and elevated to the position of a divine African liberator. As Ajai Mansingh and Laxmi Mansingh state, "He became the nucleating agent for the jelling [sic] of the spiritual thoughts, concepts and experiences and emotional cravings of Rastas."[70] The act of deifying Selassie signals the break with the colonial establishment. It was a rejection of white European religion and the whole cultural system that it legitimated. In the place of a white "gentle Jesus, meek and mild," Rastas posit an African liberator, Haile Selassie I, "conquering lion of the tribe of Judah."

The death of Selassie represented a potentially serious blow to the Rastafarian faith, and some thought that Selassie's passing would be the death knell for the Rastafarian movement. However, Rastafari responded to the news of Selassie's death (1975) in ways that defused its potential devastating effects on the movement. Some Rastas have dismissed the reports of Selassie's death as just another malicious ploy of Babylon propagandists. Selassie cannot die and hence any report of his death is a fabrication. These Rastas point to the fact that no body has been produced and no funeral held. Others accept the fact of Selassie's departure from the human sphere, but do not speak of it in terms of death. They argue that he has just assumed a different form and moved into another dimension. Still others rationalize his passing by claiming that he was a mere "personification" or "exteriorization" of God: "His body was more a vehicular unit for the carriage of God."[71] As a result, his death is inconsequential: "Jah Live!"[72] Selassie, therefore, has a continued existence as an ever-living spirit, who through "I and I" consciousness continues to live in and with the individual Rasta.[73] Thus Selassie remains a religious and political symbol inspiring the Rastafarian struggle against the stifling presence of oppression.[74]

The theme of repatriation is associated with the rediscovery of Africa. Looking to Africa/Ethiopia serves to give the Rastas a sense of common cultural and historical identity. Drawing on Marcus Garvey's back-to-Africa campaign, the Rastas have always made repatriation one of their tenets. However, the question of repatriation only became the major preoccupation in the 1950s and 1960s. Several factors may have led to the focus on repatriation. During the first two decades of the movement there was a preoccupation with establishing and expounding the divinity of Haile Selassie. With this firmly ingrained in the movement, Rastas could then concentrate on a more practical issue—their return to their African homeland.[75] At the same time, Rastas were becoming confirmed in their conviction that Jamaican nationalism and multiracialism would not benefit the black masses and that the emerging middle-class-led political parties and trade unions were producing no perceivable change in the condition of those whom Chevannes describes as the "marginalised stratum of the working class," that is, the unemployed, the underemployed, and the unemployable.[76] Rastas therefore became convinced that there was no hope for social and economic salvation in Jamaica.[77] Massive migration to Britain and, on a lesser scale, to North America only confirmed the Rastafarian conviction of the hopelessness of the Jamaican situation and also fed their desire to leave. They were spurred on by the reports of Ghana's independence and Liberia's desire to have West Indian immigrants.

The desire for repatriation was brought to a fever pitch in 1955 by the announcement of Haile Selassie's land grant, through the Ethiopian

World Federation, to those blacks in the West who supported him against the Italian invasion and who were desirous of migrating to Ethiopia.[78] Hence in the 1950s and 1960s the fever of repatriation ran high and became the focal issue of the movement. Though repatriation remains the desire of many Rastas, the emotional intensity that the issue generated then has abated.[79]

The adoption of the Ethiopian national colors of red, black, and green is another indication of the reappropriation of Africa/Ethiopia. This adoption symbolizes Rastas' "allegiance to Africa."[80] These colors, along with gold, have become a Rastafarian trademark, appearing on houses, vehicles, clothing, emblems, and accessories. Red represents the blood of those who gave their lives for freedom, especially the black slaves; black represents African skin, holiness, fire and creativity; green is variously regarded as a symbol of Ethiopia, Jamaica, or ganja; and gold symbolizes the Rastafarian faith, hope, or Jamaica.[81] Like dreadlocks, Rastafarian colors have become distinguishing marks for the members of the movement, "clearly and unambiguously" uniting them into a "single social structure."[82] Thus these colors serve the function that membership cards serve in other organizations, declaring to the world the Rastas' African identity.

Lionism and the Exorcism of Anancyism

People create folklore to tell stories about themselves, their activities, and their personalities. The most celebrated figure in Jamaica's folklore is Anancy, the spider.[83] Quintessentially, Anancy represents the ethic of survival in a hostile environment. To quote Daryl C. Dance:

> Anancy is generally a figure of admiration whose cunning and scheming nature reflects the indirection and subtleties necessary for survival and occasionally victory in a racist society. Though most of the storytellers rejoice in his victories over the stronger animals with whom he is frequently in contest, they also recognize his immorality, his greed, his stupidity, his deceitfulness.[84]

In the face of oppression, Anancy resorts to chicanery as a means of survival, and in the process he loses his sense of dignity and moral resolve. In the presence of his superiors/oppressors, Anancy acts silly and appears weak. Anancy is therefore Jamaica's rough equivalent of America's Uncle Tom, or more exactly, of the type of African American whom W. E. B. Du Bois describes as follows:

> Today the young Negro of the South who would succeed cannot be frank and outspoken, honest and self-assertive, but rather he is daily

tempted to be silent and wary, politic and sly; he must flatter and be pleasant, endure petty insults with a smile, shut his eyes to wrong; in too many cases he sees positive personal advantage in deception and lying.[85]

In most of the Anancy stories (in Jamaica as well as in Africa, especially Ghana), the spider is at the mercy of other animals, who are physically his superior. However, he uses his subtle intelligence to outwit them and hence to survive. Sociologically, this represents the use of "tricksterisms and con-artistry" as a means of survival in an oppressive situation.[86] Anancy represents what Jamaicans call "beating the system."[87] Because of this, Anancy has become for the underclass in Jamaica "a kind of 'lovable rascal,' impersonifying [*sic*] the genius of our race to survive under Babylonian conditions."[88] Therefore, as the earlier quote from Dance indicates, Anancy, in spite of his ethics, has the status of a celebrity in Jamaican folklore and Jamaican society.

Despite Anancy's status in Jamaican folklore, Rastas reject this image as a positive representation of the African personality they wish to embrace. They point out that since his ethic is an ethic of survival, Anancy has no resolute moral standard, and he is often characterized by dishonesty, deceit, doubletalk, and backstabbing. Also, the depiction of Anancy as "a little bald-headed man with a falsetto voice and a cringing manner in the presence of his superior," is antithetical to the valorization of dreadlocks, which symbolize fearlessness and fearsomeness.[89] Of course, this apparent spinelessness, often accompanied by apparent incoherence, is part of Anancy's constrategy—what Jamaicans call "playing fool to catch wise." What is more despicable for Rastafari is that Anancy uses his conartistry not only against his superiors/oppressors, but also against his friends and family. In other words, Anancy knows no other modus operandi but conartistry or "jinnalship." Even those who are closest to him—family and friends[90]—are subjected to his underhanded antics and tactics.[91] Rastafarian lyrics are always chiding backbiters, back stabbers, and "samfie men" (con artists). These appellations are a rebuke to those who practice Anancyism.

In detesting the lack of moral resolve, the spinelessness, and the endless connivings represented by the spider folk hero, Rastas contend that "the System has made us all into Anancy,"[92] divesting the people of their sense of uprightness, strength, and communality. Anancy represents the "inherited selves—albeit our acquired (slave) selves"—foisted upon the African diaspora by the experience of colonialism.[93] Therefore, the challenge of the African diaspora is to recreate its moral, self-possessed ego. Rastas are the vanguard in responding to this challenge. By invoking the lion as the symbol of their personality and by cultivating their dreadlocks as evidence of their lion-ness, Rastas have set about expunging the Anan-cyism that characterizes much of Jamaica's social life. Forsythe defines Rastas as "simply those black people who have grown tired of playing the role as 'bald-headed anancies.'" He goes on to point out that since Rastas have no superior but Jah, "the Lion is a more fitting ideal for a people bent on a militant march forward towards their own maximum and ultimate self-realization and self-discovery."[94]

The choice of the lion as a Rastafarian symbol was doubtlessly influ-enced by the association of lions with Haile Selassie. According to Rasta-farian lore, Selassie descended from the tribe of Judah, whose emblem was the lion, was born in the line of Solomon, who decorated the Solomonic temple with symbols of the lion, and was born under the as-tral sign of Leo (July 23).[95] As part of his title, Selassie is identified as "the conquering lion of the tribe of Judah." Rastafarian tales tell of pet lions roaming freely through the imperial garden and the imperial palace. Fur-thermore, Selassie and his predecessors had a preoccupation with the lion: the lion's image is on their official seal, and lion statues "guard" the gates of the imperial palace.[96]

To proclaim their identity, Rastas surround themselves with symbols and emblems depicting the lion. They often paint pictures of the lion on their dwellings, businesses, and vehicles. Statues of lions are frequently seen guarding the entrances to their homes or communes. The lion motif is ever-present in their songs, in the visual arts, and even on their personal effects.[97] Even in their deportment, Rastas seek to convey to others their sense of lion-ness, their self-confidence and self-assertiveness. Barrett is convinced that the way they stride and their cultivation of dreadlocks are attempts to embody or "simulate the spirit of the lion."[98]

The lion is the antithesis of the Jamaican folk hero Anancy. The lion suggests nobility, self-confidence, strength, pride, and moral fortitude in the face of oppression.[99] It symbolizes "power, dignity, beauty, fearless-ness and wholesome integrity that come from self-realization."[100] The adoption of the lion symbol represents Rastas' "attempt to construct a new and noble identity."[101] As Forsythe expresses in terse Rastafarian lingo, it indicates a "return to black originality, black creativity and to the ideals of 'Everliving Life.'"[102] This new or recreated identity repudiates the acquiescing trickster identity of Anancy that is so popular in Jamaican folklore.

Cultivation of Dreadlocks

The dreadlocks hairstyle began in the 1940s. It was apparently inspired by the appearance in the Jamaican press of Africans wearing a similar hairstyle. Those whose pictures appeared have been variously identified as Gallas, Somalis, Masais,[103] or Jomo Kenyatta's Freedom Fighters.[104] Along with the implicit justification of the dreadlocks hairstyle that comes from its alleged African origin, Rastas also invoke the biblical teaching concerning the Nazarites, whom the Levitical laws forbade to trim their hair or shave (Num. 6:5), as a means of validating their hairstyle.[105]

Two theories exist concerning the origin of dreadlocks in Jamaica. The first tradition, and the one more widely circulated, traces the adoption of dreadlocks to Howell's guardsmen at his Pinnacle commune.[106] The cultivation of this hairstyle was an attempt to accentuate their fearsomeness. The other tradition traces the dreadlocks trademark to the House of Youth Black Faith (HYBF), a group of young radical Rastas who exerted considerable influence on the movement from the late 1940s to the 1960s. According to Chevannes, members of the HYBF grew their locks as a direct assault on the Jamaican social norms concerning grooming, with full consciousness that the society would regard them as antisocial, if not outright crazy. But this was their way of accentuating their sense of alienation, of not belonging.[107] Whichever tradition best accounts for the origin of dreadlocks is still a question of debate. Dreadlocks, however, have become the most salient and visible symbol of Rastafarian identity.

As with other Rastafarian symbols, dreadlocks have multiple levels of significance. Aesthetically, they indicate a rejection of Babylon's definition of beauty, especially as it relates to European features and hair quality. According to Rastas, hair straightening and skin bleaching by black people reflect a yearning for whiteness and are therefore symptomatic of alienation from one's African beauty. Against this background, dreadlocks signify the reconstitution of a sense of pride in one's African physical characteristics. As Cashmore explains, dreadlocks are "used to marry blackness to positive attributes and so to upgrade the black man and align him with elite groups—and so render white stigmatic conceptions of blacks impotent."[108] Ideologically, dreadlocks express the Rastafarian belief in and commitment to naturalness. Trimming and combing, as well as straightening, are regarded as artificial, because they change the natural looks and thus are proscribed by most Rastas. Dreadlocks thus bespeak the Rastas' uncompromising posture against the artificiality of Babylon.[109] Dreadlocks also function as a mystical link between Rastas and Jah, or "earthforce." In this context locks are a kind of receptor or "psychic antenna," as Semaj calls it,[110] connecting Rastas with their God and with his mystical power, called earthforce, which is immanent in the universe. Since they connect Rastas with earthforce, the shaking of the locks is thought to unleash spiritual energy, which will eventually bring about the destruction of

Babylon. The locks are therefore symbolic of Babylon's unavoidable doom, and the very sight of the locks is supposed to generate fear in the hearts of Babylonians, hence *dread*locks.[111]

"Ital Livity": Organic Living and Herbal Healing

Another indicator of Rastas' departure from Babylon is their commitment to ital living. *Ital* means "springing from the earth, earthy, natural,"[112] or organic. Livity is living according to the strict principles of Rastafari. Ital living is therefore a commitment to using things in their natural or organic states. One of the ills of Babylon, according to Rastas, is its departure from naturalness and its commitment to artificiality. Rastas want to escape this artificiality and return to nature. Thus the Rastafarian ideal proscribes the use of synthetic materials and chemically treated foods. I say "ideal," because the economic reality of life for most Rastas makes strict ital living difficult, if not impossible. This proscription applies to tobacco, alcohol, and most manufactured products, especially canned foods. Rastas proscribe alcohol and other drugs because they view these as part of Babylon's plan to destroy the minds of black people.

Ital living also means that Rastas are basically vegetarian, rarely eating meat and strictly prohibiting the use of pork, shellfish, and scaleless fishes, especially those that are predators. The strong disapproval of fish that are predators results from the belief that eating them would be an implicit approval of their "human predator" counterparts.[113]

Central to the ideal of ital living is the belief in herbal healing. Rastas believe that the entire universe is organically related and that the key to health, both physical and social, is to live in accordance with organic principles, as opposed to the artificiality that characterizes modern technological society. In addition to the Rastafarian commitment to a virtual vegetarian diet, there is a commitment to the use of various herbs which they believe promote human well-being. Foremost among the herbs, that Rastas treasure is ganja, which they often refer to as the "holy herb" or "wisdom weed."[114] Ganja is used in a variety of ways. It is brewed as tea, soaked in rum for medicinal purposes, smoked ritually and socially, and, as one Rasta told me, used as seasoning in a variety of dishes.[115]

The study of Vera Rubin and Lambros Comitas demonstrates that these uses of ganja are not limited to the Rastas, but are fairly widespread throughout Jamaican society.[116] The research of Kenneth Bilby has uncovered the fact that ganja has long been smoked as part of a ritual in the Kumina ceremonies.[117] However, the Rastas, more than any other group, have elevated ganja to a central place in their religious practice and have developed a well-articulated ideology justifying its use and explaining its significance.

One source of justification for ganja use is the Bible. Rastas point to Genesis 1:29 to make the argument that ganja was made by God for human use: "And God said, Behold, I have given you every *herb* bearing seed, which is upon the face of the earth, and every tree, in which is the fruit of a tree yielding seed; *to you it shall be for meat*" (King James Version).[118] To justify their claim concerning the therapeutic value of ganja, they also cite Revelation 22:2: "the leaves of the tree were for the *healing of the nation*" (King James Version).[119] Rastas also cite apocryphal sources, which indicate that ganja grew on the grave of Solomon, which is why it is regarded as the wisdom weed.[120] Rastas regard the proscription of ganja use by Babylon's government as part of its strategy of social control.

Rastas also justify their use of ganja, particularly ganja smoking, by its purported therapeutic values. First, they allege that ganja smoking is a source of illumination. It gives one access to "inner and worldly knowledge."[121] In the words of Carole Yawney, it provides "inspiration enough to penetrate to the core of whatever is currently occupying their attention."[122] One ganja smoker, who is not a Rasta, described to me how ganja smoking opens up his mind and provides him with a depth perception of his inner self.

As a source of illumination, ganja has become an instrument in the war against Babylon and Babylonian consciousness. Its use, therefore, plays a major role in the de-alienation and decolonization of the African mind: "The proper use of herbs has a central role to play in freeing the mind from the *fuckery* of colonialism. It provides the inspiration necessary to transcend alienating structures of thought. Herbs, they say, are the key to the lock of understanding; God chooses to reveal himself through herbs."[123] Discussing the same point in another context, Carole Yawney explains that ganja smoking is part of the process of mitigating the pressures and overcoming the distortions of Babylon. Ganja smoking induces a visionary state, which facilitates transcending Babylon's categories and boundaries and returning home to the reality of Jah. Yawney further underscores the role of ganja smoking in Rastas' attempts to expunge Babylon's false consciousness from their minds. She notes that smoking is usually accompanied by "reasoning," an informal, open-ended dialogue, which is a collective attempt to gain new and liberating insight in a nondogmatic manner.[124]

Ganja smoking is also a means of creating and celebrating communality: "A communion bond develops among those sharing the pipe, and it would be a transgression to leave the circle until the last draw is taken."[125] This Rastafarian perspective on ganja smoking is diametrically opposed to the official view regarding the effects of ganja use. The criminalization of ganja in Jamaica is often justified by arguing that ganja smoking predisposes the smoker to violence. The incidents of violence associated with the Rastas in the late 1950s and early 1960s were thought to have been triggered by ganja intoxication. Rastas, however, contend that the smoking of ganja induces a feeling of peace and love. In a society rife with political factions, economic disparities, and racial prejudices, Rastas prescribe the smoking of holy wisdom weed "for the healing of the nation."[126] The implication is that ganja smoking will facilitate social healing by inducing a feeling of peace and love where factionalism once prevailed. As Forsythe notes: "If you have not taken the chalice [ganja pipe], you are still at malice, and you will never enter the palace of the King Rasta Fari. The 'pulling' or 'drawing' of the chalice brings people together and thereby minimizes conflict and violence in the ghettoes."[127]

Finally, ganja smoking is regarded as a source of physical healing. Many Rastas believe that their intake of ganja (in various ways) ensures perpetual health. Marley's initial refusal to seek medical treatment at the onset of his cancer was due in part to his belief in herbal healing, particularly the curative powers of smoking ganja.

"Dread Talk": The Rastafarian Argot

What has become a distinct Rastafarian argot, aspects of which have been assimilated into the popular parlance of Jamaica, developed in the House of Youth Black Faith, according to one of Chevannes's informants. The initial impulse seems to have emerged spontaneously in reasoning sessions. However, it soon became a concerted effort to conceal the meaning of their conversations from the uninitiated, particularly from Babylon's agents and informers.[128] Eventually, "dread talk" became a weapon in the Rastafarian ideological and symbolic war against Babylon.

The Rastafarian argot is an attempt to put distance between Rastas and Babylon. What Cashmore says about its significance in England is just as applicable to Jamaica: "Language was one of the blades used by the Rastaman to cut his links with the encompassing Babylon. It aided maximal detachment from the everyday experience of white society and encouraged insularity and the development of in-group solidarity."[129] Laurence A. Breiner concurs with Cashmore:

The development of the cult-language began as a kind of preemptive alienation: a gesture of withdrawal in the face of exclusion. Especially in

the early days it was a language, like that of the exilic prophets, full of estrangement and imploded with violence. In the penal colony of Babylon,
this private language served as a psychic exercise yard, a protected arena
for assertion of self impossible in the wider society.[130]

These comments reveal that the creation of a distinctly Rastafarian lingo
is another missile in the Rastafarian arsenal to be used in the ideological
and cultural warfare against Babylon. Most directly, it betokens Rastas'
nonacceptance of one of Babylon's symbols of civility. According to Babylon's standard, the parlance of the poor is inferior to the staid and standard articulation of the educated, which smacks of British culture. Thus
one of the symbols of respectability, or of being "cultured," in Jamaica is
the ability "to speak properly," which means to show mastery of the intri-
cacies of the English (British) language, both in grammatical correctness
and impeccable diction. Rastas have repudiated this symbol of respectability and have created their own linguistic devices, which directly attack
the integrity of the English language and which make their speech almost
incoherent to the uninitiated. The very act of making changes in the accepted vocabulary and established syntax is "a conscious act of protest
against the established mores of 'Babylon.'"[131]

The Rastafarian approach to language may be regarded as an exercise in
deconstruction and reconstruction. The deconstruction part of the exercise attacks the integrity of the English language and the society that values it. The reconstruction employs various stylistic and lexical innovations
to create a linguistic medium that will express the philosophical concepts
and outlook of Rastafari. Peculiarities include changing sounds, forms
and meanings of words to reflect the Rastafarian outlook.[132] For example,
consider the word *participate*. Since in the reckoning of Rastas the sound
of the word conveys its meaning, *participate* signifies less than full commitment to the specific venture at hand. Thus, the word is changed to
*full*ticipate to indicate that Rastas' involvement is always total and not
partial. The same process is at work in the change of *dedicate* to *livicate*.
The first syllable, *ded*, sounds like "dead" to Rastas. Since "dead" signifies
something negative and the word dedicate is really positive, it has to be
changed to *livicate*. Rastas also exhibit a boundless penchant for the creation of new words. Some examples are *ital*, meaning organic, natural,
and probably vital in the sense of life giving; *livity*, meaning a lifestyle
based on naturalness; and *irie*, meaning good, fine, all right, or anything
positive or delightful.

Beyond its symbolic protest, the Rastafarian argot represents an effort to
develop a medium of expression that will convey the depth of the Rastafarian experiences and perceptions. K. M. Williams declares that it "ex-

presses the expanding self-awareness of the Rastafarian, and describes his visions, as well as the need of his everyday life."[133] According to Velma Pollard, "His [Rastafarian] speech form represents an attempt to bend the lexicon of Jamaica[n] Creole to reflect his social situation and his religious views."[134] Rex Nettleford informs us that "the Rastafarians are inventing a language, using existing elements to be sure, but creating a means of communication that would faithfully reflect the specificities of their experience and perception of self, life and the world."[135] In "MABRAK," Bongo Jerry describes Rastas' intention to make over the language as an expression of their creative selves and as a reflection of their own experiences. Contending that the English language is convoluted and alienating, he portrays his hero "MABRAK" as the one who comes to right the wrong sounds and create a language that can adequately express the thoughts and feelings of Rastas.[136] Cashmore makes the same point: "Language was probably the most important symbolic device in enriching the Rastas' distinctiveness and elaborating the members' sense of identity."[137]

The ingenuity of the Rastafarian argot is reflected in its ability to encapsulate loaded and sophisticated concepts in simple expressions, which outsiders experience as linguistic crudities but which convey a whole range of meanings to the initiated. *I and I* is one such expression. I and I is indicative of the divine essence in all people. For this reason, everyone is potentially a Rasta, because everyone is born with the divine essence.[138] The true Rastas are those people who have discovered the divine principle or the God within. In Rastafarian terms, they are the ones who have "come into consciousness" of Rastafari or their divine essence.[139] I and I also connotes the oneness of all things. Since "I," in Rastafarian thought, signifies the divine principle, which is in all humanity, I and I is an expression of the oneness between two (or more) persons and between the speaker and God (whether Selassie or the God principle that rules in all creation).[140]

Rastas' insistence on using I instead of the "mi" (me) of Jamaican patois[141] expresses the dignity of the individual. Becky Mulvaney observes, " 'Me,' for Rastas, represents an expression of subservience and self-degradation. It (me) makes persons into objects, not subjects."[142] I expresses the assertion of self as an active agent instead of a malleable object. In other words, Rastas have ceased to be objects—the mi of the Jamaican patois—to be molded and defined by Babylon and have declared their determination to be subjects, creating their own reality and identity. According to I Jabulani Tafari, I and I is indicative of Rastas' refusal to be Babylon's victims despite historical and current oppression. It is a bold statement of self-assertion, which becomes a "high-calibre weapon" in the struggle against the system.[143] Breiner concurs with Tafari, arguing that the prominence of I and the creation of "I words" in Rasta language are an attempt to recapture the self as an active agent in one's self-creation and self-definition. He labels this attempt "an ingenious piece of ego assertion."[144] In the same vein, Joseph Owens writes that the Rastafarian preoccupation with I is "the awesome, fearful confrontation of a people with a primordial but historically denied racial selfhood."[145]

The Rastafarian reappropriation of Africa/Ethiopia, exorcism of Anancyism and imbibing of lionism, cultivation of dreadlocks, espousal of ital livity, and development of dread talk, are all indicative of Rastas "steppin' outa Babylon" and revitalizing their own sense of identity. Claudia Rogers captures the significance of these efforts at culture building:

> Sociologically, the development of ethnos and the maintenance of markedly different behavioral traits are of more immediate significance. They constantly re-affirm to Rastas their own African-ness, their separateness, vis-à-vis the wider society. Such patterns of behavior and attitude also become the primary means of declaring the Rasta belief in African identity to the Jamaican society, of confronting that society with an ever-present reminder that Rastas reject the categorization of "black masses" and are attempting to create yet another category for themselves. By donning "a mask of confrontation" and establishing and maintaining the overt boundaries of appearance, linguistic usage, religion, life style, and the subtle boundaries of attitudes, Rastas are attempting to reverse the syndrome of "the black man has nothing and has no chance of getting anything."[146]

Summary

The Rastafarian movement, with its ideology, symbolism, and lifestyle, constitutes a deliberate undertaking aimed at delegitimating the Jamaican sociopolitical order imposed by external powers and maintained by their local cohorts. Declaring Jamaica's social institutions and cultural values to be a contemporary expression of ancient Babylon, Rastas have embarked on the creation of a new order and a new identity.[147] Against the prevailing idea that linked Jamaicans culturally with Britain, Rastas define themselves in relation to Africa, challenging the society's view concerning what is aesthetically pleasing and culturally acceptable. In some cases, Rastas totally reverse the traditional good-bad dichotomy. What was bad, Rastas elevate to the status of good, and what the society considered good, Rastas have labeled bad or at least inferior. For example, against the notion that black is inferior, expressed in the phrase "nuthing black evah good,"[148] Rastas have celebrated their blackness and have sought to re-create themselves in the image of Africa. Against the notion that African hair is not of good quality and that wearing beards is indecorous, Rastas have cultivated long and knotted locks and have displayed them with the pride of a lion showing off its mane. In so doing they have made themselves into the picture of the "bongo man," the very image that the society rejects and fears.[149] Against the notion that to be civilized is to adopt or approximate a British accent and Western aesthetic taste, Rastas create their own argot, their own unique style of dress, and their own musical and artistic expressions. For Rastas, liberation begins with the reconstitution of self and of cultural identity in the face of prolonged assaults from the oppressive, racist forces of domination.[150]

The Ethos of Rastafari

Structure, Ideology, and Ritual

Without the development of formal institutional structures and a hierarchical organization, one would have expected the Rastafarian movement to have met its demise a long time ago. However, Rastafari has survived both repression and attempts at cooptation to become a movement with an appeal to disparate peoples around the world. In this chapter I argue that instead of an overarching formal organization, the Rastafarian movement has developed a distinctive ethos, the essential elements of which are informal networks, a shared ideological orientation, and common ritual practices. These elements reveal the internal dynamics of the movement and are among the important factors accounting for Rastafari's entrenchment in Jamaican society.

Reticulate Structure

The Rastafarian movement is characterized by much fluidity and heterogeneity and lacks an umbrella organization under which all elements of the movements are subsumed. It also lacks a formally established creed and an executive or clerical leadership structure to ensure orthodoxy. Instead, the movement consists of various "groups, quasi-groups, and individuals, who while sharing the same core beliefs, nevertheless remain separate and independent."[1] The relationship between these groups and individuals centers around personal relationships and networks.[2]

This lack of formal structures has led some scholars to refer to the Rastafarian movement as amorphous, acephalous, polycephalous, or fissiparous. The terms *amorphous* and *acephalous* seem to run counter to one of the basic sociological axioms, which states that human activities and relationships always exhibit some structure or pattern. The activities and relationships of Rastafari are no exception. As I will demonstrate shortly, the Rastafarian movement has developed its own complex of enduring forms of social organization.[3] The terms *polycephalous* and *fissiparous* better describe the nature of the movement, but do nothing to isolate its distinctive features, especially when compared to other groups in Jamaican society. These terms could just as well be ascribed to Christianity in Jamaica, which is every bit as polycephalous and fissiparous as Rastafari.

In light of its weblike or network configuration, I characterize the Rastafarian movement as reticulate. Carole Yawney, who has been doing ethnographic research on the movement since the 1970s, indicates that the Rastafarian movement consists of a loose aggregation of groups connected to each other by personal networks. Yawney further points out that this kind of reticulate, "decentralized multi-group formation is prevalent in the Caribbean, Latin America, and Africa."[4] Barry Chevannes's research confirms this point. The Rastafarian movement, he argues, is characterized by the same multigroup formations seen in other Jamaican folk religions, especially in Revivalism, Pukkumina, and the Native Baptist movement. The unifying element in these religions is a "fairly uniform system of beliefs."[5] Therefore, while the movement has not developed the formal institutions and organizational structures that Weber sees as the indicator of routinization, it has nevertheless developed its own mode of social formation—an ever-expanding network of relationships that reaches not only across Jamaica but, in many cases, extends to other parts of the world.

Researchers have identified various levels of participation within the Rastafarian movement. Many Rastas (probably the majority) fall into the category described by Velma Pollard as "own-built" Rastas.[6] These are persons who affirm the consciousness of Rastafari and share the foundational intellectual orientations and attitudes of the movement but do not identify with any particular Rastafarian group or organization. For these adherents, Rastafari is a way of life. Belonging to an organized group of Rastas is irrelevant. What is important is that one comes to I-and-I consciousness and fashions one's lifestyle according to the precepts of Rastafari. At this individual level, Rastafari religiosity approximates Troeltsch's description of mysticism as a radical individualism that deemphasizes dogma, sacraments, and social organization.[7] It focuses instead on the individual's mystical links with Jah and the cosmic energy which Rastas call *earthforce*. This individualism makes Rastafari attractive for many, especially those who are leery of institutionalized religion. It enables them to establish a religious/cultural identity without the baggage and constraints of hierarchical structures.

The relationships of other Rastas center around informal associations called "houses" or "yards,"[8] which are small independent groups of Rastas who gather frequently to smoke ganja and to reason about their faith and about current or historical events that affect their understanding of their place in the world. "Houses" express the idea that each gathering of Rastas is to be guided by the spirit of fraternity and by freedom of participation.[9] A Rastafarian house may emerge wherever several Rastas (usually males) attach themselves to a "leading brethren";[10] they frequently gather at his house or in his yard to partake of the sacramental herb and to engage in the dialectical discourse called reasoning.

Leading brethren are often regarded as elders. However, eldership is not a formal position that is attained through election, but rather an "inspirational position," which is informally conferred on those who meet at least two criteria. Elders must have a record of uncompromising commitment to and defense of the principles of Rastafari, a commitment that often leads to confronting the establishment and paying for it by going to jail. Elders must also have the ability to "speechify," that is, the ability to expound the philosophy of Rastafari, to interpret historical and contemporary events through the Rastafarian prism, and thus to inspire the brethren to greater understanding and fortitude.[11] Eldership is therefore not an ecclesiastic office with binding powers. Instead, the authority of eldership lies in the elders' ability to exercise the power of persuasion through words. That is why Homiak describes the Rastafarian elder as "principally a man of words."[12]

Membership, like eldership, has no formal requirements. By virtue of their Rastafarian consciousness, Rastas attach themselves to one or more houses of their choice from which they are free to leave at any time.[13] While there are no formal rules governing a house, Rastas and especially the elders are desirous of projecting a positive image to the community in which they live. Consequently, there are times when individuals are expelled from and forbidden to visit a yard because of "bad behavior" or "lack of livity."

Various groups of Rastas have emerged over the years. Some groups take the form of communes, organized around and dominated by a particular leader or group of elders. The first and probably the best known commune was Pinnacle (discussed in chapter 2), established and dominated by the charismatic Leonard Howell. After the demise of Pinnacle, Wareika Hills, to the northeast of Kingston, became famous for its Rastafarian communes. Various rituals, especially the ritual drumming called Nyabinghi, were developed in the Wareika Hills communes. At the end of the twentieth century, the best known commune was that of the "Bobo Dreads" in Bull Bay to the east of Kingston. The Bobo Dreads, named for the white head wrap that they wear, are the followers of Prince Emmanuel, who after being dislodged from various locations in Kingston, finally moved to Bull Bay, where he established the "City on a Hill" on captured government land.[14] Prince Emmanuel's charismatic authority is based on his claim to be the third person of the Rastafarian trinity, the other two being Haile Selassie and Marcus Garvey.[15] Rastas have also formed various voluntary organizations (sometimes legally registered) dedicated to the accomplishment of particular goals. Some Rastas refer to these as mansions, because compared to the houses which include maybe ten to fifteen Rastas, the mansions often have hundreds of members.[16] Conversely, as I discovered during my research, many a high-sounding Rastafarian organization exists in name only with no definite location or membership, except the person who conceived it in the first place.

These more formal groups fall into two categories: "churchical" and "statical." The churchical are so designated because of their emphasis on the development of Rastafarian religiosity and the cultivation of an African cultural consciousness and lifestyle. Prince Edward's Ethiopian National Congress, Henry's Peacemakers Association, Abuna Fox's Church of Haile Selassie, the Twelve Tribes of Israel, the Rastafarian Theocratic Government, and the Sons of Negus are examples of churchical Rastafarian organizations. The statical organizations gain this designation from their commitment to more political and social goals. For example, a goal of the Rastafarian Movement Association is to organize all Rastas to seize power in Jamaica through the political process. Ras Historian, the leader of this organization, told me in an interview, "Politics is wha wi a deal wid" (Politics is what we are dealing with). In the 1970s, the Rastafarian Movement Association was active in organizing mass meetings, marches, and cultural events. In addition, it published a newsletter with information of interest to or concerning Rastas.[17] The Mystic Revelation of Rastafari, founded by the famous Rastafarian drummer Count Ossie, provides another example of a statical organization. This group seeks to organize Rastas to effect repatriation through rational means, rather than waiting for the mysterious arrival of ships. It also has a commitment to the development of the creative arts and to the creation of educational opportunities for young people in the inner city of Kingston, Jamaica.[18] In the early 1970s, Count Ossie, with the assistance of the Jamaican government, established a community center at the Mystic Revelation's Adasta Road headquarters in an East Kingston ghetto to accomplish its goals. The distinction between churchical and statical is more a matter of emphasis, since both functions are often present in a single organization.

Establishing the group memberships of individual Rastas can be quite a complicated exercise. Individual Rastas often belong to more than one Rastafarian organization, and membership in a commune is marked by fluidity. A member of the Rastafarian Theocratic Government may also belong to the Rastafarian Movement Association and vice versa. In the case of Rastafarian communes, there are various patterns of participation.

Some reside in the commune on a permanent basis. Others alternate between the commune and some other place of residence. Some will belong to a certain commune today and will move to another tomorrow. Yet others are just visiting the commune and may reside there for a brief or extended period. In addition, Rastas also hold membership in organizations that are not necessarily Rastafarian in nature, but that prove attractive to Rastas because of their relationship with Africa or their commitment to African causes. For example, many Rastas belong to the Ethiopian Orthodox church, and others hold membership in the Ethiopian World Federation. When I visited the Ethiopian Orthodox church in Kingston, about a fourth of the congregants were Rastas.

The decentralized nature of the movement is probably a logical outcome of what Ernest Cashmore calls its "epistemological individualism,"[19] or what Breiner terms the "authoritative individuality"[20] that pervades Rastafari. Epistemological individualism or authoritative individualism is rooted in the philosophical concept of I and I, which leads to a fierce freedom and a radical democracy, which, in turn, is resistant to centralization.[21] As noted in the previous chapter, the basic notion of I and I is that the principle of divinity inheres in each individual, and hence truth is equally accessible to all. A Rasta is one who has consciousness of the God within, and thus he is directly linked with the source of truth and life.[22] Therefore, there is no need for teachers to impart God's truths nor priests to mediate between God and human beings. To know what is right and how to live and act, a Rasta just needs to get in touch with the God within. This epistemological individualism leads to "a highly democratic process of interrelationships,"[23] or what Breiner calls the "rule of democratic, and charismatic fluidity in Rastafarian groupings."[24] The locus of authority is in each individual. Any agreement among Rastas must be arrived at intersubjectively through the process of reasoning (discussed later in this chapter).

Interestingly, the issue of centralization has repeatedly come up for discussion among Rastas. But even in these instances, the emphasis seems to fall on "greater cooperation and communication" rather than on the development of hierarchical structures.[25] In the early 1980s, an organization called the Rastafari International Theocracy Assembly was formed. The purpose of this organization is to bring a united front to the diverse "houses and ranks of Rastafari, so that coherent inity [unity] might manifest as a result of this coming together."[26] As in the case for most Rastafarian organizations, obtaining information about Rastafari International Theocracy Assembly is difficult, partly due to an oral culture that puts little premium on documentation and partly due to inconsistent media coverage. However, the organization has had a number of meetings to

discuss issues and problems facing the movement and to devise collective strategies to address those issues and alleviate those problems.
While the stated goal of Rastafari International Theocracy Assembly is to
bring some level of organizational cohesiveness to Rastafari, in practice, it
is really a forum for socially mobile Rastas to discuss positioning themselves in the modern world. It has little significance for those at the grassroots.

Some researchers have been surprised to discover that despite the decentralized nature of the movement, Rastafari is not in organizational
chaos, but actually possesses the essential unity and identity necessary for
it to be recognized as a single social group. Although scattered throughout the island, many Rastas do know one another and are in frequent contact. Yawney points out that one of the unifying elements of the movement is the vast network that exists among various groups of Rastas and
that is maintained through "intervisiting."[27] This network disseminates
information concerning Rastafarian activities and announces the time and
place of Nyabinghi assemblies.[28] Through this informal network, Rastas
are able to share information and, probably more important from a sociological point of view, to maintain a sense of belonging to a larger collec-
tivity. In addition to networking, Rastafarian unity and identity are established and perpetuated through sharing the same "system of beliefs and a
state of consciousness"[29] and through participating in the ritual activities
referred to collectively as "grounding."

Ideological / Symbolic World View

Rastas would probably oppose the description of Rastafari as an ideology
or system of beliefs. They would declare that Rastafari is not an "ism" but
a way of life. They would contend also that Rastas do not deal with belief,
which implies doubt, but with knowledge, which implies certainty. Furthermore, Rastafari has no unequivocal Rastafarian creedal statement or
Rastafarian dogmatics (in the Weberian sense). However, Rastafari has developed identifiable ideological orientations, which inform the movement
as a whole and guide the action of individual Rastas.

Noting the heterogeneity of Rastafarian beliefs, Yawney nevertheless
identifies four orientations, which she believes characterize the Rastafarian movement as a whole: Ethiopianism, biblicism, anticolonialism,
and I-and-I consciousness.[30] I would argue that the core of the Rastafarian
world view to which all Rastas give assent is twofold: a common sense of
evil and a common sense of identity / solidarity. As discussed in the previous chapter, this sense of evil is summed up in the term *Babylon,* which is

the recognition that blacks have been the victims of a white conspiracy, which has manifested itself in colonialism, neocolonialism, imperialism, and racism. It is also a rejection of the values and institutions of Jamaican society as inimical to the well-being of the people of African heritage. The common sense of identity/solidarity is powerfully expressed at one level in the concept of I and I, which is an assertion of the godlikeness and dignity of every individual, notwithstanding the inferiority that Babylon brainwashing seeks to foist upon people of African heritage. At another level, the common sense of identity/solidarity is expressed in the Rastas' embrace of their African past, their recognition of the historic suffering of Africans at the hands of the colonial masters, their shared sense of acute pain, which comes from living in the underside of Jamaican society, and their common struggle for liberation from oppression and injustice.

Instead of elaborating these orientations in lengthy intellectual treatises, Rastas have encoded their ideology in certain evocative symbols. Abner Cohen defines symbols as "objects, acts, concepts, or linguistic formations that stand *ambiguously* for a multiplicity of disparate meanings, evoke sentiments and emotions, and impel to actions."[31] Both Cashmore and Paget Henry have observed that marginalized peoples, especially minority groups who lack access to political and economic power, often turn to "symbolic strategies"[32] and "symbolic processes"[33] in attempts to articulate their grievances and to effect social change. This use of symbolic strategies is particularly true of the Rastafarian movement. As Cashmore indicates, "Through symbolic strategies the Rastas were able to exteriorize their implicit critique of society," and their "symbolic activity articulated a concern not purely with incumbents of power positions but with power arrangements themselves."[34]

In chapter 3, I discussed Rastafari as a movement of people responding to the Babylon experience. I described various elements of the new cultural reality (or revitalized African identity) that Rastas have created and by which they define themselves. As noted, all of these elements— dreadlocks, Ethiopian colors, dread talk, ital living, as well as the term Babylon itself—are encoded with symbolic significance, the essence of which is a rejection of the Babylonian character of Jamaican society and a commitment to the struggle for selfhood and dignity through the development of an African-centered cultural identity.

Thus despite the heterogeneity of the Rastafarian movement there is an ideological/symbolic ethos that provides its members with what Yawney calls a "rich complex of meaning and symbols" through which they can filter the world they experience and by which they can shape their response to the pressures they feel.[35] Yawney further observes, "The Rastas seem to have evolved a dynamic model of the universe in terms of which members of the lower class, the dispossessed and oppressed, often illiterate, have been able both [to] construct a more satisfying and meaningful lifestyle for themselves, and to enrich their understanding of what is happening to them and why."[36] This ideological/symbolic matrix functions as a lens through which Rastas experience and interpret the world. In the words of one Rasta, "We were just blinded by European thought—but *Ras Tafari brought us new sight.*"[37]

Beyond being a prism through which the world is perceived and as an instrument in the struggle for change, the Rastafarian complex of symbols serves as the unifying element in the Rastafarian movement. Again, Cashmore is right on target:

> Bonds were expressed through symbolic procedures and such expressions served to consolidate and reinforce the feeling of belongingness and unity. It was these bonds which held the Rastas together as a movement and not as an aggregation of individuals sharing similar social positions.[38]

In place of membership cards or confessed commitments to a creedal statement, evocative and provocative symbols, which express a common sense of evil and of identity/solidarity, have become the badge of membership in the Rastafarian movement. These symbols have unified and solidified the movement into a potent force in Jamaican society.

Ritual Activities

In addition to the informal network and the ideological/symbolic matrix, certain rituals serve to shape and perpetuate Rastafarian religiosity and sociality. These rituals fall under the general rubric of what Rastas call grounding. John Paul Homiak defines *grounding* as "informal instruction in Rasta precepts and ideology; the ritual process (reasoning) by which circles of like-minded brethren are formed and maintained."[39] Homiak's definition places grounding within the context of the yards or houses I described earlier. However, while these "circles of like-minded brethren" provide the day-to-day context in which Rastafarian religiosity is formed and sustained, the periodic gathering called Nyabinghi I-ssembly or Groundation is another ritual event in which grounding takes place.

Grounding, in the context of the yards, takes place when a few Rastas gather to smoke ganja spliffs, or to "draw the chalice,"[40] and to reflect on their faith or on any current or historical event that affects their lives. This is the most informal level of grounding, and it can take place anywhere and anytime without any prearrangement. However, for many, grounding is a daily activity, which takes place in the yards of leading brethren or elders. In addition to these daily gatherings, some circles of Rastas hold periodic all-night gatherings, some as often as once a week and others once a month or "as the spirit moves."[41] Rastas who ground in other yards on a daily basis may visit these all-night gatherings as part of the intervisitation discussed earlier. These gatherings are somewhat more formal, and in addition to ritual smoking and reasoning, drumming, chanting, and sometimes "speechifying" and feasting are often elements of the grounding.

As indicated, ganja is smoked in these Rastafarian gatherings as a sacrament, which is believed to be the source of social and spiritual healing and insights. Rastas contend that the "herb" (ganja) is for "the healing of the nation." They further contend that the smoking of ganja "dispels gloom and fear, induces visions, and heightens the feelings, creating a sensation of fellow love and peace."[42] As noted in the previous chapter, ganja smoking is regarded as a source of inspiration or as an inducer of a visionary state of consciousness.[43] It lifts the users beyond the ordinary pace of life and sharpens their perceptions so they can penetrate truths hitherto not perceived or apprehended.[44] More specifically, ganja smoking facilitates the transcending of Babylon's boundaries and the apprehending of new perspectives and possibilities. The pressures and distortions of Babylon separate the individual from the real source of life and knowledge; ganja smoking aids in dissolving the barriers and in hastening the return home to the reality of Jah. Therefore, it is in the visionary state induced by ganja smoking that Rastas come to I-and-I consciousness, "the merging of the individual with all life forces, the realization that all life flows from the same source, and the collapse of the distance between internal and external, subject and object."[45]

As Homiak's definition indicates, an open-ended and informal discussion, known as reasoning, is an essential part of grounding. Yawney describes *reasoning* as an open-ended, dialogical discourse between two or more brethren, which is aimed at the exploration of intersubjectivity, that is, gaining "access to *one visionary stream*, to the condition of I and I consciousness."[46] The idea of intersubjectivity, as it relates to Rasta reasoning, speaks to the Rastafarian conviction that truth resides in each individual because the divine "I" is in each person. Therefore, reasoning, assisted by the inspiration of ganja, stimulates the intersubjective exploration of truth. Stated another way, in the process of reasoning , all the I's present are able to explore the same truth, which inheres in each of them.

Reasoning is a very intense activity, which can go on for hours in a dialogical manner until those involved arrive at a consensus.[47] Yawney claims, "Two brethren may reason together, each prompting the other to *higher and higher I-ghts* [heights], accreting layer upon layer of meaning until a satisfactory view of reality is reached."[48] Despite the Rastafarian insistence on knowing in contrast to believing (which implies doubt, in their estimation) and their elevation of the conclusions arrived at during reasoning sessions to the status of knowing, no conclusion or consensus is ever elevated to the status of a binding creed. Each conclusion is subject to modification or further elaboration at future sessions.[49]

What is most important about these reasoning sessions, from a sociological point of view, is that they function in much the same manner as do catechism or Bible study in a church. They induct the initiates into the movement and confirm old adherents in the principles and precepts of Rastafari. It is noteworthy that new members of the movement are usually recruited in the context of the yard, through their involvement in ganja smoking and reasoning. The outcome of this collective activity, therefore, is the inculcation in Rastas of a common orientation to the world.[50] Reasoning, therefore, provides the balance that tempers the individualism of the movement, that is inherent in their concept of I and I. Reasoning allows Rastas to come together to pursue common understanding or to reach consensus on particular issues.[51] According to Yoshiko Nagashima, through this ritual process " 'communitas' can be actualized."[52] Hence the purpose of grounding is to "ground the nation" of Rastafari to the "essential foundation."[53] Through this process, Rastas become steeped in the principles of "rastology."[54]

Grounding also takes place at periodic movement-wide conventions variously called "Nyabinghi" (or "Binghi," for short), "I-ssembly" (Assembly), "Rasta Convention," "Nyabinghi Convention," or "Nyabinghi I-ssembly." The term *Nyabinghi* was adopted from an East African group of the same name, which is reported to have been a secret society led by Haile Selassie. The motto of this group is said to have been "death to the white oppressors." By calling these meetings Nyabinghis, Rastas are expressing their conviction that the activities at these gatherings serve to unleash earthforce, the cosmic energy that pervades the universe, against those who have historically oppressed African people.[55]

The where and when of the origin of the Nyabinghi I-ssembly is subject to conflicting claims. The Rasta convention called by Prince Emmanuel Edwards in 1958 and the one convened by Claudius Henry in 1959 are often cited as the beginnings of the Nyabinghi I-ssemblies. However, Verena Reckford cites a 1949 gathering at a Rastafarian camp in Wareika Hills as the "first really big congregation of Rastafarians."[56] Homiak's research seems to support Reckford's findings. Though Homiak gives no specific dates, he indicates that Rastafarian "grounation" (groundation) took place in Rastafarian camps and yards prior to Edwards's convention in 1958.[57] The discrepancy may be due to the differences in the kind of publicity these events drew. The 1949 Nyabinghi was held in the relative seclusion of Wareika Hills without press coverage. Reckford seems to have come to the knowledge of this gathering during her fieldwork among those who participated, especially Count Ossie, whose drummers, along with some Burru players, provided music for the occasion.[58] In contrast, the 1958 and 1959 conventions were held in the city of Kingston with much fanfare and much media attention.[59] So while the 1958 and 1959 conventions came to be regarded as the beginning of the Nyabinghi I-ssemblies, they appear to have been the continuation of something started earlier. Their significance comes from the fact that they brought to public awareness a Rastafarian activity which had developed in the relative seclusion of the Rastafarian "cloister."

Nyabinghi I-ssemblies are held according to the Rastafarian calendar of holy days. These are the Ethiopian Christmas on January 7, the anniversary of Haile Selassie's visit to Jamaica on April 21, African Liberation Day (founding of the Organization of African Unity) on May 26, Selassie's birthday on July 23, the Ethiopian new year on September 11, and the anniversary of Selassie's coronation on November 2.[60] At these times, Nyabinghi I-ssemblies are convened. Who convenes an I-ssembly and where it is held are determined in the give-and-take decisionmaking process within the movement. However, the conveners always seem to meet two conditions. They must have reputations as exemplars of Rastafarian "livity, that is, strict uncompromising lifestyles. They must also have the economic means to make substantial contributions as the sponsors of the I-ssembly. An elder wishing to convene an I-ssembly usually announces his intention at one of the bi-monthly meetings of elders, which are called "First Light Reasoning." If he secures the support of the other elders, information concerning planning for the I-ssembly is then disseminated through the personal network of the movement.[61]

The early Nyabinghi I-ssemblies were usually held in and around Kingston. However, since 1970, Nyabinghi I-ssemblies have become rural events. As Homiak indicates, the shift is related to demographic changes affecting the movement, specifically the dislocation of Rastas from West Kingston by the demolition of Back O' Wall in 1966.[62] Many of the dislocated settled on the periphery of the city or moved to deep rural areas, taking the I-ssembly with them.[63]

Now, an I-ssembly lasts anywhere from three to seven days and is marked by a festive atmosphere, intense activities, and ecstatic emotions.[64] Large numbers of Rastas from all over the island descend on the site of the I-ssembly, sometimes in colorful motorcades. The daytime is occupied by feasting, ganja smoking, and reasoning in groups that gather informally. At night, everything shifts into high gear. The congregants gather around huge bonfires or in booths covered by leaves or thatch, and they are treated to all-night drumming, chanting, dancing, and speechifying. Of course, no Rastafarian gathering is complete without the ritual smoking of ganja. These all-night sessions are intense with many participants displaying an array of ecstatic emotions.[65]

While the early Nyabinghi I-ssemblies were regarded as a preparation for repatriation, and while present-day participants are frequently reminded that they are "sons and daughters of Zion" called out of Babylon, preparation for immediate departure to Africa is no longer the central focus. The Nyabinghi I-ssemblies, their ritual activities, and the ritual calendar have become the major means of facilitating solidarity in the Rastafarian movement as a whole.[66] The functional significance of the I-ssembly to the Rastafarian movement is multivalent as aptly summarized by Homiak. First, it is a celebration and reinforcement of the oneness among Rastas and the oneness of Rastas with Jah. The mass gathering and participation in the same activities generate a feeling of oneness akin to Durkheim's *conscience collectif*. Second, the I-ssembly is an occasion for the revitalization of the Rastas' African roots. A Nyabinghi I-ssembly is therefore a "source of cultural and spiritual upliftment." Third, the I-ssembly is also an occasion for the valorization of the strict ital livity (natural living) and precepts of Rastafari and for the purging of Babylon's influence from one's life. Fourth, the I-ssembly gains further significance from the role it is assigned in the destruction of Babylon. According to Rastas, the ritual activities of the I-ssembly are a means of channeling earthforce against the oppressive agents of Babylon. For example, the drumming and the chanting are often accompanied by ritual stomping and wild tossing of dread-locks. These are symbolic acts aimed at destroying Babylon. Finally, the I-ssembly provides an arena for the dramatization of contending claims for leadership within the movement. Since leadership is based on the individual's reputation and facility with words, at these mass gatherings various elders seek to enhance their status and authority by giving lengthy accounts of their history of uncompromising opposition to Babylon and by demonstrating their ability to interpret historical and contemporary events from the perspective of Rastafari.[67]

The foregoing discussion has demonstrated that, with all its plurality, Rastafari is a cohesive movement characterized by structured relationships, a distinctive ideological/symbolic ethos, and routine ritual activities, all of which serve to solidify and perpetuate the movement.

"Coming in from the Cold"

Rastafari and the Wider Society

The relationship between the wider Jamaican society and the Rastafarian movement has progressed through three identifiable phases: (1) resistance and repression, (2) accommodation and assimilation, and (3) cooptation and commodification. Prior to 1960 the relationship was primarily one of Rastas confronting the society and the society responding by repressing Rastas. Although resistance and repression continued into the 1960s and thereafter, during the 1960s, tensions started to ease, as the dominant powers pursued a policy of accommodation, which was supported by many Rastas. At the same time, elements of the Rastafarian perspective were being embraced by segments of the society. Since the early 1970s, Rastafari has been recognized as a positive force in Jamaican society and has become the object of cooptation by political and commercial interests.

Resistance and Repression

The Rastafarian phenomenon is "an integral aspect of the larger matrix of black religious nationalism, folk revivalism, and Jamaican resistance to the plantation economy and state."[1] As such, Rastafari is rooted in the rejection of the legitimacy of the Jamaican social system and in resistance to its values and social arrangements. Owing to the Rastafarian doctrine of nonparticipation in Babylon and because of the communal living arrangements of some Rastas, the movement has been sometimes characterized as passive or escapist. However, during the first three decades of its existence, Rastas used a variety of means to confront the Jamaican establishment, including street meetings, at which they denounced the system. George Eaton Simpson made his initial observations, which provided the data for the first academic treatment of the movement, at these meetings in the early 1950s. He identifies six themes enunciated by Rastafarian preachers at these street meetings: the wickedness of white people, the superiority of black people, Jamaica's false prophets (preachers and politicians), the oppressiveness and hopelessness of Jamaica's social system, retribution to white and black oppressors, and repatriation to Africa, the homeland of black people.[2] In the elaboration of these themes, Rastas sought to confront the colonial system and its local cohorts. Leonard Howell's preaching was laced with contempt for the Jamaican government. He called for blacks to rise up in violence against its custodians and even urged his followers not to pay taxes to the then-colonial government, informing them that their only allegiance was to Haile Selassie.[3]

Rastas also confronted the dominant powers of the society in public marches and symbolic "captures" of government property. The 1940s and 1950s saw a proliferation of these marches by which Rastas sought to express their disapproval of Jamaica's social, economic, and political system and their desire to be repatriated to the homeland of their African ancestors. Sometimes, these marches had no specific purpose other than to demonstrate Rastafarian defiance toward the custodians of power. They would march without acquiring the necessary permits, apparently hoping to provoke a police reaction.[4]

The smoking of ganja provided another means of resisting the civil authority. Although the government's prohibition of ganja use was well known, the House of Youth Black Faith (HYBF), for instance, heightened the tension with the colonial government by institutionalizing ganja smoking as the most sacred ritual activity of Rastafari, arguing that it is a herb "for the healing of the nation" (Rev. 22:2) and that "every herb bearing seed" (Gen. 1:29) was made for human consumption.[5] In addition, HYBF often went out of its way to provoke confrontation by ordering its members to carry ganja on their persons, especially at their meetings, so that if they were searched by the police, the only case that could be brought against them would be for possession of the holy herb, or wisdom weed.[6]

Though not widely used, violent confrontation periodically appeared in the Rastafarian arsenal of resistance. Of course Rastafarian rhetoric against Babylon has always been laced with violent images, such as the frequent invocation of "blood and fire" against Babylon's agents and "baldheads."[7] Early Rastafarian leaders, particularly Howell, advocated the violent overthrow of the colonial system.[8] On at least two occasions, the violence of words found more concrete expressions. The first occasion involved the Rastafarian leader Claudius Henry and his son, Ronald. In 1959 the Jamaican security forces discovered a cache of small arms at Claudius Henry's Rosalie Avenue headquarters. Though Henry claimed these were for ritual purposes, his claim was called into doubt shortly thereafter, when his son, Ronald, was implicated in a "guerrilla" operation designed to effect a coup d'etat. Though Ronald's commitment to Rastafari was questionable, and though the plot was not engineered by Rastas, several Rastas were actively involved with the plotters. The other incident, which has become known as the Coral Garden Massacre, took place in 1963 in a tourist area of Montego Bay. According to Derek Bishton, this incident was triggered by efforts to prevent Rastas from using a footpath across the property of Rose Hall Great House, which was being renovated as a tourist attraction. While the Rastas had used this path for years without incident,[9] the authorities seemed bent on creating a "sanitized tourist zone" in which the sight of Rastas was unacceptable. When the police were called in to settle the matter, some Rastas were pushed too far and expressed their anger by setting fire to a gas station, killing an attendant in the process. In the ensuing confrontation with authorities, three Rastas, two policemen, and three other people were killed.[10]

While early writers, such as Simpson, Lantenari, and Patterson, from their academic distance described Rastafari as a movement of discontented and maladjusted ghetto youths displaying an escapist syndrome, those who were custodians of the status quo rightly perceived that Rastafari was a challenge to the uneasy peace of the colonial establishment and later of the newly independent Jamaica (1962). As early as the 1930s, a retired magistrate, C. A. Bicknell, expressed concern about Rastafarian propaganda, which envisioned a "black war in Jamaica." About the same time, Major B. F. Cawes read *The Promised Key*, a Rastafarian text popularized by Howell, and wrote of the bitterness and hatred it encouraged among the lower classes.[11] The forebodings of these representatives of the ruling class were of course colored by the fact that the 1930s were characterized by broad social unrest and popular discontent as shown by the widespread labor strikes of 1938.[12]

Feeling challenged, the dominant classes and the civil authorities resorted to one of the classic weapons in the arsenal of social control: labeling. The initial move, therefore, was to characterize the Rastafarian movement as a "criminalised subculture"[13] and its members as a dangerous, lunatic fringe. Newspaper columnist Clinton Parchment summed up the attitude of the middle class (and probably of the majority of Jamaicans) toward the Rastas in a 1960 article. "It is self-evident," he claimed, "that the majority [of Rastas] are lazy, dirty, violent and lawless scoundrels mouthing religious phrases to cover up their aversion to work and their ill habits." He proceeded to declare that "the banning of the sect and the repression of their habits is something that no Jamaican government with claims to public spirit ought to hold back from."[14] Parchment's perspective is representative of the general perception of Rastas as a menace and a threat by reason of their perceived criminality and mental deficiency.

After the Coral Garden incident, a newspaper article asked, "What is it like to live on an island where an estimated 60,000 *lawless men*—most of them thought to be *mentally deficient*—aim at the destruction of the island's Government?"[15] Apparently, from the perspective of those who represented the status quo, anyone who dared to challenge the "civilized" colonial institutions and values of Jamaica or to advocate repatriation to the "dark continent" of Africa must either be a criminal or suffering from delusions of grandeur.[16]

Since the "Rastafarian menace" was a threat to the stability and good name of the country,[17] the government deemed it necessary to counter that threat. Having thus labeled the movement, the protectors of society initiated a campaign of repression directed at Rastas because they regarded "misconduct and disorder" as "organic Rastafarian attributes."[18]

The repression started as soon as the movement came to the attention of the authorities, and it grew in intensity as the movement gained strength and notoriety. In the early days, Howell was the focus of attention. In 1934, he and his associate Robert Hinds were arrested on the charge of sedition. Howell was convicted of trying to incite "disturbance and violence among ignorant people."[19] In conjunction with Howell's arrest and conviction, the religious activities of Rastas were severely restricted in St. Thomas and Portland, where Howell had significant followings. The Pinnacle commune, which Howell established after serving his first prison term, was subjected to repeated raids by the police. The establishment of Pinnacle was symbolic of Howell's break with and rejection of the values and legitimacy of the dominant society. It was also an act of retreat in order to pursue the Rastafarian lifestyle without confrontation with the establishment. However, the authorities regarded Pinnacle as a guerrilla or "terrorist base camp"[20] and proceeded to conduct a relentless campaign of harassment against its members.[21] On one occasion about seventy Rastas were arrested on ganja and assault charges; twenty-eight of them received jail terms. Howell was again imprisoned for two years.[22] Finally, in 1954, the police raided and demolished Pinnacle, arresting and imprisoning many of Howell's followers and dispersing others. The government later confined Howell to a mental institution.[23]

The 1950s and 1960s saw waves of repressive measures against Rastas. The first wave came against bands of Howellites who appeared in Kingston after the demolition of Pinnacle. Many were arrested for ganja possession and others for rioting or assembling with the intent to riot.[24] The next wave came after the Rastafarian gathering convened by Prince Emmanuel Edwards in 1958. The effusive enthusiasm of the Rastas and their vitriolic tirades against the "system" during the convention put the police on alert. Some attendees of the convention engaged in skirmishes with the police, the most serious of which was the forced removal of about three hundred Rastas from Victoria Park, which they had occupied as a symbolic capture of the city of Kingston.[25] Following the convention, Rastas were routinely searched and arrested. Edwards's camp in Back O' Wall was raided and razed. All of the occupants were arrested but were later acquitted.[26] In May 1959, after a fracas which started between a policeman and a Rasta in a downtown Kingston market, the police descended on the Rastafarian enclave in Back O' Wall, arresting Rastas, ransacking their dwellings, beating some, and forcibly shaving the locks of others.[27]

What has been dubbed the "Henry affairs" marked the high point in the tension between the establishment and the Rastafarian movement. The incidents involving Henry and his son created a wave of hysteria comparable to that created by the Morant Bay Rebellion almost a hundred years earlier (1865),[28] and the establishment unleashed its wrath against the Rastafarian movement. In addition to sentencing Henry to a long jail term and executing his son for murder, the police stepped up their harassment of Rastas. A 1960 university report describes the harassment of Rastas in the aftermath of the "Henry affairs": "The police have carried out extensive raids, made numerous arrests, and, in the heat of the moment, have indulged in many arbitrary acts against Ras Tafarians."[29] According to Barry Chevannes' characterization, "a wave of intimidation, shaving of locks, arrests, beatings and imprisonment descended on all Rastafari, in unprecedented scale and scope."[30] Feeling the heat of arbitrary intimidation and imprisonment, some Rastas approached the University College of the West Indies (now University of the West Indies) to investigate and disseminate the truth concerning Rastafari, which they believed would show that they were neither lunatics nor pathological criminals, but peace-loving and hard-working people.

Although the university study indicated that Rastas were not the menace they were portrayed to be and recommended rehabilitation instead of repression to resolve the "Rasta problem," the tension between the movement and the establishment remained high. Thus when the Coral Garden Massacre occurred in 1963, the government responded by ordering the arrest of Rastas en masse.[31] A leading politician called on the general citizenry to assist in efforts against Rastas. He asked everyone "to report any unusual movement of Rastafari people when they are going in ones or twos or in groups, wherever they suddenly appear in suspicious circumstances."[32] Since the incident at Coral Garden was attributed to ganja intoxication, the repressive measures taken against the Rastas went hand in hand with the suppression of ganja cultivation and use. The Dangerous Drug Laws were amended to impose more severe penalties for the cultivation, trading, or use of ganja. The prime minister, Alexander Bustamante, declared his resolve to deal with the ganja menace: "Wherever ganja is grown, whether on the hills, on the plains, in the forests, or on platforms between trees or in pots, I intend to see that there is no resting place for these evildoers until this country is rid of this menace."[33]

The continued association of violence, ganja, and Rastas led to the destruction of Back O' Wall in 1966. In the 1960s Back O' Wall, sometimes called Shanty Town, was the most depressed and depressing slum in Kingston. As part of its move against increasing violence and other criminal activities, the government ordered it bulldozed. The Rastas who had lived there since their dispersal from Pinnacle were again displaced.[34] This was the last major assault against the perceived Rastafarian threat.

Accommodation and Assimilation

A 1960 study of the Rastafarian movement by a group of university scholars marked the beginning of rapprochement between Rastas and the wider Jamaican society. Approaching the university and asking for a team to study and document the truth concerning the movement proved to be an astute, if not strategic, move by the Rastas. For the first time, Rastas attempted to speak with a common voice and to defend their legitimacy and right to exist without persecution. Even more important, the Rastas probably knew that within the establishment, the university was the staunchest critic of Jamaica's Eurocentrism and the most open to new ideas. Therefore, Rastas felt that if they were going to get a favorable portrayal in the society, it would most likely come from the university intellectuals.[35] The study was authorized by the university with the support of the Jamaican government. The final report took on the character of a public policy document.

This report, which was prepared by M. G. Smith, Roy Augier, and Rex Nettleford, without sanctioning the Rastafarian movement portrayed it in a favorable light. The study counteracted the caricature of the movement as a group of criminals and lunatics who preyed upon society. It pointed out that, with the exception of a few who used the guise of Rastafari to engage in criminal activities, Rastas were peaceful, nonviolent citizens.[36] The study further indicated that Rastas had justified grievances, which were fueled by the economic and social marginalization faced by the urban unemployed and underemployed. These grievances, the report claimed, would lead to greater instability and perhaps revolutionary violence if they were left unaddressed.[37] The report recommended that rehabilitative measures be taken to alleviate destitution in the urban ghettos, that the government investigate the possibility of repatriation to Africa,[38] and that the Ethiopian Orthodox church be invited to establish a branch in Jamaica.[39] The obvious conclusion of those who conducted the report was that Rastas were not sociopaths or psychopaths but were instead suffering Jamaicans responding to the pressures of marginalization.[40]

As is evident in the discussion of the confrontation between Rastas and the civil authorities, the tension between the two did not dissipate overnight with the publication of the university report. In fact, the report received scathing reviews in the press. The university scholars were labeled as Rastafarian sympathizers who were "whitewashing" the dangerous dissidents, and the report was criticized as lacking in academic value and as a waste of taxpayers' money.[41] However, the study was ground breaking; as the first attempt by the society to take a serious look at Rastafari, it represented the beginning of the debunking of the myths concerning the dementia and inherent criminality of Rastas.[42] Even more important, it set in motion a series of events, promoted by the government and supported by Rastas, which facilitated the move toward rapprochement. Several of these events stand out: the mission to Africa to explore the possibility of repatriation, the visits of African dignitaries including Haile Selassie, to Jamaica, and the establishment of the Ethiopian Orthodox church in Jamaica.

Implementing one of the recommendations of the university study, the government sponsored fact-finding missions to Africa in 1960 and 1962. The missions were composed of Rastas, members of "African consciousness" organizations, and civic leaders. The purpose of the missions was to determine which African states would allow Jamaicans to repatriate. The delegations visited Ethiopia, Nigeria, Ghana, Liberia, and Sierra Leone and met with high-level government, civic, and religious leaders. On returning to Jamaica, the Rastas on these missions maintained that the African governments were committed to the repatriation of Jamaicans whose forebears were displaced by the Middle Passage. However, the majority report of the first mission, written by journalist Vick Reid, concluded that, while there was an outpouring of goodwill from the African states visited, they were only interested in receiving professionals and other skilled persons who could contribute to the building of their postcolonial societies.[43] Since most Rastas were unskilled or semiskilled, they were effectively excluded as candidates for migration to Africa. In 1964–1965, a delegation of Rastas made another mission to Africa in the hope of pushing their repatriation agenda. Though the Rastafarian delegates were well received in the countries they visited, their mission failed to lead to an official policy of repatriation by either the African governments or the Jamaican government.

Nettleford argues that because the government was pursuing a policy of migration, as a result of which thousands of Jamaicans had moved to the United Kingdom and the United States, it felt constrained to deal with the Rastafarian call for repatriation to Africa. So without accepting the Rastas' arguments and demands for repatriation, it could pursue the possibility of Jamaicans moving to Africa within its broader migration policy.[44] Another view, however, suggests that the government never took the call for repatriation seriously and never pursued it with any vigor. Instead the missions were intended to expose Rastas to the harsh realities of Africa in order to dampen their desire for repatriation.[45] Whatever the motivation of the government, and although no repatriation took place under government sponsorship, the missions did indicate that Rastas were not criminals to be hounded, but Jamaicans whose problems and aspirations needed to be addressed by the wider society.

Following the university report and the missions to Africa, a parade of African dignitaries made official visits to Jamaica. Of course, the highlight was Haile Selassie's visit in 1966. During this visit, Rastas received prominence and visibility hitherto unimaginable. To begin with, it took Mortimer Planno, an eminent Rastafarian elder, to quiet the large crowd that flocked to the airport to welcome the emperor. Many had broken through the police line and were surrounding the plane. Repeated attempts by government officials failed to bring them under control, and the emperor could not deplane. Planno's appeal from the steps of the plane finally brought the crowd under control. Rastafarian representatives were invited to participate in state ceremonies and found themselves socializing and dining with the upper and middle classes at Kings House (the residence of the governor general). In addition, the Rastas sought and received a private meeting with Selassie. Most important, the exposure and dignified conduct of the Rastas during the visit of Haile Selassie marked another step in the rapprochement between Rastafari and the establishment. As John Paul Homiak contends, the visibility of Rastas at important state functions "conferred a sort of 'warrant of credibility' on the movement."[46]

Some scholars argue that the visits of African dignitaries, particularly Selassie, were calculated to mute the desire for repatriation and induce the acceptance of Jamaica as home. For example, Nettleford characterizes these visits "as a necessary exposure to combat the frustration born of ignorance and even to cure the Rasta desire for Africa by an overdose."[47] Homiak concurs: "The invitation by the Jamaican government to Emperor Selassie which eventuated in his historic 1966 visit was calculated to quell the demands for repatriation and to promote the 'rehabilitation' of the brethren, i.e., to de-program Rasta[s] on the Back-to-Africa issue."[48]

Certain incidents associated with these visits give merit to such claims. For example, a speech by a Nigerian government official to a group of Rastas in 1962 seemed designed to encourage the acceptance of Jamaica as home. He congratulated his audience on having achieved independence and encouraged them to make their contributions as "citizens."[49] What is more, during the Selassie visit, the phrase "liberation before repatriation" emerged. Reportedly, this was a "directive" from Selassie for Rastas to free the people of Jamaica before returning to Ethiopia.[50] The credibility of this directive seems to be buttressed by the fact that, after the visit, there was a noticeable cooling of the repatriation fervor that had been evident in the movement for more than a decade.

As another gesture of accommodation, the government invited the Ethiopian Orthodox church to establish congregations in Jamaica. This was one of the recommendations in the university study and hence a part of the program of rehabilitating Rastas.[51] It was hoped that this denomination would provide a "positive functional haven for those Jamaicans who wish to assert strongly their African origins" yet "at a more conventional and established Christian level."[52] In other words, the invitation to the Ethiopian Orthodox church was a political ploy aimed at "incorporating Rastafarians under the Christian umbrella."[53] The first congregation of the Ethiopian Orthodox church was organized in 1970. By 1982 the denomination had spread to several towns beyond Kingston, secured a sizable following, and participated in the ecumenical activities of the Jamaica Council of Churches.[54] Rastas have identified positively with this church, and many have become members. However, many who have become members refuse to compromise their staunch Rastafarian convictions and often create heterodoxy in the church.[55]

The fact-finding missions to Africa, the visits of African dignitaries, especially Haile Selassie, and the establishment of the Ethiopian Orthodox church in Jamaica were all efforts aimed at addressing the "Rasta problem." The significance of these efforts lies mainly in the fact that they brought Rastas into increasingly amicable social intercourse with the guardians of the society, thus changing the nature of their relationship from resistance and repression to one of accommodation.

While the gestures of reconciliation between Rastas and the civil authorities were playing themselves out, two other significant processes were also developing. The first process involved a growing alliance between Rastafari and the progressive elements of the Jamaican intelligentsia, while the second involved a noticeable diffusion of Rastafarian consciousness and social traits among the poor and the young in the society.

Between 1962 and 1972, there was an increasing radicalization of the middle-class intelligentsia as a result of its disillusionment with the new independent government's inability to address the issues of poverty and cultural identity.[56] This radicalization crystallized into the Jamaican version of the Black Power movement. These radical intellectuals, some of whom faced the brunt of British racism as they trained in the corridors of Oxford and Cambridge, found a ready critique of Jamaican society and a more acceptable view of life in the ideology of Rastafari. One of these intellectuals, Walter Rodney, who was a Black Power activist at the University of the West Indies, gives this appraisal of Rastafari:

> It was to the Rastafarian movement and its predecessors that Africa was our spiritual homeland and that our "sojourn" in Jamaica should be used to develop her traditions and civilisation as far as was possible in "Babylon" that is Jamaica. That was the only way in which Black men could find themselves.[57]

Rodney continues:

> In our epoch the Rastafari have represented the leading force of this expression of black consciousness. They have rejected this philistine white West Indian society. They have sought their cultural and spiritual roots in Ethiopia and Africa.[58]

Rodney's observations underscore the fact that Rastafarian ideas on "black power and majority control" had begun to take center stage in local intellectual discussions. As an observer of the Rastafarian movement during this period, Theodore Malloch came to this conclusion: "Some intellectuals in the Caribbean have understood the crux of the Rastafarian argument—that Jamaica tacitly denies its spiritual and cultural African past. These persons believe that Jamaica must accept a connection with Africa as part of its national identity."[59]

With this acknowledgment of Rastafari's social significance, the progressive elements of the Jamaican intelligentsia soon developed social and intellectual exchanges with Rastas. These exchanges resulted in the forging of alliances between the Rastas and the Black Power movement. Walter Rodney himself epitomized this exchange and the resulting alliance. The very title of his book, *Groundings with My Brothers*, is a testament to his involvement with the Rastafarian movement. Rodney defines *grounding* as "sitting down together to reason, to 'ground' as the brothers [Rastas] say."[60] When I met with Ras Historian in May 1991, he recalled how Rodney would visit Rastafarian yards and communes to teach African history. Ras Historian even claimed that he gained his moniker because of the penchant he displayed for history in Rodney's teaching sessions among the Rastas. When the Jamaican government declared Rodney persona non grata in 1968 as part of its suppression of Black Power, among the reasons it cited for his banning were "subversive activities" among people associated with the Rastafarian movement.[61]

The Abeng, a group formed in response to the banishment of Rodney, further exemplified the alliance of Rastas and middle-class intellectuals. Its membership included university professors and students, some of whom later became prominent politicians, and persons outside of the academic world, especially those of working-class and Rastafarian backgrounds. The expressed purpose of this group was to be critical of the social and political system in Jamaica.[62] Its publication, also called *Abeng*, declared solidarity with pop singers who were critical of the society, highlighted the marriage between Rastafarian ideas and reggae music, gave prominence to the issues of race, class, black nationalism, and the plight of the poor, employed Rastafari lingo liberally, and focused explicitly on issues of particular relevance to Rastas.[63] Though the group and its publication were short-lived, they served to give further credibility to Rastafarian criticism of the establishment.

The alliance between Rastas and the progressive elements of Jamaican society led to what may be called the mainstreaming of the Rastafarian perspective. Nettleford, a long-time observer of the movement, correctly points out that, by the late 1960s, Rastafarian criticisms of the society had become common fare even among those who would have looked askance on Rastas in the early 1960s.[64]

Even before the alliance of Rastafari and radical intellectuals, Rastafari was gaining ground in the consciousness of the poor and the young throughout the society. As Yawney observes, Rastas had "found ways to impose their transcendental framework of reality on the surrounding environment."[65] "By the late sixties," writes Nettleford, "there was much more widespread embrace of Rastafarian attitudes, ideals and even practices."[66] Nettleford goes on to cite several examples of the diffusion of Rastafari in the wider society: the popularity of "long and carefully unkempt hair," the donning of multicolored clothing believed to be African, defiance of "ganja laws," firm and fervent affirmation of Africa and blackness, condemnation of neocolonialism, repeated calls for an end to police brutality against the poor, criticisms of the white orientation of the society, and a reevaluation of colonial history.[67] As someone who became socially and culturally aware in the late 1960s and early 1970s, I can recall some young persons being criticized as "Rasta-minded," because they were expressing ideas, wearing accessories, or using words and expressions that were recognized as Rastafarian in origin.

Both Nettleford and Chevannes argue that the diffusion of Rastafari among the poor is related to the fact that Rastas and the rest of the poor share the same folk ethos. According to Chevannes, there is a continuity between Rastafari and the world view of the Afro-Christian traditions ingrained in the masses.[68] Nettleford maintains that "a closer look at the Rastafarian practices reveals that much in their way of life is in any case based on a moral code akin to that of the subculture."[69] Because Rastafari fit into the mold of the subculture, it is not surprising that the poor who inhabited that subculture eventually accepted elements of what was initially considered distinctively Rastafarian.

Although the 1960s started with the Rastas marginalized, maligned, and repressed, by the end of the decade, the movement was enjoying a great measure of acceptance from the wider society. By that time, the movement was not only accommodated but had began to exert tremendous influence on the social discourse and popular culture of Jamaica.

Cooptation and Commodification

The 1970s marked the beginning of a new era in the dynamics of the relationship between the Rastafarian movement and the rest of the society, an era of cooptation and commodification. With Rastafari becoming more diffused in the society, the point of view of the sufferer/Rasta became an item to be exploited by politicians in their quest to outdo their rivals. At the same time, Rastafarian images, symbols, and creativity became commodities to be peddled for commercial gain.

During the general elections of the 1970s (1972 and 1976), the battle for the heart and soul, not to mention the votes, of the people was waged around the manipulation of Rasta/African symbolisms. The visit of Haile Selassie, the Black Power movement, and the unmistakable stamp of Rastafari on the popular culture (clothing, accessories, music, and speech) had all spoken eloquently of the closeness of Africa to the hearts of the masses.

In 1972 the People's National Party (PNP), through its use of Rastafarian symbols and language and its espousal of issues close to the hearts of Rastas, conducted an election campaign that suggested an alliance with Rastas and the rest of the Jamaican lower classes.[70] This alliance was symbolized by Michael Manley's adoption of the name "Joshua" and by his carrying of a rod allegedly given to him by Haile Selassie on Manley's visit to Ethiopia in 1970. During the 1972 campaign, a pamphlet printed and distributed by the controversial Rastafarian leader Claudius Henry proposed a trinity of Henry (Moses), Manley (Joshua), and Selassie ("lord of lords").[71] The implication was clear. The Rastas have traditionally interpreted biblical references to the plight of the ancient Israelites in Egypt and Babylon as references to the suffering of the African diaspora. Now, "Joshua" would lead the modern "Israelites" to the "promised land" of equality and prosperity.[72]

The "rod of correction," as it was called, was a symbol of the authority that Selassie invested in Manley, empowering him to deal with the corruption in Jamaican society.[73] Additionally, a rod, or walking stick, is one of the trademarks of distinguished Rastafarian elders. The rod also has significance for African and Afro-Christian sects in Jamaica, since their leaders, called "shepherds," often carry rods as symbols of their authority. In 1972, even the leaders of the traditional Christian churches saw the rod as a religious symbol that signified the need for a correction of the society's moral and spiritual bankruptcy, which was charged to the Jamaican Labour Party (JLP) government.[74] With this potent symbol, Manley traveled around Jamaica promising to break the back of exploitation and corruption and bring justice and equity to the Jamaican masses.

In addition, several slogans of the People's National Party were taken both from the Rastafarian argot and from popular reggae songs with Rastafarian connotations. For example, the expressions "peace and love," "one love," and "hail de man," which were on the lips of most PNP campaigners and supporters, are readily recognized in Jamaica as Rastafarian greetings.[75] Manley once referred to the rod of correction as "I-rod," Rastafarian argot for "my rod."[76] "Better Must Come," which was the rallying cry of the PNP in 1972, was a popular reggae song. The PNP also enlisted popular Rastafarian musicians and singers, including Bob Marley, to travel on their bandwagons and to perform at their political rallies. In addition, the PNP made unabashed use of many songs that were critical of the social and economic situation in Jamaica. Many of these songs were clothed in Rastafarian rhetoric or had Rastafarian implications. "Beat Down Babylon," a song banned by the governing party, "When Jah Speaks," "Repatriation," and "Dem Ha Fe Get a Beatin," all exploding with Rastafarian overtones and undertones, were blared from PNP loudspeakers across the island.[77]

The Jamaican Labour Party tried to neutralize the PNP strategy by also using songs with Rastafarian themes, by claiming to capture the rod of correction, and by employing Rastafarian language in their speeches. Hugh Shearer, the prime minister and leader of the JLP in 1972, said at a rally before the election date was set, "Only one man can call election and [he] is *I-man*."[78] Edward Seaga, who was elevated to the leadership of the JLP by 1976, opened the 1976 campaign with a speech that read as though it were scripted by a Rasta. Among other things, he asserted, "Them going to get a beating," a clear allusion to Peter Tosh's "Dem Ha Fe Get a Beatin," a song used by the PNP in 1972. He continued, "But I want him [Manley] to know that Eddie is trodding creation, and the kingdom over which he rules no longer exists, because 'Jah Kingdom Gone to Waste.' . . . Youthman and daughta should know which is their party."[79] In addition to using such Rastafarian expressions as "trodding creation," "Jah kingdom," "youthman," and "daughta," the very tone of the speech was a simulation of dread talk, which had become "street talk" by the 1970s.[80] "Jah Kingdom Gone to Waste" was Ernie Smith's hit song, which the JLP adopted as its theme song in 1976. The song contains exclamations of "Oh Jah" and after describing the "dread" conditions of Jamaica, concludes with the words, "Jah sey dat no right."[81] By using this song, the JLP sought to highlight the failures of the Manley government over the previous four years and to claim that they would be better stewards of "Jah kingdom."

Whether the invoking of Rastafarian symbols and perspectives was an expression of genuine concern for the issues that affected Rastas and the black masses or just a political ploy is difficult to ascertain. After winning the 1972 election, the PNP did make some halfhearted gestures to deal with issues that concerned Rastas. For example, the government sought to develop greater ties with Africa, met with Rastas to discuss repatriation, declared its intention to review the ganja laws, and even pardoned some Rastas who were serving time on ganja charges.[82] Still, ganja remained illegal, and many Rastas continued to be prosecuted for its possession. Interestingly, Seaga, long recognized as a promoter of Jamaican culture, was involved in the recording and promotion of reggae. However, neither the PNP nor the JLP seem to have had any deep commitment to the tradition of protest enshrined in the Jamaican popular music. This was quite evident in the fact that while they were exploiting reggae to their own ends, they were also banning songs they deemed subversive or disruptive to the stability of the society.[83] Sometimes, the songs were merely an embarrassment to politicians or their political party and therefore hurtful to their egos to have them played on the air. For many years, some Rastas argued that they were exploited for political gain, which has strengthened their view that politics is really polytricks.

Whatever the motivations of the politicians might have been, the prominence of Rastafarian symbols, language, and themes in these elections was of sociological importance. Rastafari had clearly become something that could be exploited for political gain. Prior to this, Rastafari was something to be repressed, rehabilitated, or contained, so that it would not disturb or corrupt the "civilized" society. But when, in the elections of the 1970s, politicians adopted its language, symbols, and themes in their efforts to appeal to the poor in the society, Rastas gained unprecedented exposure, attention, and respect. A wide cross section of the society, especially the young, came to regard them as the vanguard of social and cultural change and embraced their lifestyle and artistic productions as the most genuine cultural expressions of Jamaica.

In addition to the diffusion of Rastafarian influence in the wider society and the notoriety gained from the exploitation of Rastafarian images by politicians, the embrace of Rastafarian symbols and artistic creativity as authentic Jamaican culture was partly due to the international recognition of reggae. By the early 1970s, such reggae artists as Desmond Dekker, Bob Marley and the Wailers, and Jimmy Cliff were gaining some popularity in England, and their songs were appearing on the British pop charts. When this occurred, those Jamaicans who had formerly dismissed Jamaican popular music as "uncultured" had no recourse but to turn around and embrace the music, since their artistic taste was formed by what the British considered acceptable.[84] This opened the way for the commodification of Rastafari in general and reggae in particular. Since then, people at all levels of the society have sought commercial gain by exploiting the Rastafarian image.

By the early 1970s, individuals aspiring to careers as singers had come to realize that projecting a Rastafarian image was part of the formula for having a profitable career. The artists who took on the image of the sufferer/singer were often not Rastas, but sensing that the commercial world was attracted to the Rastafarian elements in the music, they "locksed" (adopted the dreadlocks hairstyle) and invoked Rastafarian ideology in their lyrics to boost their chances of economic success.[85] For many, the key to success lay in clothing themselves in the Rastafarian image, employing Rastafarian language, and espousing Rastafarian ideas.[86] This wearing of the Rastafarian mask became so pervasive that Rastas often bemoaned the fact that many jump onto the Rastafarian bandwagon for monetary gain "without walking in the integrity of the priest."[87] Interestingly, Cedric Brooks, a renowned Rastafarian musician, cites Bob Marley as an example of an artist who exploited the Rasta image for a long time before he came to the true consciousness of Rastafari.[88]

Importantly, middle-class entrepreneurs have built thriving businesses exploiting Jamaican popular music. For example, Byron Lee, a local musician and producer, who once referred to the emerging local music as "buff-buff" because of its dominant bass line, has become a millionaire through exploiting the same music.[89] Chris Blackwell, the Jamaican-born British producer and promoter, has been able to build his Island Records empire through signing the cream of the reggae singers and promoting them around the world.[90]

Today, the commodification of Rastafari and reggae is exemplified in what Nettleford calls "culture tourism," the packaging of Rastafari as a tourist item.[91] Above everything else, reggae has become the most salable element of Jamaican folk or popular culture. The promotion of this Rasta-derived musical form as Jamaica's cultural product finds its highest expression in the yearly music festival called Reggae Sunsplash. Started in 1978, Reggae Sunsplash was for many years the biggest tourist attraction of the summer season, until it was superseded by JamFest in the 1990s. Sunsplash is a week-long music festival (as is JamFest) promoted by a group called Snergy with support from the government and the Jamaica Tourist Board.[92] In July or August each year, plane loads of reggae fans from all over the world—there are charter flights from as far away as Japan—descend on Jamaica to listen and dance to reggae music under the stars at the Bob Marley Entertainment Centre or some other venue.[93] The scheduling of these festivals at this time of the year is calculated to boost tourism, which generally is leanest during July or August. In 1988, John Jackson, an economist and research analyst, conducted a study to deter-mine the financial contribution of Reggae Sunsplash to the Jamaican economy during its first ten years. He concluded that between 1978 and 1988, the festival contributed an average of US $10–12 million each year to the Jamaican economy. In 1989, the festival brought US $17 million to the economy, and was projected to bring in US $20 million in 1990.[94] Both Sunsplash and JamFest remain strong tourist attractions. Although I have seen no recent calculation of the annual earnings of events, the fact that tourism is the largest section of the Jamaican economy suggests that they continue to be significant contributors to the economy.

For those not able to make the trip to Reggae Sunsplash or to JamFest, smaller festivals at various international venues bring the spice of Ja-maican culture to the world. Obviously, reggae has not only become en-trenched in the Jamaican popular culture but has gained a significant in-ternational following and has taken its place among the world's popular music. An indication of the esteem that reggae has achieved internation-ally is its inclusion as a category in the prestigious Grammy Awards.

In addition to reggae, the wares being hawked in Jamaica as tourist items reflect a pervasive Rastafarian influence.[95] In 1991, 1998, and 1999, I carried out research at Jamaica's craft markets in Kingston, Montego Bay, and Ocho Rios, as well as at numerous streetside stalls across the island. In these markets and at these stalls, one is first confronted with the ubiqui-tous Rastafarian colors: black, red, green, and gold. On closer examina-tion, one finds Rastafarian motifs everywhere: in the wood carvings, in the paintings, in the T-shirts, and in every imaginable accessory, from hats and handbags to necklaces and earrings. Noting that all of the carvings of human heads in a particular stall in the craft market in Montego Bay had dreadlocks, I inquired of the proprietor why all of the carvings portrayed Rastas. Without thinking, he responded, "A wi kultra; a wha di people want" (It is our culture; that is what the people want). On further inquiry, I discovered that the carvers were not necessarily Rastas, though many of them were, but people who embraced Rastafarian art as Jamaican culture and who were aware of the economic value of the Rastafarian image.

Some observers of the movement argue that cooptation by political and commercial forces has dulled the militancy of the movement and has short-circuited its potential as an agent of social change. Carole Yawney maintains that the adoption and promotion of Rastafarian cultural forms by the establishment has tempered the Rastas' trenchant criticism of the society, without providing solutions to the social and economic problems that once fed its militancy and criticism.[96] Carl Stone, a famous Jamaican pollster and political scientist, believes that historically the significance of the Rastafarian movement lies in the fact that it originally represented a potential political alternative to Jamaica's two-party system. He argues that the cooptation of the movement by the political establishment is now so complete that it has lost this potential.[97] Colin Prescod concurs, arguing that cooptation has "diverted the development of Rastafarianism."[98]

These perspectives have an element of truth. However, the cooptation and commercialization of Rastafari have also served to further entrench it in Jamaican society. These processes have facilitated the elevation and confirmation of Rastas as cultural heroes and their artistic productions as the most authentic expressions of indigenous Jamaican culture.[99] Concomitantly, they have all but buried the negative stereotypes formerly attached to Rastas. By the middle of the 1970s, the persecuted had become the peacemakers. Formerly, when there was violence in the ghettos, the police turned out in force to round up and harass Rastas. Now, politicians assemble Rastafarian musicians and poets to hold peace concerts. When a state of emergency cast a dark mood over the country in 1976, Prime Minister Manley organized a Smile Jamaica concert, with Bob Marley as the star attraction. When political factionalism escalated into "warfare" in the slums of Kingston in 1978, both political parties organized a Peace Concert, which featured all of the famous Rastafarian musicians who had emerged out of the ghettos. The highlight of this concert came when Marley called Manley and Seaga on stage and made them hold hands above his head as a gesture of reconciliation. By the end of the twentieth century, there was hardly a national celebration at which reggae and Rastas were not featured prominently. Klaus de Albuquerque is correct in his assertion that the relationship between the Rastafarian movement and the rest of the society has undergone considerable change: "The interaction . . . has brought about the Rastafarianization of Jamaica . . . and the Jamaicanization of the movement."[100] Nowhere is this more evident than in Jamaica's popular culture, which is the subject of the next chapter.

Rastafari Rules

Bearers of Jamaican Popular Culture

Beginning in the 1960s, Rastafari has become a ubiquitous presence in Jamaica's popular culture. This presence is observable in the visual arts, performing arts, literature, and music. This chapter will be primarily concerned with demonstrating how Rastafari has become the dominant influence in Jamaican popular music. I am concentrating on music because this is the element of Jamaican culture on which Rastafari has made its boldest marks and which is most fully documented. However, the Rastafarian contribution to Jamaican culture goes far beyond music. Therefore, before turning to the exploration of how Rastafari has factored into the development of popular music, I will outline briefly some of the other areas of artistic life on which the influence of Rastafari is evident.

In the visual arts, Rastafari and Rastas are subjects for artistic contemplation, and Rastafarian artists bring their own consciousness to their artistic endeavors. What is called the Jamaican Art movement started in the 1920s under the influence of Edna Manley, wife of Norman Manley, a Jamaican nationalist who was a leader in the Jamaican independence movement and the trade union movement. The Jamaican Art movement had nationalist motivation and reflected nationalist sentiments. Though Edna Manley was a white British woman, her art is in tune with the prevailing nationalist sentiments. Her subjects are often black, and her work expresses the longings and yearnings of the black populace for social, political, and racial uplift. Her famous sculptures, *Negro Aroused* and *Prophet*, exemplify her concern with the struggles of black Jamaicans.

Though Rastafari emerged at about the same time as the Jamaican Art movement, Rastas did not appear as subjects in the first two or three decades. However, by the mid-1950s, Rastafari began to emerge as a subject of interest to artists. A 1955 painting by David Miller, Sr., entitled *Rasta: Don't Touch I* signaled this artistic attention to Rastafari. Soon Rastas began to appear in the works of the famous Jamaican painter Carl Abrahams and others. By the late 1960s and early 1970s, artists who were influenced by Black Power and the growing African nationalism began to

use Rastafarian imagery to express their black consciousness. Painter Os-
mond Watson is the epitome of this trend. While Watson never professed
to be a Rasta, such pieces as *Ecce Homo*, portraying a dreadlocksed Jesus;
Peace and Love, depicting a Rasta in a meditative mood; and *Rainbow Triptych*, picturing a black Madonna, Jesus, and other saintly figures as Rastas,
are all believed to be somewhat autobiographical, reflecting Watson's consciousness of his African divine self (I-and-I consciousness).[1]

While Rastafari was becoming a frequent subject of non-Rastafarian
artists, a number of Rastas were emerging on the Jamaican art scene. Historically, Rastas have shown a predilection for involvement in arts and
crafts. This allows many to escape working in Babylon's economic structures, which they view as oppressive and exploitative. Also, strong visual
imagery and symbols form a part of the Rastafarian ethos. Thus art in the
service of religious and cultural convictions has always been essential to
Rastafari. Hence, the emergence of Rastas as artists was just a matter of
time. Eventually, such artists as Ras Dizzy, Leonard Daley, and Everald
Brown came to infuse their art with the "dread" consciousness that is
characteristic of Rastafari. Rastafarian painters and sculptors now explore
themes of blackness, African redemption, the apocalyptic destruction of
Babylon, and the divine self.[2]

The permanent collection of Jamaica's National Gallery, which is displayed in chronological order, is a good indicator of Rastafari's imprint on
Jamaican visual art. In the paintings prior to the 1960s, the colors black
and white predominate, with an occasional splash of red and green. Since
the 1960s, red, green, and gold have been used with growing liberality,
with many pieces depicting or alluding to Rastafari. *Rainbow Triptych*
(1978) epitomizes the Rastafarian presence. This piece shows various faces
of Rastafarian men and women appearing in stained-glass windows. One
frame is dominated by a black Madonna and another portrays a dreadlocksed Jesus. All of this is depicted in a profusion of Rasta colors.[3]

Rastafari has also made its mark on literature and the performing arts.
Contemporary Jamaican literature gives extensive treatment to Rastafarian themes. Writers and poets, Rastas and non-Rastas alike, have reflected
on the phenomenon of Rastafari and on other phenomena using the
prism of Rastafari.[4] *The Joker of Seville and O Babylon* by Nobel laureate
Derek Walcott, *Brother Man* by Roger Mais, and *The Children of Sisyphus* by
Orlando Patterson are examples of novels reflecting on the phenomenon
of Rastafari.[5] *The Penguin Book of Caribbean Verse in English* features such
famous Rastafarian poets as Mutabaruka, Bongo Jerry, Oku Onoura, and
Mikey Smith. These are performance poets who are highly acclaimed in
Jamaica and Jamaican communities abroad. The Penguin collection also
features poems by non-Rastas such as Louise Bennett and Linton Kwesi

Johnson, which deal with Rastafarian themes, reflect Rastafarian influence, or employ Rastafarian parlance.[6] Prominent non-Rastafarian poets, such as Lorna Goodison, Andrew Salkey, and Denis Scott, often allude to or explore Rastafarian themes, and they make liberal use of Rastafarian language and philosophy in their writings.[7] Increasingly, younger writers, such as poet Kwame Dawes and novelist Collin Channer, draw inspiration from Rastafari and reggae.

Although not much research has focused on the influence of Rastafari on the performing arts, the available evidence suggests that the stage also has come under the sway of the Rastafarian phenomenon. Such theatrical productions as *Summer Dread*, *I-Man*, and *Court of Jah* explicitly tap into or celebrate Rastafari.[8] In other productions with less obvious Rastafarian imprints, Rastafarian ideas, language, and music abound. The Rastafarian-influenced reggae music is an integral part of Jamaican theater, a frequent theme being the struggle of the reggae artist, often a Rasta, as he rises from poverty to worldwide fame. Additionally, the limited film production in Jamaica often makes use of Rastafarian characters and reggae music. Of course, the most famous film to do this is *The Harder They Come*, a 1972 feature-length film about the exploitation of a rising reggae star and his experiences after he turns to violence. *The Harder They Come* is credited with making reggae and Rastafari known around the world.

The presence of Rastafari in the artistic/cultural life of Jamaica is nowhere more obvious than in the popular music. Here we see the greatest concentration of the Rastafarian creative genius and observe its most significant imprint on the popular culture. I will devote the rest of this chapter to exploring the development of Jamaica's most widely recognized cultural product, reggae, as an example of the influence of Rastafari on culture formation in Jamaica. I will also outline the social reactions to the development of Jamaican popular music in order to trace its elevation to the status of national culture.

Rastafari and Jamaican Popular Music

The imprints of Rastafari are all over reggae, stylistically and lyrically. As Verena Reckford states, "Not only have the instrumental and vocal styling of reggae directly been influenced by Rasta Music, but the lyrics of most reggae songs and dance movements as well."[9] Agreeing with Reckford, Yoshiko Nagashima maintains, "The genuine fruit of Jamaican pop music has been yielded through the filter of the Rastafarian Movement."[10] To understand the relationship between Rastafari and reggae, we must first understand the evolution both of Rasta music and of Jamaican popular music.

Rasta Music: Nyabinghi

Traditional Rasta music, called Nyabinghi drumming, is played on a three-drum set called the *akete*, which provides the accompaniment at Rastafarian religious assemblies. Nyabinghi drumming emerged in the ghettos of West Kingston in the 1940s and 1950s. Kenneth Bilby and Elliot Leib inform us that this was the meeting place of various Afro-Jamaican folk styles brought to the city by rural migrants. They describe the folk music scene as "a cauldron of competing cultural and musical styles and forms, all of which were interacting and influencing one another."[11] In this mix were Burru (an African-derived style of drumming), Kumina, Revival, Pukkumina, and Jonkunu.[12] Of course, these were complemented by more popular forms such as mento, calypso, a variety of Latin styles (brought back by migrant workers from Cuba and Central America), jazz, and rhythm and blues. Identifying the degree to which each of these forms influences Nyabinghi drumming is a difficult task. However, the evidence suggests that Kumina and Burru were the main influences, with Burru predominating.

Rastas, while acknowledging and embracing the Burru influence, tend to reject or downplay the Kumina influence, presumably because of their distaste for its association with spirit possession and communication with dead ancestors, both of which Rastas abhor.[13] However, using historical and ethnographic evidence, Bilby and Leib have demonstrated that Howell and his followers integrated elements of Kumina, especially drumming and dancing, into their ritual practices at Pinnacle. Interestingly, the majority of Howell followers at Pinnacle followed him there from St. Thomas, the Kumina stronghold in Jamaica.[14] When Bilby and Leib did their ethnographic research in 1986, they found a group of Howellite Rastas near Spanish Town, who were still playing the Kumina rhythms using the two-drum set of Kumina (the bandu and cyas), instead of the Nyabinghi three-drum set adopted from the Burru (bass, fundeh, and repeater), which dominates in the Rastafarian movement. Bilby and Leib argue that the many Howellites who settled in West Kingston after the destruction of their Pinnacle commune brought with them their Kumina drumming, which later blended with Burru to create Nyabinghi. This leads the researchers to the conclusion that, even if Kumina had no direct influence on Nyabinghi drumming, its "invigorating rhythms" had already "meshed with those of Buru [sic]" and therefore have indirectly found their way into Rasta music.[15]

The connection between Nyabinghi drumming and Burru is more well established. Burru is a form of African drumming, which was very popular during slavery. Its survival was seemingly facilitated by the fact that slave masters often allowed Burru drum corps to play in the fields while others were working, because they had discovered that it "buoyed up the spirits of the slaves and made them work faster and so speeded up production."[16] Due to their concentration on music, Burru drummers had few agricultural skills, and so after emancipation (1834), they gravitated to the urban areas, mainly Kingston and Spanish Town. They seemed to have survived by working at odd jobs, while continuing to practice their art. At Christmas time, they would go from house to house displaying their virtuosity on the drums and singing their own compositions. Their songs addressed topical issues and exposed the "sins" of people in the community: "If a shop sold stolen goods, a critical song was sung in front of the shop. If a man committed adultery, the affair would be sung about."[17] Interestingly, this parallels a practice that still goes on in West Africa. At the end of each year, a troupe goes from house to house singing about the evil deeds of the residents, who are forbidden to retaliate.[18] Reckford points out that this "was a sort of purification rite which absolved the village of its 'sins' before they entered the new year."[19] The Burru people (they were identified as a distinct group) seemed to have retained some memory of the original African practice. Burru drumming and dancing also were used ceremonially to receive back into the community those who ran afoul of the law and consequently spent time in prison. This practice was observed particularly in West Kingston, which had a great concentration of Burru people during the formative years of the Rastafarian movement.[20]

The West Kingston slums have always been one of the haunts of Rastas, and they became even more of a focus after the police destroyed Howell's commune at Pinnacle. Many of the residents of Pinnacle gravitated to West Kingston where they built shacks on "captured" government land. The sharing of the same space by the Rastas and the Burru people led to a mutual exchange, a gradual merging, and finally, the virtual absorption of the Burru by Rastafari, with the Burru adopting the Rastafarian world view and the Rastas adopting and adapting Burru drumming.[21] Reckford describes the process this way:

> The Burru people had no religion of their own so to speak. Rastas had no music. The Burru people comprised a slowly disappearing group by the beginning of the forties, while the Rasta group was growing in numbers. The exchange of music for doctrine in the later [19]40s resulted in merger of the two groups and the almost total extinction of the Burru people as a social group.[22]

The dynamics behind the merging of the two are obvious. The anticolonialist, anti-European stance of the Rastas proved attractive to the Burru who were steeped in an African art form (drumming). Rastas, bent on ridding themselves of the trappings of Europe and on recreating themselves in the image of Africa, readily embraced this surviving African form.[23]

Of all African-derived musical forms surviving in Jamaica, Burru was probably the purest. Rastas were convinced that this form had remained uncorrupted or undiluted by Babylonian influences, and hence they appropriated it.[24] Rastas adopted the three-drum set used in Burru drumming: the bass, the fundeh, and the repeater (or 'peta). The bass and fundeh carry the rhythm of a piece, with the bass providing the foundation of the music and the fundeh setting the tempo or carrying the "lifeline." The repeater is the lead drum and supplies the melodic component. The playing of the repeater requires great skill, the drummer often improvising complex patterns with considerable virtuosity.[25]

The appropriation of Burru drumming and its development into a distinctly Rastafarian form is attributed to Count Ossie (Oswald Williams), an eminent Rasta and distinguished Jamaican musician. During the 1940s, he was grounding with other Rastas in the Dungle, a slum area built on a dump site in West Kingston.[26] A Burru player called Brother Job sometimes played his drum when the Rastas met for their reasoning sessions. The Rastafarian concern for the development of their own African culture led to the embrace of Burru drumming. Under the tutelage of Brother Job, Count Ossie became the first and most renowned virtuoso of Rasta drumming. Having mastered the Burru patterns, Count Ossie conducted his own experiments and made adaptations and innovations to suit his own taste and express his Rastafarian "vibrations."[27]

The akete (the Rastafarian three-drum set) soon became a staple at reasoning sessions and Nyabinghi I-ssemblies. As Reckford points out, the diffusion of the use of the akete throughout the Rastafarian movement was facilitated by the Rastafarian informal network kept alive by intervisitation. In describing how the network facilitated the spread of Rasta music, Reckford observes, "Brethren came and went as the spirit or occasion moved them. There was a great deal of dialogue and the exchange and transportation of ideas was strong. This was one of the means by which Rasta Music spread from camp to camp, parish to parish, in Jamaica."[28] Count Ossie's dwelling place, initially in the Dungle and later at Adastra Road in East Kingston, became famous for the musical ferment it generated. Of course Ossie and the group of drummers who gathered around him visited other camps and displayed their talents. They also played at the periodic Rastafarian mass gatherings known as Nyabinghi I-ssemblies, thus further popularizing Nyabinghi drumming.

Jamaican Popular Music

Historically, the colonial forces have actively suppressed genuine African cultural forms because of their potential to generate resistance and rebellion. However, the colonial powers did allow what Garth White calls some "denuded forms" (masquerades or Jonkunu) to exist for entertainment purposes. White further points out that wherever certain attenuated forms managed to weather the storm of suppression to assert themselves, "the white[s], shouldering their 'burden,' often took over these watered-down forms under the pretext of 'polishing' them up, pushing the black practitioners out of the picture and thus, in addition to their general exploitation of his labour, virtually using his 'last resort' against him."[29] In spite of the colonial efforts to suppress the African-derived musical expressions, some of these musical forms survived slavery and made it into the post-emancipation and post-independence eras. Traditionally, the African presence was most evident in the music of the African and Afro-Christian religions, such as Kumina, Myalism, Pukkumina, Revivalism, and the Native Baptist movement, and in more secular forms such as Jonkunu, Burru, and a variety of work songs. While the African presence still persists in these forms, in recent times it has expressed itself in what has become Jamaica's popular music.

Mento, which flourished during the second quarter of the twentieth century, may be regarded as the first attempt at developing an indigenous popular music in Jamaica. Mento is an ingenious blend of the various musical forms transported to Jamaica. Of course, the African presence is foremost, mediated through Kumina, Myalism, and Revivalism. The European presence comes in the form of British popular and religious music. Other influences come from Trinidad calypso and Latin American rhythms. The Latin influence was mediated by returning migrant workers, who had sought their fortunes in Central America, and by Cuban immigrants, who settled in Jamaica in the 1920s.[30]

Mento music was mostly played at community functions in the countryside. Initially, it had little following in the urban setting. It was particularly frowned on by "society people" (the middle and upper classes), because of its reputation for lewd and risque lyrics and because of its lower-class origins.[31] However, mento eventually gained some popularity among the Kingston nightclub crowd (of middle and upper class) in the 1940s. This breakthrough was brought about by such artists as Lord Fly and Lord Flea, who toned down the lewdness in mento to make it palatable to the nightclub patrons.[32]

The early 1960s saw the emergence of a new form of Jamaican popular music called ska. It fused mento with American rhythm and blues, which had become popular in Jamaica in the 1950s. Stephen Davis and Peter Simon explain the music:

> The music was vibrant and loping, the dancers at the sound systems made up a dance to it and called the dance *ska*, and in time that became the name of Jamaican R&B. Ska. Cheerful, riddled with funky brass sections, disorganized, almost random. Ska was mento, Stateside R&B, and Jamaicans coming to terms with electric guitars and amplification.[33]

The sound systems—mobile musical sets that play recorded music through huge speakers at dances—were largely responsible for the emergence of ska as a popular musical form. By the 1950s, sound systems had emerged as a major form of entertainment for the urban poor, who were unable to afford the price of hiring live bands for their parties. Initially, these systems played mostly rhythm and blues imported from the United States, with an occasional mento record interspersed here and there. But at least three factors coincided in the early 1960s to stimulate the development of the local recording industry and the emergence of ska. The sound systems faced the perennial difficulties of importing records in sufficient numbers to meet the local demand. To complicate this problem, the late 1950s and early 1960s saw a decline in the output of rhythm and blues in the United States, making fewer records available for import. At a more social-psychological level, the movement for political independence, which was afoot at that time, spilled over into the cultural arena, stimulating local musicians to create a music that would reflect their social location and cultural realities.[34] In this context, some owners of sound systems began to experiment with producing their own music for the dance hall crowd. When these productions were received enthusiastically by the dance hall fans, local producers, musicians, and singers rushed to cash in on the popularity of the emerging sound.[35]

The word *ska* seems to have come from the stabbing manner in which the guitar or piano played the rhythm. Jackie Mittoo, a noted ska keyboardist, claims that the name evolved from the people's call for "staya, staya" (the "chopping" staccato played on the guitar or keyboard) at live performances.[36] This piano or guitar chop or "riff," accenting the afterbeat, became the distinctive feature of ska. White explains, "The Jamaican musicians accentuated this afterchord so that it really became a backbeat or afterbeat. Or to put it another way, the piano or rhythm guitar emphasized the *and* of one-*and*-two-*and*-three-*and*-four-*and*."[37]

In the middle of the 1960s, ska evolved into a new form called *rock-steady*. Musically, rock-steady was much like ska. However, the pace was considerably slower, the bass guitar and drums were more prominent,

and fewer horns were evident. The latter may have been an economic ne-
cessity due to the prohibitive prices of horn instruments.[38] The slowing
down of the music consequently modified the popular dance. In fact, the
music took its name from the slow, steady manner in which it was danced.
Ska was a fast dance, which placed emphasis on foot movements. Rock-
steady, in contrast, was slow with minimal foot movements. As Malika
Whitney and Dermott Hussey explain, "It was more laid back, giving rise
to 'renting a tile,' a style of dance where movement is restricted to mark-
ing time on the spot, and resolving one's frustrations there."[39]

The last phrase in Whitney and Hussey's explanation reveals that the
stylistic changes were more than artistic innovations. The rock-steady
dance movements dramatized the social tensions in Jamaican society and,
particularly, the social stress and strain of the urban ghettos. Sebastian
Clarke captures this blending of art form and simmering social anxiety:

> When the rhythm slowed, paradoxically, the tension increased, and the
> body was now responding to an inner rhythmic drive. The tension of the
> external society was internalized by the dancer and expressed physically.
> Thus in rock steady, the dancer could remain on his spot of earth, and
> shake his shoulders, make pounding motions with his arms and hands (at
> an invisible enemy, or an anonymous force), without recourse to or con-
> sciousness of a partner. The internal tension was demonstratively and
> explosively expressed. Because the movement was stylized, its external
> appearance alone could be interpreted as tension-releasing, violence sim-
> mering at the surface.[40]

This interpretation is quite fitting because the social milieu of the mid-
1960s, in which rock-steady emerged and to which it responded, was
marked by heightened tensions and heightened consciousness of the inequalities in the society.[41] This was the era of the "rude boys," who celebrated violence as a means of survival in a society rife with inequities.
Many rock-steady songs reflected on the rude boy theme, often extolling
their exploits and their grittiness.

By the late 1960s, Jamaican popular music evolved into what we know
today as reggae. The derivation of the word *reggae* is shrouded in specula-
tion. Ernest Cashmore's suggestions vary from the Bantu word *ragga* with
y added on a whim, to the Indian word *rafa*, to *rico*, a reference to Rico
Rodriques, a local musician, to *ragga-ragga* or *streggae*, both words meaning unkempt, ill-clothed, or ragged in Jamaican patois.[42] Toots Hibbert,
whose song "Do the Reggay" is the first known use of the word, claims
that reggae means "regular," a reference to the fact that the music emanates from regular people and portrays their experience of suffering, past

and present.[43] Many Rastas contend that reggae comes from *regal,* and thus its meaning is "music of or for the king" (Selassie).

Reggae music researcher Garth White points out that reggae is the result of an intermingling of a variety of musical influences: "Listening to the range of reggae, one can detect the rhythms of the ancient ancestral cults [particularly Kumina and Burru] and Jonkunu masquerades, strains of revivalist religion, the uses of European instruments and melodies and the effect of exposure to music from all over the world."[44]

Of course, reggae evolved from and is a further refinement of ska and rock-steady, which preceded it. White goes on to describe how reggae differs from ska and rock-steady: "Basically in reggae a half-note is added to the classic afterchord [of ska]—one-and-two-and-three-and-four-and— becoming 'one-and*a*-two-and*a*-three-and*a*-four-and*a*.' This produced the characteristic 'reggae' or 'sken-ay' sound."[45] This description is particularly applicable to the rhythm section of reggae, but that is only one element of the music. The reggae rhythm is played on guitars, keyboards, and percussion instruments and accents the second and fourth beats of the bar. A second element of the music is the bass. Reggae has speeded up the tempo, which was slowed in rock-steady, and made even more pronounced the heavy bass introduced by rock-steady. The dominant bass often plays its own melody, leading some reggae enthusiasts to listen and dance only to the bass section. The melody or tune, the third element of reggae, consists of short phrases, which are adapted to the lyrics and which are often repeated.[46]

Rastafarian Influence on Jamaican Popular Music

Part of what accounts for the evolution of popular music into reggae is the increasing incorporation of Rastafarian elements. According to Whitney and Hussey, "The new music combined all the styles which had gone before, but with a spiritual content only partially evident during the rock steady period. The growing Rastafarian faith gave the music a new urgency, a new spirit."[47] As White's research demonstrates, the influence of Rastafari on Jamaican popular music goes back to the ska era. He writes, "From the earliest times in recent popular music history, Rastafarian music and philosophy has wielded a mighty influence, much to the chagrin of many older upper- and middle-class Jamaicans."[48] Many of the musicians who oversaw the creation of the local music were Rastas, and they brought their religious and ideological perspective to their music. The most distinguished of these were Don Drummond and Count Ossie.

Drummond was a leading member of the Skatalites, an instrumental band widely regarded as the creators and most successful exponents of the ska sound. The Skatalites provided the musical accompaniment for most of the famous ska singers. Drummond was an accomplished trombonist and a musical genius. In addition to his involvement with the studio work and live performances of the Skatalites, he wrote and recorded numerous instrumental pieces. His black consciousness, formed by his Rastafarian faith, is readily apparent in such titles as "Marcus Garvey," "Addis Ababa," "Far East," "Fidel," "Man in the Street," and "Johnny Dark."[49] White concludes that Drummond's music summed up and expressed the anguish and apocalyptic apprehensions associated with Rastafari:

> This apocalyptic mood, this "blue" pervasive sense of dread—a "brooding melancholy which seems always on the verge of exploding, but which is under some sort of formal control" was well suited to the developing Rastafarian ethos. Tunes like "Snowboy," "The Return of Paul Bogle," and the "Reburial of Marcus Garvey" underlined the connection between the leading musicians in the popular field and the Rastafarian faith.[50]

The influence of Count Ossie on the developing popular music is even more distinct. During the 1950s, Count Ossie formed a drum troupe. At first the group was famous only on the ghetto dance scene, but with its performance on the talent show "Opportunity Knocks," it began to broaden its sphere of influence. Then in the early 1960s, Count Ossie made his indelible mark on the local music. He arranged and, along with his drummers, provided the instrumental accompaniment for "O Carolina," recorded by the Folkes Brothers.[51] This was the first time that the distinctly Rastafarian rhythms appeared on a recording.[52] The song became the first big hit of the ska era and marked the beginning of the conscious incorporation of Rastafarian rhythms into Jamaica's popular music. Reckford comments, "Ever since *Carolina* Rasta ridims [rhythms] have been used by other local musicians to create on. Rasta music continued as the creative force through the *Rock Steady* period and in the *Reggae* period where it now flourishes."[53]

Count Ossie's original group disbanded. He later formed another group called Count Ossie and the Mystic Revelation of Rastafari. In this group, other instruments were added to the traditional Rastafarian drums. Through stage performances and recordings, this group disseminated Rastafarian music and lore throughout Jamaica and abroad. It performed at colleges in the United States and represented Jamaica at the Caribbean art and music festival called Carifesta.[54]

Probably even more important than Ossie's performances and record-

ings was the fact that his Adastra Road compound in East Kingston became the venue for local musicians to exchange ideas in "jam sessions":
"Among them were 'Bra' and Bunny Gaynair, Little G. McNair, Tommy
McCook, Roland Alphonso, Cedric Brooks—all saxophone players. Then
there were people like Viv Hall, trumpet, Ernie Ranglin, guitar, Donald
Drummond, trombone."[55] These are all recognized pioneers of Jamaican
music, who increasingly incorporated the "ridims" of Rastafari in the
emerging popular music.

At first the Rasta presence in popular music was felt through the style of
the drums in the rhythmic accompaniment. However, as the experiment
with Rasta music progressed, other instruments came to imitate the
whole range of the Rastafarian sound:

> The bass guitar line and traps imitated the patterns of the Rasta bass
> drum. Later on the fundeh ridim could be heard in the "Skengay" pat-
> tern of the rhythm guitar. It then left the lead guitar to imitate the adven-
> turous repeater drum. This took some time coming, but it did. Nowa-
> days not only the lead guitar, but the electric organ, horns and piano
> imitate the repeater.[56]

So that is why one often hears the comment, "Reggae is Rasta music." Of
course reggae is not coterminous with the Rastafarian ritual music, called
Nyabinghi. The difference is so great that some fundamentalist-minded
Rastas shun reggae as "devil" music, while others fear that the simulation
of Rasta music on modern instruments compromises its authenticity.[57]
Furthermore, Jamaican popular musicians are not afraid to incorporate
other influences that suit their musical fancy. However, the dominant element in reggae remains the rhythms worked out in Nyabinghi drumming.

Along with its influence on the instrumental quality of Jamaican popular music, Rastafari has infused the lyrical content of reggae with its philosophy. Some observers, including Cashmore, make the point that ska
and rock-steady were void of social consciousness, being preoccupied
with evoking sexual images and sensual fantasies, whereas "reggae signified a concentrated attempt to provoke social consciousness."[58] This perspective seems to be derived more from an observation of the "sexual sug-
gestiveness" of the swirling pelvic movements of the dances to ska and
rock-steady than from a careful analysis of the lyrics of the songs. While
sexual images and sensual fantasies were in the lyrics of many songs, from
the beginning, the popular music continued the folk tradition of using
songs to make social and political commentary. White, who is probably
the most respected authority on Jamaican popular music, points out that
"critical social commentary and protest were in the music almost from its

inception."[59] White goes on to cite two pieces, "Babylon Gone" and "Another Moses" by Count Ossie, as examples of songs from the ska era that made social commentary from the Rastafarian perspective.[60]

If the presence of Rastafarian social protest in ska can be compared to the budding of a plant, we can say it blossomed and bloomed in rock-steady and came to maturity in reggae. Describing the rock-steady era, Whitney and Hussey say, "The Rastafari and 'Rude Boy' sentiments of protest and rage that were instrumentalized by Drummond and the Skatalites, took a lyrical form. Political protest by song became popular while other songs continue to speak of the people's hardships."[61] In rock-steady, the militant Rastafarian disdain and criticism of the status quo "became even more menacing and laced with 'dread' than ska had been."[62] As already indicated, rock-steady appeared in the midst of the political and social tensions of the 1960s. At the same time, there was a coalescing of youth, music, and Rasta, all taking a posture of contempt for the status quo and demanding changes in the social system. The three leading members of the Wailers—Bob Marley, Peter Tosh, and Bunny Wailer—best exemplify this coalescence. Here were three young men from Trench Town, a most notorius ghetto in Jamaica. They were self-taught musicians trying to make a living on the recording scene. Gradually, they came to the consciousness of Rastafari and eventually became its best-known international spokespersons.

The most disturbing phenomenon of this period, from the perspective of the status quo, was the emergence of the rude boys. As White points out, the term covers a wide range of individuals, "from the anarchic and revolution-minded youth of the poorer classes to the young political 'goons,' mercenaries of the two existing political parties and Rasta-spawned 'cultural' rude boys who rejected the aping of white standards and continued existence of 'white bias.'"[63] Despite the differences, rude boys were united in their attitude of defiance and posture of toughness. The lyrics of rock-steady songs were preoccupied with the rude boy phenomenon, sometimes cautioning the rude boys, at other times berating them, but most of the time celebrating their grittiness (unyielding courage) in the face of official actions against them.[64]

In the lyrics of reggae, the perspective of Rastafari has exerted its fullest influence. Since the late 1960s, the Rastafarian point of view has come to dominate the lyrical content of reggae music. When observers of the music identify it as protest music, they are referring to the strident criticisms directed at Jamaican and Western establishments and its militant call to "Get up, stand up. Stand up for your rights."[65] We should not, however, make the mistake of characterizing reggae as exclusively protest music or its lyrical content as exclusively Rastafarian philosophy. Reggae

lyricists touch on the whole range of human experience, and as White informs us, "This music sees no theme as outside its scope and in the framework of that relentless beat addresses itself to key issues of life both
within and outside of Jamaica."[66] However, the issues facing the poor of
African descent, interpreted from a Rastafarian perspective and expressed
in Rastafarian terms, constitute the dominant element in reggae lyrics.
With all of the heterogeneity of the Rastafarian movement, two things
characterize all Rastas: a conviction that Jamaica's social system is indefen-
sible and destined to doom and a commitment to recoup and promote
proudly their African heritage. What John Sealey and Krister Malm call
the "dread tunes" became imbued with this Rastafarian posture:

> "Dread tunes" reject middle-class and white values and praise the black
> African homeland. To make their music more fearsome, Rastafarians
> brought back into the their music the original, threatening and heavy
> drumming of Africa. . . . It describes, in music and words, a powerful
> protest against poverty, unemployment and inequality in the society and
> contains the message of the Rastafarian religion.[67]

The exponents of reggae in general, and the Rastas in particular, infuse
their songs with these sentiments, regarding themselves as "fighting
against the system."[68] In this regard, White describes reggae as a musical
weapon, "a musical hand-grenade, to be used against those seen as the oppressors and agents of Babylon."[69]

Of course, social criticism through the medium of music did not originate with Rastas. Social criticism of the Jamaican society is characteristic
of most local musical expressions. Sometimes, it ridicules "high" society
or presents satirical commentary on its pretentious values. At other times,
it is just an ejaculative cry brought on by the harsh realities of life on the
margins or by what Whitney and Hussey call "the permanent trauma of
poverty."[70] What Rastafari has brought to this tradition is philosophical
depth, a serious ideology that repudiates the values and institutions associated with Western civilization and that explains the roots of the contradictions that pervade Jamaican society. By the late 1960s and early 1970s,
Rastafari had become the mold in which criticism of Jamaican society was
fashioned and the grid through which it was sifted and analyzed.

The foregoing considerations lead to the conclusion that Rastafari has
been a dominant force in the development of Jamaican popular music.
The Rastafarian contribution is readily evident in the musical characteristics and the lyrical content of reggae. The rhythmic quality, especially
the dominant bass line of reggae, is acknowledged by all as derived

from Nyabinghi drumming, which in turn was derived from Burru and Kumina. Furthermore, many of the instrumentalists who fashioned the indigenous musical sound that eventually became reggae were of the Rastafarian faith. In this respect, Don Drummond and Count Ossie were key players. Also evident is the role of the Rastafarian philosophy or world view as the "philosophical guiding force" in the lyrics of reggae.[71] Whether or not the singers and songwriters are committed Rastas, their lyrics are saturated with the Rastafarian perspective and clothed in Rastafarian language.

Social Reaction to Jamaican Popular Music

From the beginning, the "new sounds" found ready acceptance among the masses of poor Jamaicans. Ska, rock-steady, and reggae became the mainstays of the sound systems that played at community dances. The ready, almost instinctive, acceptance of the emerging local music by the poor was probably due to the fact that the music gave expression to the experience and point of view of the poor, especially the urban underclass. It sometimes expressed their stoic response to their experience of being excluded and their undying hope for better fortunes. Reggae singer/lyricist Jimmy Cliff poignantly expresses their stoicism as "sitting here in limbo" and their hope as "waiting for the tide to flow."[72] At other times, the music articulates "the oppressive world and environment of the masses,"[73] raises questions about the political and cultural integrity of the status quo, and declares their resolve to have their "piece of the pie, right here, right now."[74] The African elements in the music strike responsive chords in the hearts of a people who have struggled for centuries to keep the African presence in their song. The embrace of Jamaican popular music by the masses of the poor is unreserved and enthusiastic.

The initial response of the privileged and the guardians of Jamaican society ran the gamut from disdain to near-paranoia. Disdain was born of the mentality of the black and brown middle class that Chevannes describes as mostly European in all respects, except for the color of their skin.[75] This mentality "embraced anything white and metropolitan and conversely rejected anything that was reminiscent of the black past."[76] Therefore, ska, by displaying continuity with African rhythms, grated on the "refined" sensibilities and European aesthetics of the Jamaican middle class. This emerging cultural expression was dismissed as mere "noise." As mentioned earlier, Byron Lee, a middle-class musician and entrepreneur, referred to the emerging local music as "buff-buff" because of the

prominence of the drum and the bass. In the early days, local radio sta-
tions all but ignored the local music, giving instead a steady diet of
rhythm and blues and rock and roll.[77]

Despite their disdain, members of the middle class, and particularly the
government, could not ignore the new musical ferment. Its popularity
among the masses and its lyrics, which railed against Jamaica's social system, made them uncomfortable, to say the least. In Clarke's words, "Once
the articulation of the oppressive world and environment of the masses
came into focus, middle-class Jamaicans felt threatened and apprehensive.
The status quo was being vigorously questioned."[78] In many instances,
the government's response was to ban the songs it considered disruptive
to social order. When these songs became jukebox and dance hall hits all
across the island, the police frequently raided the dance halls and clashed
with the patrons.[79]

The Jamaican establishment eventually came to embrace reggae, with
all of its Rastafarian overtones, as Jamaica's most genuine indigenous cultural expression and as a cultural commodity. This has led Malloch to observe that "dreadlocks and reggae music have become a mainstay of Jamaican and Caribbean culture."[80] With the national embrace of reggae
has come the elevation of Rastas to the status of culture bearers and cultural heroes. Bob Marley, the most famous exponent of reggae music, exemplifies this elevation. Like most other artists engaged in the development of Jamaica's popular music, Marley emerged from the ghettos of
West Kingston. By the early 1970s, the Wailers, the group led by Marley,
had imprinted itself on the Jamaican public as the leading voice of the
ghetto. In fact, the original name of the group was the Wailing Wailers,
signifying that their music was a plaintive cry born of the ghetto experience. Such Wailers classics as "Concrete Jungle," "Trench Town Rock,"
"Duppy Conqueror," "No Woman No Cry," "We an' Dem," "Babylon
System," and others tell tales of the suffering, the defiance, and the hope
of ghetto dwellers. As Whitney and Hussey observe, "It was as if the people had entrusted their consciousness to the Wailers. They raised the life
in Trench Town, Kingston 12, to the forefront of awareness in Jamaica
and internationally."[81]

The emergence of Bob Marley and the Wailers as the leading reggae
group was due to an auspicious combination of a number of factors: the
musical creativity of the group, the ability of Marley and other lyricists to
tap the folk wisdom of the common people and to interpret their experiences to the world, and the successful collaboration between promoter
Chris Blackwell and Marley. Prior to meeting Blackwell, Marley and the
Wailers had many hits on the local recording scene, but remained strug-

gling artists. Whether it was because of his perspicacity or his penchant for a gamble, Blackwell signed the Wailers to the Island Records label in 1972 and gave them £4,000 and virtual artistic freedom to make an album. The result was *Catch a Fire*, which signaled the coming of age of reggae (on both the local and international music scenes). *Catch a Fire* received critical international acclaim and opened the world's pop stages to the curious group of Rastas from Kingston's worst ghetto. They plied their hypnotic rhythms and revolutionary lyrics about life on the margins and the injustices in the world. The collaboration between Blackwell and the Wailers made Marley into an international star, and even though he died in 1981, Marley is probably still the most widely known Jamaican.

With Marley's international success, the society came to embrace him as a cultural hero and reggae music as Jamaica's contribution to the world. After all, reggae music was replacing rum and limbo as the things for which Jamaica was known and was enhancing its status in the world.[82] Any lingering doubt concerning Marley's status dissipated when he was awarded the Order of Merit, Jamaica's third-highest honor, and further granted the respect of a state funeral at his premature death.[83] For a man who had made a career of "wailing" against the system and who once sang, "Mi no have no friend inna high society,"[84] these were incredible honors.

The kind of esteem in which the public held Marley was reflected in the outpouring of respect during the period of national mourning that followed his passing. Whitney and Hussey describe it: "On the morning of May 21, 1981, they all came to pay their respects, the well-heeled and the barefooted. They had filed by in numbers like the stones in the Great Wall of China. For three days the procession seemed endless."[85] The politicians were not to be outdone. At the funeral, Michael Manley and Edward Seaga, Jamaica's two leading politicians, both eulogized Marley, highlighting his contribution to the popular art form. According to Seaga, "His music did more than entertain. He translated into music, in a remarkable style, the aspirations, pain and feeling of millions of people throughout the world. As an individual, Bob Marley was the embodiment of discipline and he personified hard work and determination to reach his goals. He left us with a rich heritage of popular Jamaican music."[86] Manley was equally eloquent: "He is a genius. He's one of those extraordinary figures that . . . comes along perhaps once in a generation; who, starting with a folk art, a folk form, by some inner magic of commitment, sincerity of passion and of just skill, turns it into a part of the universal language of the arts of the world."[87]

Whitney and Hussey comment on how Marley's funeral symbolized the turnaround in the manner in which Rastas and Jamaican popular music are regarded: "A swarm of international journalists and photographers, some of whom may have once filled their news reports with stories about what they referred to as Rastafarian riff raff, were now elbowing for the best vantage point to record the last important event in the life of the front line man."[88]

Today, Marley is probably more alive in Jamaica's national consciousness than during his lifetime. His birthday, February 6, has become a de facto public holiday, having been declared Bob Marley Day.[89] Each May, his passing is commemorated with special events. During my trip to Jamaica in 1991, the Ministry of Culture and the Bob Marley Foundation sponsored a concert at the Ward Theatre to commemorate the tenth anniversary of his death. A Marley monument stands in front of the National Arena. The Marley Museum at his Hope Road residence receives a constant stream of visitors from around the world. Marley's mausoleum has become one of the most visited shrines in Jamaica. And Marley's music is as popular as ever, selling more than three million albums by 2000. At the turn of the century, the British Broadcasting Corporation played "One Love" as the anthem of the twentieth century, and *Time* magazine named Marley's *Exodus* as the album of the century.[90] As Rita Marley says, "Jah live, Bob lives, his music lives—Rastafari lives forever. . . . Bob is with us continually."[91]

The Rastafarian contribution to the evolution of Jamaica's indigenous culture is quite remarkable and has led Laurence Breiner to conclude that the movement is "the most energetic and creative segments [sic] of the Jamaican society," providing the masses of Jamaicans with "the only coherent culture to which they have access."[92] Velma Pollard and Yoshiko Nagashima concur. For Pollard, Rastafari "has moved like yeast through the Jamaican society, infusing all these expressions [artistic and cultural] with its power."[93] According to Nagashima, the "revitalization of hitherto repressed and seemingly moribund African [Afro-Jamaican] tradition in general is a reflection of the precious outcome of Rastafarian culture."[94] The Rastafarian contributions to and influence on the visual arts, the performing arts, literature, and particularly music have brought them widespread acceptance and have conferred legitimacy on the movement.

Summary

In this chapter, I have demonstrated that Rastas have emerged as the most creative segment of the Jamaican population, making imprints on the popular culture in a variety of ways, but most significantly in the area of popular music. The evidence, I conclude, suggests that Rastafari has assured itself of perpetuity by etching itself in Jamaica's national consciousness and by becoming embedded in the social and cultural fabric of Jamaican life. Hence, we can speak unequivocally of the routinization of Rastafari in Jamaican society.

Summary and Conclusions

The primary purpose of this study has been to identify and explain the factors that have led to the routinization and entrenchment of the Rastafarian movement in Jamaican society. In the process of doing this, I have argued that the theory of charisma and routinization, as articulated by Weber, is in need of modifications at some points. In this final chapter, I will summarize my findings and indicate their implications for the theory of charisma and routinization. I will also reflect briefly on the future of the Rastafarian movement with regard to its organization and its status in Jamaican society.

Charisma, Routinization, and Rastafari

Rastafari, at its very core, is a response to colonialism and its impact on the lives of Afro-Jamaicans. In the broader sociohistorical context, the movement emerged against the background of the miseries and atrocities experienced by the majority of Afro-Jamaicans since their removal from Africa in the seventeenth and eighteenth centuries. In the more immediate context, the movement was an attempt to deal with the economic hardship, political disfranchisement, and cultural imperialism of the 1920s and 1930s. Though novel in some respects, Rastafari has deep roots in the African and Afro-Christian traditions that preceded it. In particular, Rastafarian messianism, biblical apocalyticism, and Ethiopianism have their roots in ideas that have long been current in the folk tradition and in the tradition of resistance in Jamaica.

The crowning of Haile Selassie as emperor of Ethiopia was the catalyst that brought to the fore the deep-seated attitudes of many Afro-Jamaicans toward Jamaica's colonial establishment. It also heightened their desire for liberation from oppression and alienation. The Rastafarian movement, therefore, emerged because some Afro-Jamaicans perceived the crowning of an African monarch as the sign that their liberation from colonial oppression was imminent. Shortly after Selassie's crowning, some people started proclaiming him as divine and calling on others to reject the authority of Jamaica's colonial government and to give allegiance to Selassie alone. In time, Leonard Howell distinguished himself as the most forceful and persuasive personality.

Though this study has focused primarily on routinization, the phenomenon of Rastafari also has some implications for Weber's theory of charisma. By placing the emergence of Rastafari within the social and historical context of the experiences of the Afro-Jamaican masses, I wish to demonstrate that the context in which charismatic movements are likely to arise is too narrowly depicted by Weber. Instead of seeing charismatic movements as generated by merely extraordinary events or situations, we should see them as convergences of historical and social forces. In this light, equal emphasis should be placed on charisma as a collective social phenomenon as on charisma as the extraordinary qualities or exceptional powers of individuals. Weber himself indicates that for authority to be considered legitimate, those who submit to it must believe it to be so. From this perspective, charismatic leaders have only as much authority as their followers accord them. Therefore, those who recognize and submit to charismatic leadership are just as responsible as the leaders themselves for the creation of charismatic movements.

By pointing to the sources that helped to shape the character and message of Rastafari, I hope to correct the impression given by Weber that the teachings of charismatic leaders are completely novel. My contention is that the teachings and pronouncements of charismatic leaders must resonate with and have some measure of familiarity to those whose loyalty they solicit. Such familiarity is usually achieved by the charismatic leaders tapping into ideas and invoking symbols that have currency in the culture or subculture.

Furthermore, the emergence of Rastafari raises the question of the possibility of multiple charismatic leaders arriving at the same conclusions, advocating the same goals, and hence all contributing to the emergence of a single movement (a possibility not explored by Weber). Though the career of Leonard Howell is more fully documented than that of other early advocates of Rastafari, all historical studies of the emergence of Rastafari indicate that shortly after the crowning of Haile Selassie several persons, independent of each other, started proclaiming his divinity and enunciating the fundamental principles of Rastafari. If charismatic movements are collective social phenomena generated by convergences of social and historical forces, then it is quite likely that multiple charismatic personalities may emerge with similar ideas and similar agendas in those contexts that give rise to such movements.

With regard to the routinization/entrenchment of Rastafari in Jamaica, three contributing factors have been explored in this study: the movement's own internal development of an ethos, the rapprochement between the movement and the wider society, and the influence of Rastafari on the evolution of popular culture in Jamaica.

Though the movement has not developed the centralized and bureaucratic organization traditionally viewed as the most salient feature of routinization, it has evolved a reticulate type of organization, an intricate network of houses and mansions, connected and kept alive by personal relationships and intervisitation. The movement also exists within what I have labeled an ideological/symbolic/ritual ethos. The core of Rastafarian ideology is a common sense of evil, expressed in the concept of Babylon, and a common sense of identity and solidarity, centered around Rastas' attempts to recreate themselves in the image of Africa. This ideology is powerfully expressed in evocative symbols (Babylon, Zion, I and I, dreadlocks, the lion, Ethiopian national colors, and so on) instead of in elaborate treatises or carefully crafted creedal statements. Rastafarian rituals center around the concept of grounding, the establishing and strengthening of adherents in the principles of Rastafari. These include daily reasoning and the ritual smoking of ganja in the houses and mansions of Rastafari, periodic all-night sessions among circles of Rastas, and movement-wide I-ssemblies held according to the Rastafarian calendar of holy days.

The second factor facilitating the routinization/entrenchment of Rastafari was the gradual rapprochement between the movement and the rest of the society. Initially, the movement's antiestablishment posture was met by official repression. However, after a 1960 study by a group of university scholars defused some of the negative misconceptions about Rastas, the government began to pursue a policy of rehabilitation/accommodation, which led to greater social intercourse between Rastas and the rest of the society and an attendant lessening of the tensions the movement had occasioned in the society. At the same time, the Rastafarian perspective was gaining favorable attention among the radical intellectuals, the poor, and the young in the society, which led to a gradual assimilation of some of the elements of Rastafari by the wider society. Eventually, the cooptation of Rastafarian symbols and language by the political establishment and the commodification of the Rastafarian image and creativity by commercial interests from the 1970s onward served to confer legitimacy on the movement. More specifically, Rastafari has become the recognized voice of the poor and dispossessed and the creative edge of Jamaica's indigenous culture.

This leads to the third factor in the routinization of Rastafari. Rastafari has made an imprint on all areas of artistic and cultural endeavor in Jamaican society: literature, poetry, painting, sculpture/carving, theater, dance, and music. The contribution of Rastafari to the recent development of Jamaican culture has been so far-reaching that Rastas have been recognized as the most creative segment of the Jamaican society, and their artistic/cultural products have been lauded as Jamaica's only coherent indigenous cultural expression. Above all, reggae music, which imitates the rhythms of the Nyabinghi drums and which is infused with the language and ideological perspective of Rastafari, exemplifies the Rastafarianization of Jamaica's popular culture.

The entrenchment of Rastafari has several implications for the theory of routinization. First, the phenomenon of Rastafari indicates that a movement's ability to gain perpetuity and become a part of the social landscape is not solely dependent on the formalization of leadership and administrative structures. Observers of the movement have repeatedly underscored that the Rastafarian movement has not evolved any formal structures within which leaders are chosen, decisions are made, and the affairs of the movement are administered. Instead, the movement has developed a reticulate organizational structure, with unity and solidarity being facilitated by intervisitation, by sharing the same ideological/symbolic points of reference, and by participating in the same ritual activities.

Second, in addition to how a movement negotiates the problems of succession, economic support, and organization, routinization is also contingent on how it negotiates its relationship with the rest of the society, especially the dominant powers in the society. This point is almost self-evident, especially for a new movement emerging as an alternative to the established institutions and values of the society. While it cannot be determined beforehand what the society's reaction to the new movement is going to be and how that reaction may stifle or facilitate the development of the new movement, the dialectic of the relationship between the two is bound to affect the fate of the new movement. In some instances, the repression of the new movement by the establishment may be so rigorous as to bring about the death of the movement. In other instances, repression may only serve to strengthen the resolve of those involved in the movement and to attract others to it. In some instances, the acceptance of the movement by the wider society may lead to its domestication and finally to its demise as a force for social change. At other times, acceptance may confer credibility and legitimacy on a new movement, leading to its embrace by more and more people within the society and eventually to the mainstreaming of its perspective. As I outlined in chapter 5, the Rastafarian movement seems to have run the gamut from weathering the storms of repression to gaining accommodation and, eventually, to achieving credibility and legitimacy.

Third, the phenomenon of Rastafari also shows that, in the absence of formal leadership and organizational structures, a movement may work its way into the fabric of society by becoming the impetus for the artistic/cultural development of that society. The artistic innovations of the Rastas in Jamaican society and their elevation to the status of culture bearers serve to underscore the fact that the social significance of a new movement may not lie in the formal structures it evolves, but in its ability to affect the subsequent artistic/cultural development of the society.

Any theory of routinization, therefore, must take into consideration the development of social structures other than those considered formal or bureaucratic. It must address the dialectic of the relationship between the new movement and the rest of the society, and it must factor in the ability (or the lack thereof) of the new movement to become a force for social/cultural change in the society.

The Future of the Rastafarian Movement

The influence of Rastafari on Jamaican society and its growth into an international movement have been phenomenal, especially considering its humble beginnings. However, in recent years there have been questions concerning the future of the movement. Will Rastafari ever develop centralized bureaucratic structures and become an organized political force? Is the dynamism of the movement abating, thus signaling its decline and eventual demise? Definitive answers to these questions will have to await the further disclosure of the historical process. Nevertheless, I wish to reflect on them in light of my perception of the present state of the Rastafarian movement.

The answer to the first question will depend in part on whose assessment of this lack of centralized leadership prevails among the majority of adherents to Rastafari. Some Rastas and some experts on Rastafari see this lack of centralized leadership as a positive characteristic of the movement. According to I Jabulani Tafari, "One of the reasons for the survival of Rastafari in Jamaica has probably been the fact that I and I didn't have any formal centralized structure, but came into the faith and expressed the Rasta conception through various mansions and houses."[1] By this statement, Tafari is implying that the movement has maintained its appeal because of the attractiveness of its "ethical value of complete freedom from the force of man-made rules."[2] As I noted in chapters 3 and 4, the Rastafarian principle of I and I engenders a radical philosophical individualism. To those wary of being dominated by Babylon's systems and agents, this individualism is particularly attractive. As Yoshiko Nagashima indicates, "The individual is liberated from the feeling of bondage . . . to associate freely with any larger or smaller group or become independent."[3] This kind of freedom of association and participation provides a haven for those who want to belong without institutional commitments.

At the same time, other Rastas and other experts on Rastafari recognize the limitations that come with a lack of centralized organization and leadership. Among these limitations are the difficulty of acting as a united force, the difficulty of securing formal recognition (from the government), and the inability to protect the Rastafarian image and creativity from exploitation by outsiders. Educated Rastas, who seem to value the political clout that would come with a united front and with formal recognition, are the ones most concerned about these limitations. Therefore, they have made some attempts to unify the movement. The Rastafarian Movement Association of Ras Historian and the Ethiopian International Unification Committee organized by attorney Michael Lorne are examples of such efforts.[4] They have also initiated efforts to secure from the Jamaican government a formal recognition of Rastafari as a socially acceptable religion.[5] Since the 1980s, a group named the Rastafarian Centralisation Organization (RCO) has been meeting to discuss the issue of and strategize for the unification of the various elements of Rastafari. Furthermore, inspired by a Catholic commission, which recommended that the Rastafarian movement in England be recognized as a valid religion, some Jamaican Rastas sought to gain admission (without success) to the Jamaica Council of Churches in the early 1980s.[6] The problem with Rastafarian organizations such as the Rastafarian Centralisation Organization is that they are initiated with much enthusiasm and fanfare and then they disappear from the public radar because no one is willing or able to do the systematic, sustained grassroots organizing that is necessary for long-term success.

I have no way of predicting whether the radical individualism of the movement will continue to resist centralized organization and leadership or whether the appeal of political clout, the need for social recognition, and the desire for economic profit will lead to centralization. However, from my contact with Rastas during the 1990s, I have detected a growing conviction among Rastas—mostly the young and the better educated—that, if they are going to gain the recognition they demand and effect the changes they envision in the social institutions of Jamaica, they will have to become a rationally organized movement with centralized leadership. For example, at a special groundation held at the University of the West Indies in Mona, Brother Samuel, a young Rasta, related to me that the elders (older, influential Rastas) have resisted any attempt to organize the movement in a rational manner. He claimed, however, that the younger Rastas realize that different times call for different strategies and that for the movement to receive the recognition it deserves, it has to organize itself.[7] Part of the impetus for more rational and centralized organization among the educated comes from their desire to have the same kind of respectability and clout that their non-Rastafarian colleagues and counterparts enjoy in Jamaican society. With the passing of the first and second generations of elders, who were the "leading lights" of the movement, and with more educated Rastas becoming prominent in the movement, there are likely to be continued calls for unification or centralization.

With regard to the second question raised above, some observers of the movement have expressed the idea that Rastafari is in a state of decline. Eron Henry contends that "Rastafarianism has lost its light and is now in a state of eclipse," despite the "epochal" impact it has had on Jamaican society.[8] Arthur Kitchen, an intellectual of Rastafarian persuasion,[9] has noted that the Rastafarian penetration of all occupational ranks and other facets of Jamaican society has been accompanied by shifts in the movement, which have led to questions concerning the direction in which Rastafari is going. As examples of these shifts, Kitchen mentions both the move from an emphasis on immediate repatriation to an emphasis on social and economic rehabilitation and the absence of militancy and open agitation, which have historically characterized the movement.[10] To some, these shifts indicate that Rastas are capitulating to the wider society and are therefore losing their distinctive edge. The Reverend Samuel Vassel, with whom I have had a number of discussions concerning the movement in general and this study in particular, contends that social acceptance has led to the "Babylonization of Rastafari." When I interviewed Vassel in May 1991, he agreed with Henry and Kitchen that Rastafari lacked the militancy it has historically displayed and was also no longer the magnetic attraction it was for Jamaican youth in the 1960s and 1970s. Furthermore, during the decade of the 1990s, several notable Rastas, including Tommy Cowan and Judy Mowatt (of the I/Threes), converted to evangelical Christianity. This defection raises further questions about the possible demise of Rastafari.[11]

My response to these concerns and observations is threefold. First, we may characterize the lack of dynamism in the Rastafarian movement in the 1980s and 1990s as the price of success. Mayer Zald and Roberta Ash have observed that when new movements have gained some measure of success and "have found a niche for themselves" in the society they once opposed, they are likely to become "becalmed," which is characterized by a lack of activism, by conservatism, and even by attrition.[12] Therefore, it should not be surprising that the mainstreaming of Rastafari, especially in the artistic/cultural arena, should be accompanied by a noticeable decrease in the vigor with which the movement formerly confronted the wider society.

Second, the perceived lack of militancy on the part of Rastas may also indicate the extent to which Rastafari has become a familiar presence on Jamaica's social scene. Before 1970, the very proclamation of oneself as a Rasta was a militant and challenging gesture. The wearing of dreadlocks, the repeated enunciations of "blood and fire" and other vitriolic outbursts by Rastas, and the combative lyrics of the popular songs were likely to create panic in non-Rastas and to set the establishment on alert. Today, dreadlocks have become a trendy hairstyle among many non-Rastas, verbal outbursts by Rastas are regarded as comical (non-Rastas are also likely to clothe their verbal outbursts in Rastafarian terms), and protest in reggae lyrics is commonplace, hardly regarded as anything but an outlet for pent-up frustration.[13] The movement has therefore become less threatening as it has become more familiar to the wider society.

Third, social movements are often subject to a pattern of ebb and flow, and being in the ebb phase does not necessarily indicate that a movement is destined for death. Historically, the Rastafarian movement has shown a pattern of militancy and retrenchment. The emergence of the movement in the early 1930s was accompanied by public agitation, especially in Kingston and St. Thomas. The main focus of the early agitation was the condemnation of Jamaica's colonial government and the proclamation of the divine kingship of Haile Selassie. Early persecution led to a kind of retreat, as in the creation of Howell's commune at Pinnacle. The mid-1950s to the early 1960s saw another period of activism, which focused mainly on the demand for repatriation to Africa. Public marches, mass conventions, and refusals to cooperate with the law enforcement and judicial systems were the main activities of this period. Most of the 1960s was a period of cooling off as the movement and the wider society brokered a kind of truce. The late 1960s through the 1970s marked a third period of militancy, aimed at expunging Eurocentrism from the Jamaican psyche and infusing it with a sense of African history and culture. In that period, the hypnotic rhythms and the scathing lyrics of reggae became the catalyst and medium of protest. The 1980s and the 1990s can be characterized as an ebb phase, and signs of renewed strength and militancy are on the horizon in the early twenty-first century.

One sign is the effort of some Rastas to effect changes in the legal and political structures of the society. Using the arrest (December 1996) and conviction (1997) of Dennis Forsythe, who is a Rasta and an attorney, on possession of ganja and ganja paraphernalia, Rastas and their liberal supporters spearheaded a high-level campaign for the legalization of ganja in the late 1990s. Forsythe's case was eventually considered by Jamaica's constitutional court, which ruled that section 21 of Jamaica's constitution allows for the possession and use of ganja for religious observances. Probably as a response to the case and the decriminalization campaign it sparked, the Jamaican government empaneled a commission to study the existing laws concerning ganja and to recommend whatever changes it considers necessary.[14] In 2001, the panel, headed by University of the West Indies professor and expert on Rastafari Barry Chevannes, recommended the eventual decriminalization of ganja. So far, the Jamaican Government has not indicated if it will accept the commission's recommendation and start the legislative process that will lead to the decriminalization. Such a process will not only face opposition from civic and religious organizations in Jamaica, but also from the U.S. government, which will consider any move toward the decriminalization of ganja as a dereliction of duty in the war against drugs.

Renewed Rastafarian activism is also seen in the decision of a group of Rastas to contest political elections in Jamaica. In doing so, they claim that Rastafari remains the only viable hope for social justice in Jamaican society. During the 1997 general election in Jamaica, they entered four candidates, and though these candidates garnered little electoral support, the group declared its intention to continue its participation in the electoral process.

The reemergence of a strong Rastafarian militancy in Jamaican popular music, after the dominance of sex and violence in the dance hall era (1980–mid-1990s), is another sign that Rastafari may be ready to reassert itself more forcefully in Jamaican society. Popular artists, such as Luciano and Sizzla, infuse their lyrics with Rastafarian spirituality and cultural awareness. Others, such as Anthony B and Buju Banton (shedding his reputation for "slackness"), have emerged as serious social and political critics. Anthony B's "Fire Pon Rome" is a bold, scathing, and frontal attack on political corruption and economic exploitation in Jamaica.[15] He even calls the names of prominent politicians and businessmen, whom he sees as responsible for poverty and oppression in Jamaica.

Renewed Rastafarian militancy has also emerged in reaction to the conversion of some prominent Rastas to evangelical Christianity. In the late 1990s, there was a strident rhetoric of "bun Jeezas" (burn Jesus) emanating from fundamentalist Rastafarian circles. Prominent Rastas also wrote editorials suggesting that the so-called converts were never genuine Rastas and calling into question the Rastafarian credentials of professing Rastas whom they viewed as too enmeshed in Babylon.[16]

The next phase of Rastafarian militancy is likely to be presided over by the intellectual elite, which developed in the movement over the last twenty years of the twentieth century. The voices of these educated Rastas are becoming the leading voices in the movement, and their concerns are beginning to shape the agenda for the future. This agenda is likely to be marked by more political pragmatism than the Rastafarian movement has exhibited to date.

In conclusion, Rastafari has become a "part of the taken-for-granted landscape" of Jamaican society.[17] It has weathered the storm of repression and has emerged as a legitimate religious and cultural expression of a people bent on rediscovering their African heritage after prolonged oppression and Europeanization. Furthermore, it has become the sociocultural force exerting the most significant impact on the evolution of Jamaica's indigenous popular culture. Where the movement goes from here will depend largely on how it faces the challenges and existential problems of the twenty-first century. Whatever the trajectory of Rastafari in the future, the history so far has been an amazing transition from Rastas being social outcasts to being the bearers of Jamaica's popular culture.

Appendix

A Review of the Literature on Rastafari

For its first twenty years, the Rastafarian movement did not attract much scholarly attention. Since 1953, however, the movement has been receiving increasing scholarly treatment. From my reading of the literature, several distinct approaches and emphases have become evident. These approaches see Rastas as (1) millennial escapists, (2) social change agents, (3) a dynamic community, (4) people returning to authentic, ancient roots, or (5) social/political activists. To consider every significant piece of the literature would make this review too voluminous. Therefore, I will present a sampling of those treatments that I consider the best examples of each approach or emphasis in order to provide the newcomer to the study of Rastafari with an introduction to the range of literature on the movement.

Rastas as Millennial Escapists

Between 1953 and 1969, researchers mostly focused on deprivation theory to explain the phenomenon of Rastafari. Both George Eaton Simpson, whose research first introduced Rastafari to the scholarly community in the 1950s, and Leonard Barrett, whose research on Rastafari in 1965 was the first attempt at a comprehensive treatment of the movement, view the Rastafarian movement in terms of millennial/messianic cultism. From this perspective, these scholars emphasize the oppressive social situation from which the movement originated and view the Rastafarian ideology/theology and agitation as escapist or at best adjustive. In Simpson's words, the movement is a compensation for the "deprivation of [a] lowly social situation."[1] But the compensatory measures, manifested in "political withdrawal combined with verbal aggression" and in a desire to repatriate to Africa,[2] are escapist rather than creative. Simpson's basic claim is that the Rastafarian posture results from an acceptance of the dominant values of the society coupled with frustration at the prospects of achieving success under the existing system. The Rastafarian posture is therefore an avenue for the release of pent-up frustrations.[3]

While Barrett's work is based on more substantial ethnography (providing a wealth of descriptive information on the history, doctrines, and social organization of the Rastas), and while it recognizes the role of Rastafari in creating a more positive self-image for its members, Barrett follows Simpson in casting the movement in terms of millennial messianism and in concluding that it is escapist. Barrett argues that the Rastafarian posture of nonparticipation in the political and social processes of Jamaica is dysfunctional, because it does nothing to change the oppressive situation that Rastas are protesting.[4]

The University of the West Indies' study of 1960, while not a theoretical work, implicitly accepts the deprivation premise (probably influenced by Simpson). The study concludes that the Rastafarian movement, rooted and thriving in the urban slums, is a response to the poverty, the unemployment, and the lack of acceptable physical infrastructures that characterize these areas.[5] However, the university report does not follow Simpson with regard to his claims that Rastafarian ideas are fanciful and farfetched. Its analysis of the social and economic conditions under which Rastas lived in West Kingston in the 1950s and early 1960s and its recommendations to the Jamaican government are implicit admissions that Rastas had legitimate grounds for complaint against the dominant powers in the society.[6] As a public policy document, the study recommends that steps be taken to remedy the conditions under which Rastas live and that their concerns be addressed. Among the recommendations are the exploration of the possibility of repatriation to Africa, the building of low-income houses, the provision of public utilities, and the offering of social services.[7] Despite the positive intentions of the university scholars, their recommendations seem to have been born of the conviction that the Rastafarian movement was socially pathological and had the potential to generate serious social upheaval. In fact, the report specifically claims that the movement is malleable material for Marxists and other radicals desirous of fomenting revolutionary activities.[8] Thus the recommendations must be seen as an effort to rehabilitate or repatriate Rastas before they become more socially dangerous.

Sociologist Orlando Patterson and anthropologist Sheila Kitzinger have more social-psychological interpretations of the movement. Both seem to subscribe to an interpretation of millennialism as a psychosocial pathology or a sign of "group neuroses."[9] For Patterson, Rastafari is a psychological reaction to cultural alienation born of unsuccessful social mobility, urban ghettoization, and economic deprivation. Barred from the fruits of the society, Rastas have developed a kind of "sour grape syndrome," which manifests itself in an aggressive denunciation of Jamaica and an avid desire to emigrate.[10] Therefore, the expression of a desire for repatriation among Rastas is, from a psychological point of view, really a desire to participate in the benefits of the society. In other words, the Rastas' expression of a desire to repatriate should be interpreted as a coded way of saying they wish to be made full participants in the privileges of mainstream society.[11]

While claiming to recognize the potential of Rastafari as a political force, Kitzinger categorizes the movement as a "last ditch effort" to preserve some sense of identity in a society which has made them outcasts.[12] But while the Rastafarian faith serves as a coping mechanism in a desperate situation, it does nothing to address the objective structures that create and maintain the situation. Rastafarian beliefs, political stance, and lifestyle only serve to make Rastas further marginalized.[13] Kitzinger's conclusion is that "repressed psychological drives," resulting from marginality,[14] "provide the basis for faith and action for the Rastafari."[15]

The scope of this review will not permit me to do an extensive critique of the millennialist approach to Rastafari. However, I would like to raise a few points. On the positive side, the studies that I have just reviewed are significant in that they introduced Rastafari to the scholarly community and provided the initial data on the movement. Furthermore, they are correct in identifying the economically underprivileged sector of Jamaican society as the strata from which Rastafari emerged and in which it thrives. However, these approaches suffer from at least three critical problems: limited data, myopic focus, and theoretical rigidity. A number of the early treatments of Rastafari were based on limited data. For example, Simpson's data were obtained by observing Rastafarian street meetings and visiting several Rastafarian yards in Kingston over a brief period of time. The university report, for all of its acclaim, was limited to Kingston (mainly West Kingston) and based on research that lasted only a month.

Along with the limited data, there is a narrow focus on certain aspects of the movement. Even when researchers (like Barrett, Kitzinger, and Patterson) acknowledge the complexity of the Rastafarian experience and philosophy, they manifest a tendency to focus on repatriation and political withdrawal as the most significant elements. This of course fits into their millennialist mold, but it not only ignores the complexity of the movement but also fails to grapple with the significance of Rastafari as a call for social change and as an attempt to reconstruct an African identity for people of African ancestry.

In the 1950s and 1960s, viewing religious movements indigenous to colonial and postcolonial societies in terms of millennialism and escapism seemed to have been in vogue among sociologists and anthropologists.[16]

The use of the millennialist framework was supposed to be a mark of scholarly sophistication, so investigators felt compelled to filter their research through this model. The uncritical application of this approach to Rastafari results in a theoretical rigidity, which forces the movement into a predetermined model, thus emphasizing those elements of the movement (the deprivation of its adherents and their call for repatriation) that tend to support the biases of the theory. The movement is far more complex than these researchers' analyses indicate. But the problem goes even deeper. Some scholars seem to consider an acceptance of the status quo as normal and legitimate, and thus any challenge or alternative must be considered pathological. They therefore join the status quo in viewing the Rastas as criminals, lunatics, or fanciful dreamers because of their rejection of the established values and institutions. However, the repressive actions of the guardians of the society revealed their fear of the potential of Rastafari as a vehicle for social change. The next generation of scholars would highlight such a potential.

Rastas as Social Change Agents

The growth and visibility of the Rastafarian movement during the 1960s seemed to have alerted scholars to its revolutionary potential. Professor Rex Nettleford, an astute observer of cultural and social change in Jamaica and one of the three researchers who conducted the university study of 1960, was the first to break with the millennial/escapist tradition. Focusing on the dynamic interactions between the movement and the wider society, Nettleford argues that Rastafari represents a creative and revolutionary force in a society plagued by inequalities and a denial of its African heritage.[17] As Joseph Owens comments, Nettleford's break with the previous scholarship is evident in the fact that he boldly asserts that "it is the society that is abnormal and the Rastas sane."[18]

Since Nettleford's observation, there has been a chorus of voices hailing the Rastas as social change agents. The recurring theme in these studies is the role of Rastafari in resisting colonial and neocolonial ideology and socioeconomic structures and in forging an Afro-Caribbean consciousness that reflects the Afro-Caribbean experience. Some studies focus on the historical significance or the historical trajectory of the movement. Horace Campbell and Frank Jan van Dijk represent this historical approach to Rastafari as social change agents. Others, including Maurice Bryan, Becky Michele Mulvaney, and Jack Anthony Johnson-Hill, focus on how the internal character and social dynamics of the movement embody protest and advance social change.

Horace Campbell places the Rastafarian movement in the context of the history of social and political resistance in Jamaica. As indicated by the title of his book, *Rasta and Resistance: From Marcus Garvey to Walter Rodney*, between the eras of these two formidable figures (Garvey and Rodney), Rastas bore the torch of black consciousness and carried on the struggle for political and economic power and cultural authenticity. Rastafari, therefore, falls within the tradition of radical protest by Afro-Jamaicans in the quest for social change.[19] Frank Jan van Dijk is more concerned with tracing the historical development of Rastafari within the context of Jamaican society and beyond. Using all available sources (archives, interviews, books, and so on), van Dijk seeks to present the world of Rastafari to his readers while highlighting how a despised minority resists racial, economic, cultural, and political domination to create a voice and an identity for itself.[20]

Like Campbell, Maurice Bryan also portrays Rastafari as a resistance movement and places it in the tradition of black struggle in the Americas. However, Bryan hones in on how aspects of Rastafari, such as its spirituality, philosophy, and music, continue the tradition of black struggle in the contemporary world.[21] Similarly, Becky Michele Mulvaney focuses on the protest, resistance, and call for social change characteristic of reggae to underscore the transformative impetus of Rastafari. Using Rastafarian poetry and reggae lyrics as his data, Jack Anthony Johnson-Hill also emphasizes the transformative influence of Rastafari but focuses primarily on the transformation of the consciousness of the adherents of Rastafari. The word *I-Sight* in the title of Johnson-Hill's book is indicative of the transformed self-understanding of Rastas which leads them to embrace new ethic and a new way of life.[22]

Even some scholars who first described the movement as millennial and escapist have come around to a more positive appraisal. For example, Simpson and Barrett, in more recent publications, have pointed to the impact of the movement on the wider society and to its potential as a catalyst for social change.[23]

The social change approach grounds Rastafari in the social realities that the movement has faced over the years and that have shaped its perspective on the world. At the same time, it raises questions about the inequities of Jamaican society, takes seriously the ideals of Rastafari, and gives credence to the Rastafarian demands for redress of the structural ills of the society. Today, the almost universal acknowledgment of the positive influence of the Rastafarian movement on Jamaican society gives strength to the validity of this approach. However, this perspective demonstrates a tendency to gloss over such issues as repatriation and ganja smoking. In addition, these theorists must admit that, in spite of the changes that the Rastafarian movement has effected in Jamaican society in terms of African consciousness and acceptable cultural and artistic expressions, it has done little to change the European-derived political, economic, judicial, and educational institutions. While Rastafari may rule in the culture of the streets, Europe still rules in the culture of the established institutions. Furthermore, while the social change theorists provide invaluable information on the interface of Rastafari and the wider society, they do not shed enough light on the experiences of those who inhabit the world of Rastafari. It is to the research of those who see Rastafari as a dynamic community that we must turn for such a perspective.

Rastafari as a Dynamic Community

A growing body of scholarly literature focuses primarily on the internal dynamics and inner workings of the Rastafarian movement. This body of literature places emphasis on the ideological and symbolic content of the movement, the historical evolution of various aspects of the movement, the ritual and social dynamics of the movement, and gender issues within the movement. Ernest Cashmore and Joseph Owens represent the first emphasis. Cashmore, focusing primarily on the Rastafarian movement in England, uses insights from the sociology of knowledge to focus on how the movement constructs, communicates, and preserves its world view in a hostile environment. He pays particular attention to the use of symbols (for example, Rasta colors, dreadlocks, I and I, and Babylon) as embodiments of such a world view.[24] Owens also seeks to articulate the Rastafarian world view, which he believes authenticates the religiosity of Rastafari. Without casting the movement within any sociological and anthropological framework, he provides a thematic analysis of Rastafarian beliefs.[25]

Barry Chevannes's research pays close attention to the social history and the development of various aspects of the Rastafarian movement. He traces many aspects of Rastafari to the African and Afro-Christian traditions, which preceded it in Jamaica. Particularly, he demonstrates how a number of Rastafarian beliefs and practices are taken from Jamaican folk religion, particularly Revivalists. Chevannes's research also sheds light on the emergence of certain Rastafarian distinctions. For example, he traces the institutionalization of the smoking of the ganja pipe (chillum or kochi) as a ritual activity, the establishment of dreadlocks as a Rastafarian trademark, and the development of a distinct Rastafarian argot to a group of young radical Rastas in the House of Youth Black Faith, who came to prominence in the late 1940s and early 1950s.[26]

The third emphasis is represented by Carole Yawney and John Paul Homiak. They are more concerned with the ritual and social dynamics of the movement. Yawney's major concern is how reasoning and the ritual smoking of ganja serve as media for the creation of a new consciousness that is different from and rejecting of that of the dominant society. Yawney's other concern is Rastafarian sociality. Here she highlights the polity of the yards,[27] the importance of the informal network that links yards across the island, and the subdued role that women play in the movement.[28] Homiak's investigation deals with the role of elders as inspirational leaders and as charismatic exponents and defenders of the strict, conservative principles of Rastafari, which are upheld in the Nyabinghi Order.[29] Homiak outlines the role of elders in the oral tradition of the movement, in the ritual administration of reasoning sessions, in the convening of Rastafarian conventions, and in the decisionmaking process in the movement.[30]

While various scholars have pointed to the patriarchal ethos of Rastafari, only a few have focused on analyzing the dynamics of gender relations. Maureen Rowe, Imani M. Tafari-Ama, and Obiagele Lake are most representative of those who pay close attention to this aspect of Rastafari. Both Rowe and Tafari-Ama are Rastas and therefore bring an insider's perspective to their work.

Rowe basically outlines the traditional gender roles of Rastafarian women in relation to their "kingmen"(male partners). She argues that this ascription of a subordinate status to Rastafarian women mirrors the patriarchy[31] of Jamaican society and draws ideological support from African patriarchy and the Old Testament, especially the Levitical laws. Rowe also agues that in early Rastafari, male-female relationships were on more equal terms and women participated in all aspects of Rastafari. The advent of dreadlocks with its attendant emphasis on "dreadness" and the influence of the male-oriented, macho-steeped rude boy movement on Rastafari led to both a discourse and a praxis that relegated women to the background of the movement. Developments since the 1970s, such as the entrance of more educated women (as well as men) into the movement, the willingness of more "liberated" Rastafarian men to talk about gender issues and the place of women in the movement, and the phenomenon of more single, independent women who are "trodding" Rastafari on their own terms, have created fractures in the staunch patriarchy of earlier years.[32]

Tafari-Ama takes a similar position as Rowe concerning the roots of Rastafarian patriarchy. However, she focuses more on how women wrestle with such a system and negotiate spaces for themselves within the movement.[33] This perspective on gender issues in Rastafari gives voice and agency to Rastafarian women, a perspective noticeably absent from the works that simply charge the movement with being patriarchal.

Obiagele Lake's book, *Rastafari Women: Subordination in the Midst of Liberation Theology*, is a serious critique of the position of women in Rastafari. Showing how women are relegated to the margins of the movement and how the Jamaican popular culture that has developed around or under the influence of Rastafari denigrates and objectifies them, Lake seriously questions whether Rastafari can be a serious force for the liberation of the African diaspora when it makes women into second-class citizens.[34]

Two other scholars of note who have written about women in Rastafari are Carole Yawney and anthropologist Diane J. Austin-Broos. Following through on her exploration of the internal dynamics of Rastafari, Yawney describes how women figure in the patriarchal religious and social ethos of Rastafari.[35] Austin-Broos's work compares the male-centeredness of Rastafari with the female-centeredness of Pentecostalism in Jamaica.[36]

Approaches to the study of Rastafari that focus on its internal dynamics tend to be ethnographically rich, revealing the intricate contours of Rastafari as a dynamic community. Most of the researchers I have mentioned in this section have engaged in extensive or intensive primary research (usually participant observation) on the movement as a whole or on various aspects of the movement. The result is a wealth of information on the historical evolution, the ideological sophistication, and the social dynamics of Rastafari. The major flaw in this approach is its tendency to ignore the dynamic interactions between the movement and the rest of the society. The most telling example of this tendency is Joseph Owens's work, which systematically explains the beliefs of the Rastas, but says precious little about who these believers are and how they relate to the rest of the society. The result is that his treatment reads like a systematic theology of Rastafarianism and pays little attention to the sociological and social-psychological issues facing the movement. Other studies review the historical background against which the movement emerged but fail to follow the ongoing relationship between the movement and the wider society. One notable exception is the work of Chevannes, who in an article entitled "Case of Jah versus Society: Rastafari Exorcism of the Ideology of Racism in Jamaica," demonstrates how Rastafari confronted Jamaica's Eurocentricity and became the vanguard in leading Jamaica to a sense of its African heritage and identity.[37]

Rastafari as Authentic Culture

Because of the oral culture that prevails in the movement, serious extended theorizing has been slow in coming from Rastas themselves. However, as an intelligentsia emerges in the movement, scholarly reflections have begun to appear from within the ranks. Dennis Forsythe's work represents one objective of the emerging literature: the provision of an apologia for the authenticity of the Rastafarian movement. Forsythe points out that historically, "the insider's account of Jah Rastafari has been told only in the form of song, dance, parables and symbols," but he proposes to use the biographical method to explain the phenomenon of Rastafari "in plain enough terms."[38] His account of Rastafari has a threefold purpose. First, he seeks to demonstrate that Rastafari is not a parochial religion based on the eccentricity of its practitioners in Jamaica. He does this by tracing Rastafari's "mystical roots" to ancient mysticism, particularly Egyptian mythology, the wider African religious experience, and the gnostic elements in early Christianity.[39] Second, he seeks to demonstrate that Rastafari is essentially an attempt to recreate an African cultural identity in a context that has historically imposed European definitions on the African diaspora. Rastas replace the negative associations that have been attached to Africa and Africans with a bold assertion of African beauty and dignity.[40] Third, Forsythe provides an apology for ganja use. Amassing any kind of evidence he can find (historical, personal, scientific), he argues that ganja is a therapeutic substance. Its use by Rastas, he contends, aids in the rediscovery of the African self and the universal spiritual reality and, at the same time, unleashes natural energy, which heals the body and restores it to a state of equilibrium.[41]

To Forsythe's credit, he delivers on his promise to present Rastafari in "plain enough terms." He avoids the tendency of many Rastas, who like to communicate in streams of esoteric verbiage that seem calculated to obfuscate rather than to elucidate. His account of Rastafari is passionate, yet lucid and cohesive. He manages to capture and systematize ideas carefully worked out in Rastafarian oral culture but hitherto expressed only in parables, poetry, songs, and symbols. This is the best example of systematic theorizing or theologizing coming from inside the movement. Though an insider's account like Forsythe's will obviously help in focusing sociological and anthropological investigations of Rastafari, the apologetic nature of his work has to be taken into account in assessing its analytic value.

Others from within the Rastafarian movement have joined Forsythe in reflecting on various aspects of Rastafari. In 1999, Douglas R. A. Mack, an adherent of Rastafari for more than fifty years, published a book entitled *From Babylon to Rastafari*. With much the same objective as Forsythe and using the same "biographical method," he explains the historical and biblical roots of the movement, its evolution in Jamaica, and the centrality of Haile Selassie as its guiding light. He also explains the ethos of Rastafari, including its major tenets and ritual activities.[42] Though not as rigorous as

Forsythe's, Mack's account is lucid and coherent. As someone who has witnessed from the inside the major developments (including participating in two missions to Africa to investigate the possibility of repatriation) in the Rastafarian movement since the 1960s, Mack's account rings with authenticity.

Recent years have seen a proliferation of publications on Rastafari by Rastas. While these books may not be deemed scholarly, they provide helpful insights into Rastas' attempts to assert the authenticity of their movement and its vision of the world. These recent publications fall roughly into four categories. The first includes republication or reworking of "sources" that have inspired the Rastafarian vision. Some examples are *The Holy Piby: The Blackman's Bible*, an African redemption text written in 1924 by Robert Athlyi Rogers, an African-American minister from Newark, New Jersey;[43] *The Promised Key*, written by the most well known early Rastafarian leader, Leonard P. Howell, under the pseudonym G. G. Maragh, and primarily dedicated to proving and affirming the divinity of Haile Selassie;[44] and *The Rastafari Ible*[45] and *The Kebra Negast: The Lost Bible of Rastafarian Wisdom and Faith from Ethiopia to Jamaica*,[46] both retellings of an Ethiopian legend that traces the royal line of Haile Selassie to a sexual liaison between Solomon (of the Hebrew Bible) and the queen of Sheba.

The second category consists of works concerning the person or teachings of Haile Selassie (teachings are culled from his speeches). The purpose of these works is to establish the central place of Selassie as the divine black messiah and to valorize his teachings on various subjects as a source and guide to the Rastafarian philosophy of life. Examples of books that fall within this category are *Haile Selassie and the Opening of the Seven Seals*,[47] *The Important Utterances of H. I. M. Emperor Haile Selassie I Jah Rastafari*,[48] *The Testimony of His Imperial Majesty Emperor Haile Selassie I, Defender of the Faith*,[49] and *Rasta: Emperor Haile Selassie and the Rastafarians*.[50]

The work of E. S. P. McPherson exemplifies the third category of books in the growing repertoire of Rastafarian writers. His works focus more on the social, cultural, and historical development of Rastafari: *Rastafari and Politics: Sixty Years of a Developing Cultural Ideology: Sociology of Development Perspective*[51] and *The Culture-History and Universal Spread of Rastafari*.[52] McPherson's writings tend to be in the same spirit as that of Douglas R. A. Mack.

The final category of writings being published by Rastas consists of personal reflection on various issues or poetic expressions of Rastafarian consciousness. Examples of personal reflections are *Prophet on Reggae Mountain: Meditations of Ras Shabaka Maasai, Prophet of Jah Rastafari*[53] and *Christopher Columbus and Rastafari: Ironies of History and Other Reflections on the Symbol of Rastafari.*[54] Numerous Rastafarian poets have published (and recorded) their works over the years. The most well known collections are in the series called *Itations of Jamaica and I Rastafari,* published by Mihlawhdh Faristzaddi.[55]

Like Forsythe and Mack, these works are concerned with establishing Rastafari as an authentic lifestyle with deep cultural roots. The outsider may remain unconvinced by their evidence and argument. However, these works have begun to establish a body of literature by Rastas, which will give researchers insights into the thinking of members of the movement.

Rastas as Social/Political Activists

Another theorist writing from within the ranks of the Rastafarian movement is Leahcim Semaj.[56] Semaj agrees with Forsythe that the essence of Rastafari is a "restructuring of identity" from an "Africentric [*sic*] perspective."[57] However, he argues that historically the effort has been religious in nature, founded on a body of myths concerning Garvey, Africa, and Selassie. As a religion, Semaj believes, Rastafari has succeeded as much as it can in Jamaica, having become an integral and vital component of the popular culture, that is, the indigenous values and expressions of the people.[58] Semaj asserts that for Rastafari to move to the level of national culture (the collective and conscious ideas on which a society is built), to the level of scientific culture (a critical assimilation of all human achievements), and to the level of universal culture (a humanistic respect for and solidarity with all human beings), it must make the transition from religion (a body of myths) to social theory (with a carefully crafted agenda for social, political, and economic activity).[59] To do this, Rastas must cease perceiving Garvey as a prophet and regard him as a social activist whose ideas must be critiqued and placed in the context of the liberation struggles faced by the African diaspora today. Rastas must also refrain from regarding the Bible as special revelation and see it as an interesting book, which sheds light on the human situation. Selassie must no longer be regarded as the Creator, but as a symbol of the God-man unity. Repatriation as a mysterious act must give way to collective activity in the context of global Pan-Africanism. Personal appearance should not only be projected in terms of its symbolic values, but also as an expression of African aesthetic pride. The use of ital (natural, organic) food and ganja smoking must not be explained in terms of biblical restrictions or prescriptions but in terms of their medicinal and health values.[60]

Whereas the objective of the writing by Rastas that I mentioned in the previous section is to demonstrate that Rastafari is a cogent world view and an acceptable lifestyle with deep historical and cultural roots, Semaj wants to go one step further and fashion the ideology of Rastafari into a rational social theory that will be able to critique and change the world. Semaj's position represents the thinking of a new breed of intellectual Rastas. They recognize that the Rastafarian mythology and lifestyle have been useful in the process of recapturing a sense of the significance of Africa to their lives. However, they are acutely aware that this does not change the configuration of power and privilege in Jamaica and the world. Therefore, Semaj and his like-minded brethren wish to move Rastafari beyond its cultural achievements and, even more, beyond its vitriolic rhetoric, to coherent social theory and concrete, rational, political actions, which will facilitate the liberation process in Jamaica and the political objectives of Pan-Africanism worldwide.

Beyond providing a window into the thinking of the new breed of intellectual Rastas, Semaj's approach reveals the impact of the academic process on their perspective. On the one hand, the impetus for the evolution of a rational social theory comes from the fact that intellectual Rastas have come to the realization that some of the mythology of Rastafari is based on unsupportable propositions or naive projections. For example, the conception of Africa as the promised land "flowing with milk and honey" ignores Africa's hardships, poverty, political clannishness, and tribalism. On the other hand, the influence of radical social theorists is apparent in Semaj's approach. He quite openly accepts Feuerbach's and Marx's notion that religion is a human creation.[61] However, instead of seeing religion as false consciousness to be destroyed in the revolutionary process, he sees religion as a malleable tool, which must be shaped to fit the demands of particular historical circumstances.[62] It is in this intellectual framework that he proposes that Rastafari make the transition from religion to social theory. Although Semaj's ambition for Rastafari to become the national and eventually the universal culture may concur with the aspirations of many Rastas, I seriously doubt that his neo-Marxist assumptions will find acceptance among the rank and file of Rastas. In fact, the Jamaican grapevine has it that Semaj is not a genuine Rasta, but an opportunistic intellectual who uses the guise of Rasta for his own economic and political aims.

Conclusion

Not all studies fit comfortably within the categories I have used here. The purpose of my arrangement is to give the reader a broad sense of the approaches and foci that appear in the growing body of literature on Rastafari. As Rastafarian studies has grown in recent times, some books attempt to present a more macro perspective, while others focus on more micro concerns. A good example of the macro perspective is *Chanting Down Babylon: The Rastafari Reader*, which is a collection of essays seeking to give an overview of the movement from multiple perspectives.[63] *Dread Jesus*, which focuses on the Rastafarian understanding of Jesus and how that understanding challenges traditional Christian understanding,[64] "Rastafari in the Promised Land,"[65] and "First Generation Rastafari in St. Eustatius" are good examples of micro perspectives.[66] Furthermore, the ballooning academic interest in Rastafari is spawning ethnographic studies of Rastafarian communities from South Africa to Cuba to Brazil to New Zealand to New York City to the Fiji islands. In the years to come, scholars in anthropology, sociology, history, comparative religions, literature, and cultural studies will no doubt add to our understanding of this socioreligious group, which started on the margins of Jamaican society but now attracts and inspires people from across the globe.

Notes

INTRODUCTION

1. The movement is named after Ras Tafari, which was Haile Selassie's name before he became emperor of Ethiopia (one of the central tenets of the movement is the divinity of Selassie). Ras is a royal title similar to duke, and Tafari is a family name. The movement is variously referred to as *Rastafari*, "Ras Tafari," or the "Rastafarian" movement. In this study, I will use the form *Rastafari* in a generic sense to refer to the totality of the experience that constitutes the movement. I will refer to the movement as the *Rastafarian movement*. When referring to an individual member or members of the movement, I will use *Rasta* or *Rastas*.

2. The movement has adherents in most Caribbean islands, North America, Brazil, the British isles, northern Europe, Africa (particularly Nigeria, Ghana, and South Africa), New Zealand, Australia, and even Japan. See Carole D. Yawney, "The Global Status of Rastafari," *Caribbean Times*, July 10, 1990, p. 24.

3. According to the dictionary, *entrench* means "to place in a position of strength; to establish firmly or solidly" (*Random House Dictionary of the English Language*, unabridged ed., 1983); or "to establish securely," often "used in the passive voice or with a reflective pronoun (an official entrenched in office)" (*Webster's New World Dictionary of American English*, 3d college ed., 1988). My use of the word *entrenchment* in this volume is intended to reflect these meanings.

4. Anthony Wallace also uses the term *routinization* to refer to the final stage of revitalization movements, although his cursory treatment of the term only lasts for a short paragraph. Therefore, he adds nothing substantive to Weber and comments that routinization usually takes place along the lines outlined by Weber. See Anthony Wallace, "Revitalization Movements," *American Anthropologist* 58 (1956): 275.

5. Max Weber, *Economy and Society: An Outline of Interpretive Sociology*, 3 vols., edited by Guenther Roth and Claus Wittich (New York: Bedminster, 1968), 1:246.

6. Leonard E. Barrett, *The Rastafarians: Sounds of Cultural Dissonance* (Boston: Beacon, 1988), 146.

7. Jack Anthony Johnson-Hill, "Elements of an Afro-Caribbean Social Ethic: A Disclosure of the World of Rastafari as a Liminal Process (Jamaica)" (Ph.D. diss., Vanderbilt University, 1988).

8. Neville Callam, "Invitation to Docility: Defusing the Rastafarian Challenge," *Caribbean Journal of Religious Studies* 3 (Sept. 1980): 28–29.

9. Ibid., 43–44.

10. As will be made clear in chapter 5, *houses* refer to small, informal groups of Rastas, which usually form around local leading Rastas. *Mansions* are intended to convey the idea of larger groups, usually communes or more formal Rastafarian organizations.

11. The reader who has no interest in the finer points of sociological theory, but who is interested in the dynamics of the Rastafarian movement itself, may skip chapter 1 and yet get a good understanding of Rastafari.

CHAPTER I

1. Lewis A. Coser, *Masters of Sociological Thought: Ideas in Historical and Social Context*, 2d ed. (New York: Harcourt Brace Jovanovich, 1977), 228.

2. Max Weber, *The Protestant Ethic and the Spirit of Capitalism*, translated by Talcott Parsons (New York: Scribner, 1958), 26–27.

3. Ibid., 27–28; Max Weber, *Ancient Judaism*, translated and edited by Hans Gerth and Don Martindale (Glencoe, Ill.: Free Press, 1952), *The Religion of India: The Sociology of Hinduism and Buddhism*, translated and edited by Hans Gerth and Don Martindale (New York: Free Press, 1967), and *The Religion of China, Confucianism and Taoism*, translated and edited by Hans Gerth and Don Martindale (New York: Collier and Macmillan, 1964).

4. Although Weber wants to emphasize the role of ideas as independent variables, he does not deny that ideas are always interactive with social structures and material circumstances.

5. Max Weber, *The Sociology of Religion*, translated by Ephraim Fischoff (Boston: Beacon, 1963), xxxii–xxxiii.

6. Hans H. Gerth and C. Wright Mills, ed., *From Max Weber: Essays in Sociology* (London: Routledge and Kegan Paul, 1948), 56–57; Coser, *Masters of Sociological Thought*, 218–19.

7. Weber, *Sociology of Religion*, 1–2.

8. Anthony Orum, *Introduction to Political Sociology: The Social Anatomy of the Body Politic*, 3d ed. (Englewood Cliffs, N.J.: Prentice Hall, 1989), 70.

9. Weber, *Protestant Ethic*, 88–90, 178, 180–81.

10. Orum, *Political Sociology*, 70.

11. Jonathan H. Turner, Leonard Beeghley, and Charles Power, *The Emergence of Sociological Theory* (Belmont, Calif.: Dorsey, 1989), 215.

12. Max Weber, *Economy and Society: An Outline of Interpretive Sociology*, 3 vols., edited by Guenther Roth and Claus Wittich (New York: Bedminster, 1968), 1:241.

13. Weber, *Sociology of Religion*, xxxiii.

14. Ibid., 46.

15. Ibid., 46–47.

16. Weber, *Economy and Society*, 1:245.

17. Ibid., 1:243–44.

18. Ibid., 1:244.

19. Ibid., 1:245.

20. Ibid., 3:1116.

21. Ibid.

22. Weber, *Protestant Ethic*, 181–82.

23. Weber, *Economy and Society*, 1:246.

24. Ibid., 1:212, 3:946.

25. Orum, *Political Sociology*, 67; Weber, *Economy and Society*, 1:112–13; Turner et al., *Sociological Theory*, 214.

26. Orum, *Political Sociology*, 67; Weber, *Economy and Society*, 1:264.

27. Weber, *Economy and Society*, 1:213.

28. Ibid., 1:215, 226–41.

29. Ibid., 1:215, 217–26.

30. Ibid., 1:215, 241.

31. Ibid., 1:241.

32. Weber, *Sociology of Religion*, 51.

33. Weber, *Economy and Society*, 3:1115.

34. Ibid., 3:1117.

35. Ibid., 3:1112.

36. Ibid., 1:242; Reinhard Bendix, *Max Weber: An Intellectual Portrait* (Garden City, N.Y.: Doubleday, 1960), 298.

37. Weber, *Economy and Society*, 1:242. In one sense, charisma inheres in the acclaim and devotion of followers as much as in the exceptional qualities of the charismatic leader. In other words, followers cocreate and maintain charismatic leaders.

38. Ibid., 3:1111.

39. Ibid., 3:1111–12.

40. Ibid., 3:1117.

41. Ibid., 3:1134.

42. Turner et al., *Sociological Theory*, 215.

43. Weber, *Economy and Society*, 1:246, 3:1121.

44. Ibid., 1:246.

45. Ibid., 1:246–50.

46. Ibid., 3:1123.

47. Ibid., 3:1121.

48. Ibid., 3:1122.

49. Ibid., 1:246–49.

50. Though not pure charisma, depersonalized charisma is still charisma in the sense that it is a quality not available to the rank and file and in the sense that it remains the source of legitimation for the exercise of authority over the masses.

51. Weber, *Economy and Society*, 3:1135.

52. Ibid., 3:1121.

53. Theodore Long, "Prophecy, Charisma and Politics: Reinterpreting the Weberian Thesis," in *Prophetic Religions and Politics: Religion and the Political Order*, edited by Jeffrey K. Hadden and Anson Shupe (New York: Paragon, 1986), 7–10.

54. Peter L. Berger, "Charisma and Religious Innovation: The Social Location of Israelite Prophecy," *American Sociological Review* 28 (1963): 948.

55. Ibid., 949.

56. Weber, *Sociology of Religion*, 47–48.

57. Weber, *Economy and Society*, 3:1132.

58. For rather extensive discussions of these theories, see Orum, *Political Sociology*; and Doug McAdam, John D. McCarthy, and Mayer Zald, "Social Movements," in *Handbook of Sociology*, edited by Neil J. Smelser (Newbury Park, Calif.: Sage, 1988), 696–737.

59. John J. Macionis, *Sociology*, 2d ed. (Englewood Cliffs, N.J.: Prentice Hall, 1989), 597–98; Orum, *Political Sociology*, 345–46; McAdam et al., *Handbook*, 696.

60. Macionis, *Sociology*, 598; McAdam et al., *Handbook*, 596.

61. Macionis, *Sociology*, 599–600; Orum, *Political Sociology*, 338–39.

62. Macionis, *Sociology*, 601; Orum, *Political Sociology*, 339–41; McAdam et al., *Handbook*, 697.

63. Orum, *Political Sociology*, 350.

64. Ibid., 246–47.

65. Weber, *Economy and Society*, 3:1120; see also 1111–12.

66. See Anthony Orum's discussion of social movements (*Political Sociology*, 332–52). Most of the social movements mentioned are represented by bureaucratic organizations.

67. Ann Ruth Willner, *Charismatic Political Leadership: A Theory* (Princeton, N.J.: Center of International Studies, Princeton University, 1968), 35.

68. Ibid., 35–36. These conditions parallel the factors identified by the structural strain theory.

69. Weber, *Economy and Society*, 3:1138.

70. Willner, *Charismatic Political Leadership*, 44.

71. Ibid., 47; Richard H. Dekmejian and Margaret J. Wyszomirski, "Charismatic Leadership in Islam: The Mahdi of the Sudan," *Comparative Studies in Society and History* 14, no. 2 (Mar. 1972): 194.

72. Willner, *Charismatic Political Leadership*, 45.

73. Curlew O. Thomas and Barbara Boston-Thomas, "Charisma and Charismatic Changes: A Study of a Black Sect," *Free Inquiry in Creative Sociology* 17, no. 1 (1989): 108–10.

74. Robert Alun Jones and Robert M. Anservitz, "Saint-Simon and Saint-Simonism: A Weberian View," *American Journal of Sociology* 10, no. 5 (Mar. 1975): 1109.

75. Ibid., 1098; Dekmejian and Wyszomirski, "Charismatic Leadership," 195.

76. Jones and Anservitz, "Saint-Simon," 1098. The emphasis is mine.

77. Anthony F. C. Wallace, "Revitalization Movements," *American Anthropologist* 58 (Apr. 1956): 270.

78. Jones and Anservitz, "Saint Simon," 1107–9.

79. Ibid.

80. Ann Ruth Willner and Dorothy Willner, "The Rise of Charismatic Leaders," *Annals of the American Academy of Political and Social Science* 358 (1965): 83–84.

81. Dekmejian and Wyszomirski, "Charismatic Leadership," 196.

82. Mayer N. Zald and Roberta Ash, "Social Movement Organizations: Growth, Decay and Change," *Social Forces* 44, no. 3 (Mar. 1966): 327–42; see also Orum, *Political Sociology,* 352-54; and McAdam et al., *Handbook,* 716–18.

83. Zald and Ash, "Social Movement Organizations," 330.

84. Ibid.

85. Orum, *Political Sociology,* 332.

86. McAdam el al., *Handbook,* 716.

87. The structural strain theorists point out that a lack of rigid social control is one of the conditions necessary for the rise and survival of new movements (see Orum, *Political Sociology,* 338). However, strict repressive actions have often served to further radicalize new movements and to strengthen the resolve of their members to resist the establishment. Furthermore, some movements have the flexibility to adapt to situations of either repression or accommodation.

88. Paget Henry, "Indigenous Religions and the Transformation of Peripheral Societies," in *Prophetic Religions and Politics: Religion and the Political Order,* edited by Jeffrey K. Hadden and Anson Shupe (New York: Paragon, 1986), 124, 129–30.

89. Barry Chevannes, "Rastafari: Towards a New Approach," *New West Indian Guide* 64, nos. 3–4 (1990): 138.

90. Jones and Anservitz, "Saint-Simon," 1119–21.

91. Long, "Prophecy, Charisma and Politics," 13. The quotation is from Max Weber, *The Theory of Social and Economic Organization,* translated by A. M. Henderson and Talcott Parsons (New York: Free Press, 1947), 363.

92. Long, "Prophecy, Charisma and Politics," 14–16.

93. Berger, "Charisma," 949–50.

CHAPTER 2

1. John Paul Homiak, "The 'Ancient of Days' Seated Black: Eldership, Oral Tradition and Ritual in Rastafari Culture" (Ph.D. diss., Brandeis University, 1985), 101–2.

2. Ibid., 132.

3. Samuel J. Hurwitz and Edith Hurwitz, *Jamaica: A Historical Portrait* (New York: Praeger, 1971), 175–78.

4. Rex Nettleford, *Mirror, Mirror: Identity, Race and Protest in Jamaica* (Kingston, Jamaica: Collins and Sangster, 1970), 171–72.

5. Aggrey Brown, *Color, Class, and Politics in Jamaica* (New Brunswick, N.J.: Transaction, 1979), 13, quoted by Theodore Malloch, "Rastafarianism: A Radical Caribbean Movement/Religion," *Center Journal* 4, no. 4 (Fall 1985): 69.

6. Leahcim Semaj, "Race and Identity and Children of the African Diaspora: Contributions of Rastafari," *Caribe* 4, no. 4 (1980): 15.

7. Ibid.

8. Bob Marley and the Wailers, "One Drop," on *Survival*, Island Records, 90088-4-7, 1979.

9. Patrick D. M. Taylor, "Perspectives on History in Rastafari Thought," *Studies in Religion* 19 (Nov. 1990): 194. Also see Monica Schuler, "Myalism and the African Religious Tradition in Jamaica," in *Africa and the Caribbean: The Legacies of a Link*, edited by Margaret Graham and Franklin Knight (Baltimore, Md.: Johns Hopkins University Press, 1979), 60.

10. Taylor, "Perspectives on History," 195.

11. Dale Bisnauth, *A History of Religions in the Caribbean* (Kingston, Jamaica: Kingston Publishing, 1989), 83. Bisnauth goes on to point out that after this insurrection the Jamaican legislature banned the practice of obeah because of its fear that it would foment revolts. Of course, myal and obeah were confused.

12. In some Afro-Christian sects in Jamaica, notably revivalism and its predecessor, the Native Baptist movement, the spiritual leader is referred to as "Daddy" or "Madda" (mother).

13. Bisnauth, *History of Religions*, 186.

14. Derek Bishton, *Black Heart Man* (London: Chatto and Windus, 1986), 10. Bishton argues that with increasing contact between Europe and Africa, the maps began to change until AETHIOPIA was replaced by Africa, in the same manner that individual countries lost their names and were renamed by the Europeans. According to Bishton, there seems to have been an ideological reason behind this, since the positive image of Ethiopia was replaced by the concept of Africa as the "dark continent" (11).

15. Fascination with the greatness of Ethiopia predates the African diaspora. There is a long history of European fascination with Ethiopia, dating back to the Greeks. With each succeeding generation, this fascination received additional embellishment. At one point, Ethiopia was believed to be the kingdom of the fabled Prester John, a supposed Christian king. The initial impulse of European exploration may have resulted from a desire to establish alliance with this supposed Christian king (ibid., 10).

16. Bisnauth, *History of Religions*, 189.

17. Bishton, *Black Heart Man*, 63, 81.

18. Peter Clarke, *Black Paradise: The Rastafarian Movement* (Wellingborough, Northamptonshire, England: Aquarian, 1986), 30.

19. The tradition of linking Ethiopian's religion and monarchy to Solomon is set forth in the Ethiopian legends of the kings, the *Kebre Negest*, which is

translated as the Greatness of Kings. See Bishton, *Black Heart Man,* 11–19, for discussion of the Sheba legend.

20. Clarke, *Black Paradise,* 34.

21. Bishton, *Black Heart Man,* 82; Bisnauth, *History of Religions,* 186. Casely Hayford expressed these ideas in a book entitled. *Ethiopia Unbound: Studies in Race Emancipation* (London: Cass, 1969), first published in 1911.

22. Leonard E. Barrett, *The Rastafarians: Sounds of Cultural Dissonance,* rev. ed. (Boston: Beacon, 1988), 76.

23. Bishton, *Black Heart Man,* 100.

24. Ibid., 100–101.

25. Taylor, "Perspectives on History," 198.

26. Robert A. Hill, "Leonard P. Howell and Millenarian Visions in Early Rastafari," *Jamaica Journal* 16, no. 1 (1983): 26–27.

27. Amy Jacques-Garvey, ed., *Philosophy and Opinions of Marcus Garvey* (New York: Atheneum, 1974), 140–41.

28. Barrett, *Rastafarians,* 7, quoting Robert Hill and Barbara Bair, *Marcus Garvey: Life and Lessons* (Berkeley: University of California Press, 1987), 20.

29. Jacques-Garvey, *Philosophy,* 68.

30. Psalm 68:31; Barrett, *Rastafarians,* 78.

31. Barrett, *Rastafarians,* 79.

32. Bisnauth, *History of Religions,* 187.

33. Hill, "Leonard P. Howell," 26.

34. The fact that no documentation has been found in Garvey's writings for this prediction have led some scholars to believe that it was fabricated by the early exponents of Rastafari. However, it is likely that Garvey made some oral declaration to that import and that it was kept alive in the memory of people steeped in oral tradition.

35. *Haile Selassie* means "power of the trinity."

36. Ivor Morrish, *Obeah, Christ and Rastaman: Jamaica and Its Religion* (Cambridge: Clarke, 1982), 69.

37. Bisnauth, *History of Religions,* 189.

38. This raises a question concerning the possibility of multiple charismatic personalities being active in the founding of a single movement.

39. M. G. Smith, Roy Augier, and Rex Nettleford, *The Rastafari Movement in Kingston, Jamaica* (Mona, Jamaica: Institute of Social and Economic Research, University College of the West Indies, 1960), 6.

40. Hill, "Leonard P. Howell," 28.

41. Malloch, "Rastafarianism," 74; Smith et al., *Rastafari,* 7.

42. Barrett, *Rastafarians,* 85.

43. Smith et al., *Rastafari,* 7.

44. Ibid., 8; Hill, "Leonard P. Howell," 36; Horace Campbell, *Rasta and Resistance: From Marcus Garvey to Walter Rodney* (Trenton, N.J.: African World, 1987), 94; Bishton, *Black Heart Man,* 117.

45. Morrish, *Obeah,* 71; Smith et al., *Rastafari,* 9.

46. Morrish, *Obeah,* 71; Smith et al., *Rastafari,* 9.

47. Barrett, *Rastafarians,* 87.

48. Members of the movement who distinguish themselves as uncompromising exponents of Rastafari are often referred to as "leading lights."

49. Barrett, *Rastafarians,* 87.

50. Hill, "Leonard P. Howell," 34.

51. Taylor, "Perspectives on History," 198.

52. Bishton, *Black Heart Man,* 111.

53. Ibid.

54. Hill, "Leonard P. Howell," 30.

55. Ibid., 35.

56. This name obviously has an East Indian origin. Reportedly, Howell adopted it through the influence of one of his lieutenants, who was an East Indian with Hindu connections (Taylor, "Perspectives on History," 199). This raises the question of East Indian influences on Rastafari, which has been discussed in the literature. For some indication of the issues involved, see Ajai Mansingh and Laxmi Mansingh, "Hindu Influences on Rastafarianism," *Rastafari* (Kingston, Jamaica: Caribbean Quarterly, University of the West Indies, 1985): 96–115 (this is a collection of essays published by *Caribbean Quarterly* as a monograph. Most of the essays were previously published in *Caribbean Quarterly* 26, no. 4 in 1980); and Kenneth Bilby, "The Holy Herb: Notes on the Background of Cannabis in Jamaica," *Rastafari* (Kingston, Jamaica: Caribbean Quarterly, University of the West Indies, 1985), 82–95.

57. Taylor, "Perspectives on History," 199; Hill, "Leonard P. Howell," 35.

58. Hill, "Leonard P. Howell," 34–35.

59. Barry Chevannes, "Era of the Dreadlocks," unpublished manuscript, n.d., 10.

60. Max Weber, *The Sociology of Religion,* translated by Ephraim Fischoff (Boston: Beacon, 1963), xxxiii.

CHAPTER 3

1. Max Weber, *Economy and Society: An Outline of Interpretative Sociology,* 3 vols., edited by Guenther Roth and Claus Wittich (New York: Bedminster, 1968), 3:1115, 1117.

2. Anthony Wallace, "Revitalization Movements," *American Anthropologist* 58 (Apr. 1956): 265.

3. Ibid., 269.

4. During the African slave trade, from the seventeenth to the nineteenth centuries, each slave ship would make a triangular journey from Europe to Africa, from Africa to the Americas, and from the Americas back to Europe. The leg of the journey from Africa to the Americas is referred to as the Middle Passage. The use of the term is often meant to suggest the physical squalor and psychic trauma faced by the human cargo during this journey.

5. I am using *delegitimation* to refer to the fact that the Rastafarian ideology, by assigning an evil status to the Jamaican establishment, has effectively

destroyed the establishment's legitimacy in the eyes of Rastas. While the rest of the society may take the inherited colonial culture and institutions for granted, they have lost that status for Rastas.

6. Ernest Cashmore, *Rastaman: The Rastafarian Movement in England* (Boston: Unwin, 1983), 129.

7. Ibid.

8. Ibid., 130.

9. Patrick D. M. Taylor, "Perspectives on History in Rastafari Thought," *Studies in Religion* 19, no. 1 (Nov. 1990): 191.

10. This stone is generally interpreted as a symbolic prophecy of Israel's messiah.

11. Dennis Forsythe, *Rastafari: For the Healing of the Nation* (Kingston, Jamaica: Zaika, 1983), 91.

12. Joseph Owens, *Dread: The Rastafarians of Jamaica* (Kingston, Jamaica: Sangster's, 1976), 69–70.

13. The Nyabinghi Order are those Rastas who take the strictest and most uncompromising stance against involvement with Babylon. In theological terms, they represent the fundamentalist element in the Rastafarian movement.

14. John Paul Homiak, "The 'Ancient of Days' Seated Black: Eldership, Oral Tradition and Ritual in Rastafari Culture" (Ph.D. diss., Brandeis University, 1985), 510.

15. Quoted in Horace Campbell, *Rasta and Resistance: From Marcus Garvey to Walter Rodney* (Trenton, N.J.: African World, 1987), 135.

16. Forsythe, *Rastafari*, 91.

17. Bob Marley and the Wailers, "Talkin' Blues," on *Talkin' Blues*, Island Records, 848243-4, 1991.

18. Owens, *Dread*, 74-80.

19. Ibid., 70.

20. Ibid., 88.

21. Ibid., 70, 71.

22. Ibid., 70, 73.

23. Bob Marley and the Wailers, "Redemption Song," on *Songs of Freedon* compilation, Island Records, 414-514 432-2, 1999.

24. Bob Marley and the Wailers, "Slave Driver," on *Talkin' Blues*.

25. Burning Spear, "Do You Remember the Days of Slavery?" (recorded at a live performance in Reggae Park, St Anns, Jamaica, May 1991).

26. Bob Marley and the Wailers, "Survival," on *Survival*, Island Records, 90088-4-7, 1979; Michael N. Jagessar, "JPIC and Rastafarians," *One World*, Feb. 1991, p. 17.

27. Bob Marley and the Wailers, "Burnin' and Lootin'," on *Talkin' Blues*.

28. Cashmore, *Rastaman*, 173.

29. Ibid., 177.

30. Bob Marley and the Wailers, "Pimper's Paradise," on *Uprising*, Island Records, 422-846211-4, 1980.

31. Bob Marley and the Wailers, "Babylon System," on *Survival*.

32. Bob Marley and the Wailers, "Crazy Baldhead," on *Rastaman Vibration*, Island Records, 422-846205-4, 1976.

33. Bob Marley and the Wailers, "Rat Race," on *Rastaman Vibration*.

34. K. M. Williams, *The Rastafarians* (London: Ward Lock, 1981), 27.

35. Marley, "Crazy Baldhead," on *Rastaman Vibration*.

36. Klaus de Albuquerque, "The Future of the Rastafarian Movement," *Caribbean Review* 8, no. 4 (1979): 44; Owens, *Dread*, 75.

37. Walter Rodney, *Groundings with My Brothers* (London: Bogle L'Ouverture, 1969), 10.

38. Williams, *Rastafarians*, 27. Ironically, Haile Selassie Secondary School was among the schools that refused to accept children with dreadlocks.

39. Bongo Jerry, "MABRAK," in *The Penguin Book of Caribbean Verse in English*, edited by Paula Burnett (London: Penguin, 1986), 70–71.

40. Marley, "Babylon System," on *Survival*.

41. Owens, *Dread*, 81, 85.

42. Bob Marley and the Wailers, "Revolution," on *Talkin' Blues*.

43. Marley, "Babylon System," on *Survival*.

44. Jack Anthony Johnson-Hill, "Elements of an Afro-Caribbean Social Ethic: A Disclosure of the World of Rastafari as a Liminal Process (Jamaica)" (Ph.D. diss., Vanderbilt University, 1988), 360.

45. Rex Nettleford, *Mirror, Mirror: Identity, Race and Protest in Jamaica* (Kingston, Jamaica: Collins and Sangster, 1970), 60.

46. Mikey Smith, "Tell Me," quoted by Johnson-Hill, "Afro-Caribbean Social Ethic," 362.

47. Marley, "Crazy Baldhead," on *Rastaman Vibration*.

48. Mikey Smith, "Dread," quoted by Johnson-Hill, "Afro-Caribbean Social Ethic," 364.

49. Bob Marley and the Wailers, "Ambush in the Night," on *Survival*, Island Records, 90088-4-7, 1979.

50. Paget Henry, "Indigenous Religions and the Transformation of Peripheral Societies," in *Prophetic Religions and Politics: Religion and the Political Order*, edited by Jeffrey K. Hadden and Anson Shupe (New York: Paragon, 1986), 135.

51. Ibid.

52. Marley, "Crazy Baldhead," on *Rastaman Vibration*.

53. Marley, "Babylon System," on *Survival*.

54. de Albuquerque, "Future," 45.

55. Linden F. Lewis, "Living in the Heart of Babylon: Rastafari in the USA," *Bulletin of Eastern Caribbean Affairs* 15, no. 1 (Mar.–Apr. 1989): 22.

56. I Jabulani Tafari, "The Rastafari: Successors of Marcus Garvey," *Rastafari* (Kingston, Jamaica: Caribbean Quarterly, University of the West Indies, 1985), 2.

57. Laurence A. Breiner, "The English Bible in Jamaican Rastafarianism," *Journal of Religious Thought* 42, no. 2 (Fall–Winter 1985–86): 35.

58. Nettleford, *Mirror, Mirror*, 47.

59. Leahcim Semaj, "Rastafari: From Religion to Social Theory," *Rastafari* (Kingston, Jamaica: Caribbean Quarterly, University of the West Indies, 1985), 22.

60. Ibid., 23.

61. Claudia Rogers, "What's a Rasta?" *Caribbean Review* 7, no. 1 (Jan.–Mar. 1977): 10.

62. Barry Chevannes, "Case of Jah versus Society: Rastafari Exorcism of the Ideology of Racism in Jamaica," *Social Movement Seminary Paper 1* (1989): 7.

63. Dennis Forsythe, "West Indian Culture through the Prism of Rastafarianism," *Rastafari* (Kingston, Jamaica: Caribbean Quarterly, University of the West Indies, 1985), 64.

64. Ibid.

65. Ibid., 62.

66. Leahcim Semaj, "Race and Identity and Children of the African Diaspora: Contributions of Rastafari," *Caribe* 4, no. 4 (1980): 17.

67. Ibid.

68. Ibid.

69. Lewis, "Living in the Heart of Babylon," 22.

70. Ajai Mansingh and Laxmi Mansingh, "Hindu Influences on Rastafarianism," *Rastafari* (Kingston, Jamaica: Caribbean Quarterly, University of the West Indies, 1985), 112.

71. Cashmore, *Rastaman*, 60.

72. Ibid., 62.

73. I and I has several levels of importance for Rastas. Here it indicates the Rastafarian belief that the divine essence inheres in all human beings and that through it they can experience unity with the Creator. Later in this chapter, I will explore the concept of I and I more fully.

74. Taylor, "Perspectives on History," 201.

75. Chevannes, "Jah versus Society," 11.

76. Ibid., 12; also see Williams, *Rastafarians*, 24.

77. In the late 1960s and early 1970s, middle-class academics and university students were converted to this point of view. Socialist politicians also became convinced that the future of the society lay in addressing the conditions that gave rise to this sentiment. Hence the People's National Party appealed to the poor using Rastafarian and revivalist symbolisms (Williams, *Rastafarians*, 25).

78. Chevannes, "Jah versus Society," 12; M. G. Smith, Roy Augier, and Rex Nettleford, *The Rastafari Movement in Kingston, Jamaica* (Mona, Jamaica: Institute of Social and Economic Research, University College of the West Indies, 1960), 12–13.

79. Among Rastas, there are divergent views about the meaning and means of repatriation. Some insist on a physical relocation to Africa/Ethiopia. For others, repatriation is the psychological and cultural reappropri-

ation of their African identity and culture. Some expect repatriation by divine intervention, some by the Jamaican or British governments as a gesture of restitution, and others by means of their own rational efforts.

80. Cashmore, *Rastaman*, 241.

81. Williams, *Rastafarians*, 15.

82. Cashmore, *Rastaman*, 160.

83. The Anancy/Spider stories are part of the African retention in the Caribbean, a carry-over from the folklore of West Africa. However, they have been modified to reflect the realities of plantation slavery and the entire colonial complex.

84. Daryl C. Dance, *Folklore from Contemporary Jamaicans* (Knoxville: University of Tennessee Press, 1985), 12.

85. W. E. B. Du Bois, *The Souls of Black Folk*, in *Writings*, edited by Nathan Huggins (New York: Literary Classics of the United States, 1986), 503.

86. Forsythe, *Rastafari*, 73.

87. Anancyism has come to describe the attitude or practice of "beating the system."

88. Forsythe, *Rastafari*, 74.

89. Forsythe, "West Indian Culture," 73.

90. One story tells of how Anancy deliberately gave all of his food to his wife and children, leaving himself with nothing. This act made him look altruistic. However, his family, seeing that he had nothing to eat, felt such a sympathy for him that each of them gave him half the portion each had received. Of course, he ended up with half of the total available ration, which was his desire in the first place.

91. Campbell, *Rasta and Resistance*, 99.

92. Forsythe, *Rastafari*, 81.

93. Forsythe, "West Indian Culture," 75.

94. Ibid., 73.

95. Forsythe, *Rastafari*, 53.

96. Ibid., 52; Forsythe, "West Indian Culture," 76.

97. Forsythe, *Rastafari*, 102.

98. Leonard Barrett, *The Rastafarians: Sounds of Cultural Dissonance* (Boston: Beacon, 1988), 142.

99. Diane J. Austin-Broos, "Pentecostals and Rastafarians: Cultural, Political and Gender Relations of Two Religious Movements," *Social and Economic Studies* 36, no. 4 (Dec. 1987): 20.

100. Forsythe, *Rastafari*, 101.

101. Austin-Broos, "Pentecostals and Rastafarians," 21.

102. Forsythe, "West Indian Culture," 73.

103. Smith et al., *Rastafari*, 9.

104. Campbell, *Rasta and Resistance*, 96.

105. Williams, *Rastafarians*, 15; Barry Chevannes, "Era of the Dreadlocks," unpublished manuscript, n.d., 15.

106. Theodore Malloch, "Rastafarianism: A Radical Caribbean Movement/Religion," *Center Journal* 4, no. 4 (Fall 1985): 74.

107. Chevannes, "Era of Dreadlocks," 15.

108. Cashmore, *Rastaman*, 158.

109. Chevannes, "Era of Dreadlocks," 15.

110. Semaj, "Rastafari," 29.

111. Rogers, "What's a Rasta?" 11–12.

112. Ibid., 11.

113. Williams, *Rastafarians*, 23–25; Rogers, "What's a Rasta?" 10.

114. Some Rastas seldom use the word *ganja*. They regard it as Babylon's derogatory label for the holy herb.

115. Rogers, "What's a Rasta?" 12.

116. Vera Rubin and Lambros Comitas, *Ganja in Jamaica* (The Hague: Mouton, 1975).

117. Kenneth Bilby, "The Holy Herb: Notes on the Background of Cannabis in Jamaica," *Rastafari* (Kingston, Jamaica: Caribbean Quarterly, University of the West Indies, 1985), 85.

118. The emphases are mine.

119. The emphasis is mine. Rastafarian biblical hermeneutics is fluid and expedient. When necessary, Rastas will yank a verse or a word out of context to prove a point. However, when the obvious meaning of a passage seems to disprove a particular Rastafarian notion, they will dismiss it as an interpolation by the white editors, especially of the King James Version. It seems the truth is what Rastas have come to intuitively. Biblical authority is invoked to legitimize preconceived notions. See Breiner's discussion of Rastafarian interpretive fluidity in "English Bible," 370.

120. Sebastian Clarke, *Jah Music: The Evolution of the Popular Jamaican Song* (London: Heinemann, 1980), 49; Forsythe, "West Indian Culture," 71.

121. Rogers, "What's a Rasta?" 12.

122. Carole D. Yawney, "Dread Wasteland: Rastafarian Ritual in West Kingston, Jamaica," in *Ritual, Symbolism and Ceremonialism in the Americas: Studies in Symbolic Anthropology*, edited by N. Ross Crumrine (Greenley, Colo.: Museum of Anthropology, University of Northern Colorado, 1978), 165; also see Bilby, "Holy Herb," 88.

123. Yawney, "Dread Wasteland," 169; also see Bilby, "Holy Herb," 88.

124. Carole D. Yawney, "Lions in Babylon: The Rastafarians of Jamaica as a Visionary Movement" (Ph.D. diss., McGill University, 1978), 213; also see Bilby, "Holy Herb," 88.

125. Yawney, "Dread Wasteland," 169.

126. Forsythe, *Rastafari*, 118–20.

127. Forsythe, "West Indian Culture," 72.

128. Chevannes, "Era of the Dreadlocks," 16.

129. Cashmore, *Rastaman*, 167.

130. Breiner, "English Bible," 38.

131. Carolyn Cooper, "Chanting Down Babylon: Bob Marley's Song as Literary Text," *Jamaica Journal* 19, no. 4 (Nov. 1986–Jan. 987): 7; Malika Lee Whitney and Dermott Hussey, *Bob Marley: Reggae King of the World* (Kingston, Jamaica: Kingston Publishers, 1984), 115.

132. For an analysis of the Rastafarian approach to language, see Velma Pollard, "The Social History of Dread Talk," *Caribbean Quarterly* 28, no. 2 (Dec. 1982): 17–40. Also see Velma Pollard, "Dread Talk: The Speech of the Rastafarian in Jamaica," *Rastafari* (Kingston, Jamaica: Caribbean Quarterly, University of the West Indies, 1985), 32–41.

133. Williams, *Rastafarians*, 22.

134. Pollard, "Dread Talk," 32.

135. Rex Nettleford, introduction to Owens, *Dread*, ix.

136. Bongo Jerry, in Burnett, *Caribbean Verse*, 70–71.

137. Cashmore, *Rastaman*, 163

138. Williams, *Rastafarians*, 22.

139. Ibid.

140. Cashmore, *Rastaman*, 67.

141. In Jamaican patois, *me* or *mi* is used as both object and subject. In Rastafarian understanding (or "overstanding," as Rastas would say), this is an indication that people conceive themselves as objects. In contrast, Rastas use *I* and *I and I* in all cases and all persons to indicate that all people are active, creative agents and not passive objects.

142. Becky Michele Mulvaney, "Rhythms of Resistance: On Rhetoric and Reggae Music" (Ph.D. diss., University of Iowa, 1985), 74.

143. Tafari, "Rastafari," 3.

144. Breiner, "English Bible," 39.

145. Owens, *Dread*, 3; Breiner, "English Bible," 39.

146. Rogers, "What's a Rasta?" 12.

147. Henry, "Indigenous Religions," 131–32.

148. de Albuquerque, "Future," 44.

149. Ibid.

150. Henry, "Indigenous Religions," 134–35.

CHAPTER 4

1. Barry Chevannes, "Rastafari: Towards a New Approach," *New West Indian Guide* 64, nos. 3–4 (1990): 137.

2. Carole D. Yawney, "Lions in Babylon: The Rastafarians of Jamaica as a Visionary Movement" (Ph.D. diss., McGill University, 1978), 102.

3. Carole D. Yawney, "Dread Wasteland: Rastafarian Ritual in West Kingston, Jamaica," in *Ritual, Symbolism and Ceremonialism in the Americas: Studies in Symbolic Anthropology*, edited by N. Ross Crumrine (Greenley, Colo.: Museum of Anthropology, University of Northern Colorado, 1978), 156.

4. Yawney, "Lions in Babylon," 107.

5. Chevannes, "Rastafari," 138.

6. Velma Pollard, "The Social History of Dread Talk," *Caribbean Quarterly* 28, no. 2 (Dec. 1982): 17.

7. See Ernst Troeltsch, *The Social Teaching of the Christian Churches,* translated by Olive Wyon (New York: Macmillan, 1931), 377–78, 745, 993.

8. Yards as a sociological category are not distinct to Rastas. They represent the practice of poor urban dwellers, who often congregate in someone's yard to share ideas or rumors, discuss politics, or engage in communal activities, such as playing dominoes.

9. Barry Chevannes, "Era of the Dreadlocks," unpublished manuscript, n.d., 13.

10. The Rastafarian argot and Jamaican patois use *brethren* as both singular and plural.

11. Chevannes, "Era of the Dreadlocks," 13; Chevannes, "Rastafari," 138.

12. John Paul Homiak, "The 'Ancient of Days' Seated Black: Eldership, Oral Tradition and Ritual in Rastafari Culture" (Ph.D. diss., Brandeis University, 1985), 355.

13. Chevannes, "Rastafari," 138.

14. Barry Chevannes, *Rastafari: Roots and Ideology* (Syracuse, N.Y.: Syracuse University Press, 1994), 171–4.

15. Ibid., 179.

16. Yawney, "Lions in Babylon," 108–10.

17. Ibid., 58.

18. Ibid., 108.

19. Ernest Cashmore, *Rastaman: The Rastafarian Movement in England* (Boston: Unwin, 1983), 126.

20. Laurence A. Breiner, "The English Bible in Jamaican Rastafarianism," *Journal of Religious Thought* 42, no. 2 (Fall–Winter 1985–86): 37.

21. Chevannes, "Rastafari," 137. There are only a few instances in which there is any semblance of hierarchical organization: the Twelve Tribes of Israel, Prince Emmanuel Edwards's Bobo Dreads, and Henry's Peacemakers Association are some examples. Even in these cases, the group is dominated more by the personality of the leaders than by rational principles.

22. Chevannes, "Era of the Dreadlocks," 12.

23. Sebastian Clarke, *Jah Music: The Evolution of the Popular Jamaican Song* (London: Heinemann, 1980), 5.

24. Breiner, "English Bible," 37. The "democracy" is mainly among men. Traditionally, the Rastafarian movement is patriarchal, with explicit ideas about female subordination. However, there is some indication that the role of women within the movement is changing. For a discussion of the traditional and changing roles of women in the Rastafarian Movement, see Maureen Rowe, "The Woman in Rastafari," *Rastafari* (Kingston, Jamaica: Caribbean Quarterly, University of the West Indies, 1985), 13–21.

25. Yawney, "Lions in Babylon," 301–2.

26. *Rasta Speaks,* June–July 1983, p. 17.

27. Yawney, "Lions in Babylon," 110.

28. Homiak, "'Ancient of Days,'" 407.

29. Chevannes, "Rastafari," 143.

30. Yawney, "Lions in Babylon," 258–60, 343.

31. Abner Cohen, *Two-Dimensional Man* (London: Routledge and Kegan Paul, 1974), quoted by Cashmore, *Rastaman*, 152.

32. Cashmore, *Rastaman*, 152.

33. Paget Henry, "Indigenous Religions and the Transformation of Peripheral Societies," in *Prophetic Religions and Politics: Religion and the Political Order*, edited by Jeffrey K. Hadden and Anson Shupe (New York: Paragon, 1986), 124.

34. Cashmore, *Rastaman*, 154.

35. Yawney, "Lions in Babylon," 9.

36. Carole D. Yawney, "Remnant of All Nations: Rastafarian Attitudes to Race and Nationality," in *Ethnicity in the Americas*, edited by Francis Henry (The Hague: Mouton, 1976), 232.

37. Cashmore, *Rastaman*, 137. The emphasis is mine.

38. Ibid., 151.

39. Homiak, "'Ancient of Days,'" 512. In the context of the yard, ganja smoking and reasoning are traditionally male activities. Women are mostly excluded from the circle in which the chalice is passed and in which reasoning takes place. Males are expected to "educate" the "sistren." Women, however, take active parts in Nyabinghi I-ssemblies, though the males dominate. See Rowe, "Woman in Rastafaris," 15–16.

40. *Spliffs* are huge, conical marijuana cigars. *Chalice* is the ritual name for either of the two pipes used in the ritual smoking of ganja. One is called the *kochi* (also *cutchie*), a kind of water pipe with a bowl on the top to hold the ganja. This is of African origin. The other is called the *chillum*, a conical or cylindrical pipe of East Indian origin. See Kenneth Bilby, "The Holy Herb: Notes on the Background of Cannabis in Jamaica," *Rastafari* (Kingston, Jamaica: Caribbean Quarterly, University of the West Indies, 1985], 87).

41. Yoshiko S. Nagashima, *Rastafarian Music in Contemporary Jamaica: A Study of the Socioreligious Music of the Rastafarian Movement in Jamaica* (Tokyo: Institute for the Study of Languages and Cultures of Asia and Africa, 1984), 115.

42. K. M. Williams, *The Rastafarians* (London: Ward Lock, 1981), 20.

43. Yawney, "Lions in Babylon," 213.

44. Williams, *Rastafarian*, 20.

45. Yawney, "Lions in Babylon," 201.

46. Ibid., 216. The emphasis is mine.

47. Yawney, "Remnant of All Nations," 239.

48. Yawney, "Lions in Babylon," 216.

49. Ibid., 216; Yawney, "Remnant of All Nations," 243.

50. Cashmore, *Rastaman*, 64.

51. Yawney, "Lions in Babylon," 102.

52. Nagashima, *Rastafarian Music*, 116.

53. Homiak, "'Ancient of Days,'" 512.

54. *Rastology* is a term used sometimes to refer to the Rastafarian world view, ideology, or theology.

55. Williams, *Rastafarians*, 18.

56. Verena Reckford, "Rastafarian Music: An Introductory Study," *Jamaica Journal* 11, nos. 1–2 (1977): 9.

57. Homiak, "'Ancient of Days,'" 361.

58. Reckford, "Rastafarian Music," 9.

59. For a discussion of the conventions and their publicity, see M. G. Smith, Roy Augier, and Rex Nettleford, *The Rastafari Movement in Kingston, Jamaica* (Mona, Jamaica: Institute of Social and Economic Research, University College of the West Indies, 1960), 14–15; and Clarke, *Jah Music*, 47.

60. Homiak, "'Ancient of Days,'" 361.

61. Ibid., 401.

62. Back O' Wall was a slum in West Kingston, which the Jamaican government bulldozed because of its association with endemic criminality. I will say more about this later.

63. Homiak, "'Ancient of Days,'" 367.

64. Williams, *Rastafarians*, 18.

65. Ibid., 20.

66. Yawney, "Lions in Babylon," 54.

67. Homiak, "'Ancient of Days,'" 362–72, 382–85.

CHAPTER 5

1. Robert A. Hill, "Leonard P. Howell and Millenarian Visions in Early Rastafari," *Jamaica Journal* 16, no. 1 (Feb. 1983): 38.

2. George Eaton Simpson, "The Ras Tafari Movement in Jamaica: A Study in Race and Class Conflict," *Social Forces* 34, no. 2 (1955): 168.

3. Hill, "Leonard P. Howell," 34; Leonard Barrett, *The Rastafarians: Sounds of Cultural Dissonance*, rev. ed. (Boston: Beacon, 1988), 85.

4. Barry Chevannes, "Era of the Dreadlocks," unpublished manuscript, n.d., 17–19.

5. Ibid., 14.

6. Ibid.

7. Baldheads are non-Rastas; the term is intended as the antithesis of "dreadlocks."

8. M. G. Smith, Roy Augier, and Rex Nettleford, *The Rastafari Movement in Kingston, Jamaica* (Mona, Jamaica: Institute of Social and Economic Research, University College of the West Indies, 1960), 9.

9. It is common practice in the rural areas of Jamaica to make footpaths as shortcuts across open land.

10. Derek Bishton, *Black Heart Man* (London: Chatto and Windus, 1986), 122; Horace Campbell, *Rasta and Resistance: From Marcus Garvey to Walter Rodney* (Trenton, N.J.: African World, 1987), 106–7.

11. Hill, "Leonard P. Howell," 34.

12. Chevannes, "Era of the Dreadlocks," 4–5.

13. Ernest Cashmore, *Rastaman: The Rastafarian Movement in England* (Boston: Unwin, 1983), 48.

14. *Daily Gleaner* (Jamaica) Apr. 30, 1960, quoted by W. Errol Bowen, "Rastafarism and the New Society," *Savacou* 5 (June 1975): 41.

15. Bishton, *Black Heart Man*, 122. The emphases are mine.

16. Campbell, *Rasta and Resistance*, 93.

17. Bishton, *Black Hearet Man*, 122.

18. Linden F. Lewis, "Living in the Heart of Babylon: Rastafari in the USA," *Bulletin of Eastern Caribbean Affairs* 15, no. 1 (Mar.–Apr. 1989): 24.

19. Ivor Morrish, *Obeah, Christ and Rastaman: Jamaica and Its Religions* (Cambridge: Clarke, 1982), 71.

20. Bishton, *Black Heart Man*, 117.

21. Yoshiko S. Nagashima, *Rastafarian Music in Contemporary Jamaica: A Study of the Socioreligious Music of the Rastafarian Movement in Jamaica* (Tokyo: Institute for the Study of Languages and Cultures of Asia and Africa, 1984), 19.

22. Morrish, *Obeah*, 71; Smith et al., *Rastafari*, 8.

23. Smith et al., *Rastafari*, 9, 11; Morrish, *Obeah*, 71–72.

24. Smith et al., *Rastafari*, 11.

25. Morrish, *Obeah*, 72–73; Smith et al., *Rastafari*, 14–15.

26. Morrish, *Obeah*, 73.

27. Smith et al., *Rastafari*, 16.

28. The Morant Bay Rebellion was a peasant revolt protesting the economic hardships of the early post-emancipation era. Paul Bogle and William Gordon, two of Jamaica's national heroes, were key players in this revolt.

29. Smith et al., *Rastafari*, 27; also see Campbell, *Rasta and Resistance*, 104.

30. Barry Chevannes, "Case of Jah versus Society: Rastafari Exorcism of the Ideology of Racism in Jamaica," *Social Movement Seminar Paper* 1 (1989): 16.

31. Campbell, *Rasta and Resistance*, 106–7; Rex Nettleford, *Mirror, Mirror: Identity, Race and Protest in Jamaica* (Kingston, Jamaica: Collins and Sangster, 1970), 79–80.

32. Bishton, *Black Heart Man*, 122.

33. *Daily Gleaner* (Jamaica), Oct. 19, 1963, quoted by Carole Yawney, "Lions in Babylon: The Rastafarians of Jamaica as Visionary Movement" (Ph.D. diss., McGill University, 1978), 53.

34. K. M. Williams, *The Rastafarians* (London: Ward Lock, 1981), 40.

35. Chevannes, "Jah versus Society," 17; Yawney, "Lions in Babylon," 52.

36. Smith et al., *Rastafari*, 27.

37. Nettleford, *Mirror, Mirror*, 44.

38. By recommending that the possibility of repatriation be investigated, the study team declared, in effect, that the doctrine of repatriation was not a fanciful dream of deluded people but a legitimate desire of a people wanting

to return to their ancestral home from which their forebears had been forcibly removed.

39. Smith et al., *Rastafari*, 33–38; Yawney, "Lions in Babylon," 52.

40. Nettleford, *Mirror, Mirror*, 54.

41. Ibid., 55–56; Chevannes, "Jah versus Society," 17.

42. Nettleford, *Mirror, Mirror*, 57; Nagashima, *Rastafarian Music*, 123.

43. Douglas R. A. Mack, *From Babylon to Rastafari: Origin and History of the Rastafarian Movement* (Chicago: Research Associates School Times Publications, 1999), 94–115.

44. Nettleford, *Mirror, Mirror*, 70.

45. Rupert Lewis, "Black Nationalism in Jamaica in Recent Years," in *Perspectives on Jamaica in the Seventies*, edited by Carl Stone and Aggrey Brown (Kingston, Jamaica: Jamaica Publishing, 1981), 68.

46. John Paul Homiak, "The 'Ancient of Days' Seated Black: Eldership, Oral Tradition and Ritual in Rastafari Culture" (Ph.D. diss., Brandeis University, 1985), 372.

47. Nettleford, *Mirror, Mirror*, 62.

48. Homiak, "'Ancient of Days,'" 328; also see Nettleford, *Mirror, Mirror*, 58–78.

49. Nettleford, *Mirror, Mirror*, 62.

50. Barrett, *Rastafarians*, 160.

51. Nettleford, *Mirror, Mirror*, 44.

52. Morrish, *Obeah*, 95.

53. Nagashima, *Rastafarian Music*, 118.

54. Morrish, *Obeah*, 95.

55. Nettleford, *Mirror, Mirror*, 109. There have been disagreements between Rastas and church officials concerning the status of Haile Selassie in the Ethiopian Orthodox church.

56. Anita M. Waters, *Race, Class, and Political Symbols: Rastafari and Reggae in Jamaican Politics* (New Brunswick, N.J.: Transactional, 1984), 94.

57. Walter Rodney, *Groundings with My Brothers* (London: Bogle L'Ouverture, 1969), 8.

58. Ibid., 61.

59. Theodore Malloch, "Rastafarianism: A Radical Caribbean Movement/Religion," *Center Journal* 4, no. 4 (Fall 1985): 79.

60. Rodney, *Groundings*, 64.

61. Waters, *Race, Class, and Political Symbols*, 94.

62. Ibid., 85–86.

63. Ibid., 96.

64. Nettleford, *Mirror, Mirror*, 61.

65. Carole Yawney, "Dread Wasteland: Rastafarian Ritual in West Kingston, Jamaica," in *Ritual, Symbolism and Ceremonialism in the Americas: Studies in Symbolic Anthropology*, edited by N. Ross Crumrine (Greenley; Colo: Museum of Anthropology, University of Northern Colorado, 1978), 176.

66. Nettleford, *Mirror, Mirror*, 46.

67. Ibid., 46–47; also see Chevannes, "Jah versus Society," 19.

68. Barry Chevannes, "Rastafari: Towards a New Approach," *New West Indian Guide* 64, nos. 3–4 (1990): 129–30.

69. Nettleford, *Mirror, Mirror,* 77.

70. Carole Yawney, "Remnant of All Nations: Rastafarian Attitudes to Race and Nationality," in *Ethnicity in the Americas,* edited by Francis Henry (The Hague: Mouton 1976), 234.

71. Ibid.

72. Waters, *Race, Class, and Political Symbols,* 124.

73. Ibid., 111.

74. Ibid., 115.

75. Ibid., 124.

76. Ibid., 115.

77. Ibid., 130–35; Yawney, "Remnant of All Nations," 235.

78. Waters, *Race, Class, and Political Symbols,* 123. The emphasis is mine.

79. Ibid., 178.

80. For a discussion of the influence of dread talk on popular Jamaican parlance in the 1970s see Velma Pollard, "Dread Talk: The Speech of the Rastafarian In Jamaica," *Rastafari* (Kingston, Jamaica: Caribbean Quarterly, University of the West Indies, 1985), 39–40.

81. Waters, *Race, Class, and Political Symbols,* 185.

82. Yawney, "Remnant of All Nations," 23.

83. Sebastian Clarke, *Jah Music: The Evolution of the Popular Jamaican Song* (London: Heinemann, 1980), 95.

84. Chevannes, "Jah versus Society," 22.

85. Clarke, *Jah Music,* 94.

86. Nagashima, *Rastafarian Music,* 161.

87. Lewis, "Living in the Heart of Babylon," 23.

88. Clarke, *Jah Music,* 95.

89. Ibid., 63.

90. Malika Lee Whitney and Dermott Hussey, *Bob Marley: Reggae King of the World* (Kingston, Jamaica: Kingston Publishers, 1984), 69–70.

91. Rex Nettleford, "The Caribbean: The Cultural Imperative," *Caribbean Quarterly* 34, no. 3 (1989): 5.

92. Leslie Miles, "Reggae Sunsplash: A Brief History," in *Reggae Sunsplash 1990: A Special Report* (Kingston, Jamaica: Daily Gleaner, 1990), 7–8.

93. Because of a suit brought by the Bob Marley estate, the original venue of Reggae Sunsplash is no longer called the Bob Marley Entertainment Centre.

94. Calvin A. Brown, "Reggae Sunsplash: A Boom for MoBay," in *Reggae Sunsplash 1990: A Special Report* (Kingston, Jamaica: Daily Gleaner, 1990), 14.

95. Not only in Jamaica, but in many other parts of the world, creating and dealing in Rastafarian paraphernalia has become a profitable business. In most large cities in North America and Britain, for example, one can purchase dreadlocksed wigs and T-shirts, necklaces, earrings, bracelets, handbags, hats,

and posters with Rastafarian colors or symbols. (Lewis, "Living in the Heart of Babylon," 23.) I often see these items being sold in the Drew University Center. The number of these items usually multiplies at the bazaar held during African-American History Month.

96. Yawney, "Lions in Babylon," 94.

97. Carl Stone, *Class, Race, and Political Behaviours in Urban Jamaica* (Kingston, Jamaica: Institute of Social and Economic Research, University of the West Indies, 1973), 153, 156, quoted by Yawney, "Lions in Babylon," 71.

98. Colin Prescod, "The People's Cause in the Caribbean," *Race and Class* 17 (1975): 72, quoted by Yawney, "Lions in Babylon," 71.

99. Laurence A. Breiner, "The English Bible in Jamaican Rastafarianism," *Journal of Religious Thought* 42, no. 2 (Fall–Winter 1985–1986): 42.

100. Klaus de Albuquerque, "The Future of the Rastafarian Movement," *Caribbean Review* 8, no. 4 (1979): 22.

CHAPTER 6

1. Interview with Veerle Poupeye, art historian and critic of Jamaican art, August 1998.

2. K. M. Williams, *The Rastafarians* (London: Ward Lock, 1981), 44; Walter Rodney, *Grounding with My Brothers* (London: Bogle L'Ouverture, 1969), 68; Wolfgang Bender, "Liberation from Babylon," in *Missile and Capsule*, edited by Jurgen Martini (Bremen, Germany: Druckerei der Universität Bremen, 1983), 22–28.

3. This observation is from fieldwork at the Jamaican National Gallery, May 1991. Many pieces on display celebrate Rastafari in both the titles and the contents: *Ras Smoke I* depicts a dread with a chalice; *The Mystic* is a portrait of a Rasta; *Hymn of Praise* shows Rastas singing with halos around their heads; *Ecce Homo* portrays a dreadlocksed Jesus in a stained-glass window wearing black, red, and green and with a golden halo; *Peace and Love* is a portrait of a dread in a meditative mood; *Homage to the Rastaman* shows the upper body of a Rasta with his hands crossed over his chest; *Ras Dizzy* is a portrait of the famous Rastafarian painter; *Nyabinghi Hour* depicts a Nyabinghi ceremony; and *The Dreads at Large* shows four Rastas hiding in the bushes.

4. Laurence A. Breiner, "The English Bible in Jamaican Rastafarianism," *Journal of Religious Thought* 42, no. 2 (Fall–Winter 1985–1986): 41; Anita M. Waters, *Race, Class, and Political Symbols: Rastafari and Reggae in Jamaican Politics* (New Brunswick, N.J.: Transactional, 1984), 177.

5. Derek Walcott, *The Joker of Seville and O Babylon* (New York: Farrar, Straus and Giroux, 1978); Orlando Patterson, *The Children of Sisyphus* (Boston: Houghton Mifflin, 1965); Roger Mais, *Brother Man* (London: Heinemann, 1982).

6. Paula Burnett, ed., *The Penguin Book of Caribbean Verse in English* (London: Penguin, 1986).

7. Barry Chevannes, "Case of Jah versus Society: Rastafari Exorcism of

the Ideology of Racism in Jamaica," *Social Movement Seminar Paper 1,* (1989), 23.

8. Seretha Rycenssa, "The Rastafarian Legacy: A Rich Cultural Gift," *Economic Report on Jamaica: Paul Cheng Young and Associates* 4, no. 1 (Aug. 1978): 24; Waters, *Race, Class, and Political Symbols,* 177.

9. Verena Reckford, "Rastafarian Music: An Introductory Study," *Jamaica Journal* 11, nos. 1–2 (1977): 13.

10. Yoshiko S. Nagashima, *Rastafarian Music in Contemporary Jamaica: A Study of the Socioreligious Music of the Rastafarian Movement in Jamaica* (Tokyo: Institute for the Study of Languages and Cultures of Asia and Africa, 1984), 162.

11. Kenneth Bilby and Elliot Leib, "Kumina, the Howellite Church and the Emergence of Rastafarian Traditional Music in Jamaica," *Jamaica Journal* 19, no. 3 (Oct. 1986): 23.

12. Kumina is a spirit-possession cult that practices mainly in the eastern section of Jamaica. It was brought to the island by Africans and is believed to have remained relatively pure. Pukkumina blends elements of African and Christian religions. Revival similarly blends African and Christian elements, but it is more distinctly Christian than Pukkumina. Drumming is a regular feature of these religious groups. Jonkunu is traditional music and dance performed during the Christmas holidays in Jamaica.

13. Nagashima, *Rastafarian Music,* 77–78.

14. Bilby and Leib, "Kumina," 26.

15. Ibid., 26–27.

16. Reckford, "Rastafarian Music," 6.

17. Nagashima, *Rastafarian Music,* 72.

18. Roger Schmidt, *Exploring Religion,* 2d ed. (Belmont, Calif.: Wadsworth, 1988), 425–26.

19. Reckford, "Rastafarian Music," 6; also see Sebastian Clarke, *Jah Music: The Evolution of the Popular Jamaican Song* (London: Heinemann, 1980), 52.

20. Reckford, "Rastafarian Music," 8; M. G. Smith, Roy Augier, and Rex Nettleford, *The Rastafari Movement in Kingston, Jamaica* (Mona, Jamaica: Institute of Social and Economic Research, University College of the West Indies, 1960) 14; Stephen Davis and Peter Simon, *Reggae Bloodlines: In Search of the Music and Culture of Jamaica* (Garden City, N.Y.: Anchor, 1977), 141.

21. Clarke, *Jah Music,* 52; Nagashima, *Rastafarian Music,* 74.

22. Reckford, *Rastafarian Music,* 8; also see Nagashima, *Rastafarian Music,* 74–75.

23. Reckford, "Rastafarian Music," 7–8.

24. Clarke, *Jah Music,* 53.

25. Michael Burnett, *Jamaican Music* (Oxford: Oxford University Press, 1982), 27; Reckford, "Rastafarian Music," 6; Davis and Simon, *Reggae Bloodlines,* 21; Clarke, *Jah Music,* 53.

26. The Dungle was a part of Back O' Wall. It was basically a tangle of

shacks built on a garbage dump. Thus the name *Dungle* was meant to suggest "dung" and "jungle."

27. Reckford, "Rastafarian Music," 8–9; Clarke, *Jah Music*, 53.

28. Reckford, "Rastafarian Music," 9.

29. Garth White, "Reggae: A Musical Weapon," *Caribe* 4, no. 4 (1980): 6.

30. Ibid., 6; Malika Lee Whitney and Dermott Hussey, *Bob Marley: Reggae King of the World* (Kingston, Jamaica: Kingston Publishers, 1984), 9; Nagashima, *Rastafarian Music*, 163.

31. Davis and Simon, *Reggae Bloodlines*, 12.

32. Whitney and Hussey, *Bob Marley*, 9-10.

33. Davis and Simon, *Reggae Bloodlines*, 14.

34. White, "Reggae," 8; Davis and Simon, *Reggae Bloodlines*, 14; Clarke, *Jah Music*, 69.

35. White, "Reggae," 8.

36. Clarke, *Jah Music*, 69.

37. White, "Reggae," 8. The emphases are mine.

38. Davis and Simon, *Reggae Bloodlines*, 16.

39. Whitney and Hussey, *Bob Marley*, 13.

40. Clarke, *Jah Music*, 81.

41. Ibid., 82.

42. Ernest Cashmore, *Rastaman: The Rastafarian Movement in England* (Boston: Unwin, 1983), 102.

43. Davis and Simon, *Reggae Bloodlines*, 17, 91–92; see also Cashmore, *Rastaman*, 103.

44. White, "Reggae," 6. This blend of diverse elements may account for why people from a variety of cultures are drawn to reggae music.

45. White, "Reggae," 9. The emphases are mine.

46. Burnett, *Jamaica Music*, 43–44; White, "Reggae," 9.

47. Whitney and Hussey, *Bob Marley*, 14.

48. White, "Reggae," 7.

49. Davis and Simon, *Reggae Bloodlines*, 21; Garth White, "The Development of Jamaican Popular Music. Part 2: The Urbanization of the Folk," *African-Caribbean Institute of Jamaica Research Review* 1 (1984): 65–66; Whitney and Hussey, *Bob Marley*, 12.

50. White, "Development of Jamaican Popular Music," 66.

51. This seems to have been the only recording by the Folkes Brothers, and their financial remuneration was inconsequential. Shaggy's recording of "O Carolina" (with some modifications) in 1993 was a huge hit, which brought to the fore the issue of who had the rights to the song. Prince Buster, the producer of the original, made claims to the rights, but the courts upheld the claim of one of the Folkes Brothers and gave him substantial royalties from the Shaggy hit.

52. Clarke, *Jah Music*, 53, 62; Reckford, "Rastafarian Music," 12; White, "Development of Jamaican Popular Music," 63; Horace Campbell, *Rasta and*

Resistance: From Marcus Garvey to Walter Rodney (Trenton, N.J.: African World, 1987), 127.

53. Reckford, "Rastafarian Music,"12.

54. Ibid., Davis and Simon, *Reggae Bloodlines,* 142; Clarke, *Jah Music,* 54.

55. Reckford, "Rastafarian Music,"12; also see White, "Development of Jamaican Popular Music," 63.

56. Reckford, "Rastafarian Music,"13.

57. Lehkem [Leahcim] Semaj, "Rastafari and Jamaican Music," *Jamaica Record,* Nov. 3, 1989, p. 7b.

58. Cashmore, *Rastaman,* 100.

59. White, "Development of Jamaican Popular Music," 64; also see White, "Reggae, 8.

60. White, "Development of Jamaican Popular Music," 64.

61. Whitney and Hussey, *Bob Marley,* 13.

62. White, "Reggae, 9.

63. Ibid.

64. Whitney and Hussey, *Bob Marley,* 58.

65. Bob Marley and the Wailers, "Get Up, Stand Up," on *Talkin' Blues,* Island Records, 848243-4, 1991.

66. White, "Reggae, 10.

67. John Sealey and Krister Malm, *Music in the Caribbean* (London: Hodder and Stoughton, 1982), 37.

68. Ibid., 37.

69. White, "Reggae, 9.

70. Whitney and Hussey, *Bob Marley,* 15.

71. Clarke, *Jah Music,* 36.

72. Jimmy Cliff, "Sitting in Limbo," on *The Harder They Come* (original soundtrack for the movie), Mango Records, ZCM 9202, 1973.

73. Clarke, *Jah Music,* 63.

74. Jimmy Cliff, "Piece of the Pie," on *The Power and the Glory,* Jimmy Cliff Oneness, C38986, 1983.

75. Chevannes, "Jah versus Society," 15.

76. White, "Reggae, 2.

77. Clarke, *Jah Music,* 62–63.

78. Ibid., 72.

79. Waters, *Race, Class, and Political Symbols,* 102.

80. Theodore Malloch, "Rastafarianism: A Radical Caribbean Movement/Religion," *Center Journal* 4, no. 4 (Fall 1985): 80.

81. Whitney and Hussey, *Bob Marley,* 14.

82. Clarke, *Jah Music,* 131.

83. Whitney and Hussey, *Bob Marley,* 23.

84. Bob Marley and the Wailers, "We an' Dem," on *Uprising,* Island Records, 422-846211-4, 1980.

85. Whitney and Hussey, *Bob Marley,* 21.

86. Ibid., 28.

87. Ibid.

88. Ibid., 30.

89. Bob Marley Day is also celebrated in North America in some large cities, such as New York, Los Angeles, Atlanta, and Toronto.

90. *Rebel Music: The Bob Marley Story*, PBS video, 2001.

91. Quoted in Whitney and Hussey, *Bob Marley*, 5.

92. Breiner, "English Bible," 42.

93. Velma Pollard, "Dread Talk: The Speech of the Rastafarian in Jamaica," *Rastafari* (Kingston, Jamaica: Caribbean Quarterly, University of the West Indies, 1985), 18.

94. Nagashima, *Rastafarian Music*, 32.

CHAPTER 7

1. I Jabulani Tafari, "The Rastafari, Successors of Marcus Garvey," *Rastafari* (Kingston Jamaica: Caribbean Quarterly, University of the West Indies, 1985), 11.

2. Barry Chevannes, "Rastafari: Towards a New Approach," *New West Indian Guide* 64, nos. 3–4 (1990): 137.

3. Yoshiko S. Nagashima, *Rastafarian Music in Contemporary Jamaica: A Study of the Socioreligious Music of the Rastafarian Movement in Jamaica* (Tokyo: Institute for the Study of Languages and Cultures of Asia and Africa, 1984), 26.

4. Chevannes, "Rastafari," 138.

5. Arthur Kitchen, "Where Is Rastafari Going?" *Daily Gleaner* (Jamaica), June 25, 1987; Lekhem (Leahcim) Semaj, "Revivalism, Mormonism and Rastafari," *Jamaica Record* (Jamaica), Mar. 17, 1989, p. 9.

6. Joy Scott, "Rastas and the Council of Churches," *Daily Gleaner* (Jamaica), Aug. 22, 1982. The Reverend Bevis Byfield, who chaired the Church and Society Commission that reviewed the Rastas' request for membership in the Council of Churches, told me that the request was denied based on a determination that Rastafari does not constitute a "church" according to Troeltsch's church-sect typology.

7. Interview with Brother Samuel, May 1991.

8. Eron Henry, "Rastafari in Eclipse," *Daily Gleaner* (Jamaica), Dec. 2, 1987, p. 8.

9. I have been told that Kitchen has ceased wearing dreadlocks. I have not been able to confirm this or to ascertain whether this indicates that he no longer adheres to the Rastafarian faith.

10. Kitchen, "Where Is Rastafari Going?"

11. *Jamaica Observer*, May 10, 1988; *Jamaica Observer*, May 1, 1999.

12. Mayer N. Zald and Roberta Ash, "Social Movement Organizations: Growth, Decay and Change," *Social Forces* 44, no. 3 (Mar. 1966): 33–34.

13. Ernest Cashmore, *Rastaman: The Rastafarian Movement in England* (Boston: Unwin, 1983), 104.

14. *Jamaica Gleaner* [online], Aug. 17, 2001 (www.Jamaica-gleaner.com/gleaner/20010817/lead/lead1.html), and *Daily Gleaner* (Jamaica), Oct. 27, 2000.

15. Anthony B, "Fire Pon Rome," on *So Many Things*, VP Records, B000001TLY, 1996.

16. Two examples are Ras Bas's article in the *Jamaica Observer*, May 1, 1999, and Abuna Foxe's "Of True and False Rastas and Haile Selassie I" (http://koti.nettilinja.fi/~hsaarist/fox.htm).

17. Neville Callam, "Invitation to Docility: Defusing the Rastafarian Challenge," *Caribbean Journal of Religious Studies* 3 (Sept. 1980): 43.

APPENDIX

1. George E. Simpson, "The Rastafari Movement in Jamaica: A Study of Race and Class Conflict," *Social Forces* 34, no. 2 (Dec. 1955): 170.

2. Ibid.; also see George Eaton Simpson, "Political Cultism in West Kingston, Jamaica," *Social and Economic Studies* 5 (1955): 133–49.

3. Joseph Owens, "Literature on the Rastafari Movement, 1955–1974: A Review," *Savacou* 11–12 (Sept. 1975): 88; George E. Simpson, *Religious Cults of the Caribbean: Trinidad, Jamaica and Haiti* (Rio Piedras, Puerto Rico: Institute of Caribbean Studies, University of Puerto Rico, 1970), 228.

4. Leonard Barrett, *The Rastafarians: A Study of Messianic Cultism in Jamaica* (Puerto Rico: Institute of Caribbean Studies, University of Puerto Rico, 1969), 15, 175.

5. M. G. Smith, Roy Augier, and Rex Nettleford, *The Rastafari Movement in Kingston, Jamaica* (Kingston, Jamaica: Institute of Social and Economic Research, University College of the West Indies, 1960), 28, 36, 37.

6. Ibid., 36–38.

7. Ibid., 34–38.

8. Ibid., 29.

9. Carole Yawney, "Lions in Babylon: The Rastafarians of Jamaica as Visonary Movement" (Ph.D. diss. McGill University, 1978), 5. See pp. 66–70 for a fuller discussion of those who see Rastafari as a manifestation of social pathology.

10. The desire to emigrate is no more characteristic of Rastas than of the rank and file of Jamaicans. Repeated waves of migration have seen hundreds of thousands of Jamaicans going to Central America, Cuba, Great Britain, and North America. Scholars have repeatedly pointed to the tendency of Jamaicans to look outward for solutions to their problems. See Barry Chevannes, "The Literature of Rastafari," *Social and Economic Studies* 26 (1977): 247. If this outward looking is pathological, then Rastas have many counterparts among Jamaicans, including Patterson himself, who is a Jamaican who migrated to the United States years ago.

11. Orlando Patterson, "Ras Tafari: Cult of Outcasts," *New Society* 4, 111 (Nov. 12, 1964): 16.

12. Sheila Kitzinger, "Protest and Mysticism: The Rastafarian Cult in Jamaica," *Journal for the Scientific Study of Religion* 8, no. 2 (Fall 1969): 242.

13. Ibid., 262.

14. Here Kitzinger speaks of a double marginality: of being outcasts from the dominant society and of being marginalized males in their domestic sphere. Jamaican society is widely regarded as matrifocal, while Rastafarianism is clearly patrifocal and patriarchal.

15. Kitzinger, "Protest and Mysticism," 259.

16. Vittorio Lantenari's study of religions indigenous to colonial and former colonial societies, which has a chapter on Rastafari, is a perfect example of this tendency. Vittorio Lantenari, *The Religions of the Oppressed: A Study of Modern Messianic Cults*, translated by Lisa Sergio (New York: Knopf, 1963).

17. Rex Nettleford, *Mirror, Mirror: Identity, Race and Protest in Jamaica* (Kingston, Jamaica: Collins and Sangster (1970), 100–101.

18. Owens, "Literature on the Rastafari Movement," 97.

19. Horace Campbell, *Rasta and Resistance: From Marcus Garvey to Walter Rodney* (Trenton, N.J.: African World, 1987).

20. Frank Jan van Dijk, *Jahmaica: Rastafari and Jamaican Society, 1930–1990* (Utrecht, The Netherlands: Universiteit Utrecht, 1993).

21. Maurice Bryan, *Roots, Resistance and Redemption: The Rise of Rastafari* (Africanstory, 1997).

22. Jack Anthony Johnson-Hill, *I-Sight: The World of Rastafari: An Interpretive Sociological Analysis of Rastafarian Ethics* (Latham, Md.: Scarecrow, 1995), originally a dissertation entitled "Elements of an Afro-Caribbean Social Ethic: A Disclosure of the World of Rastafari as a Liminal Process (Jamaica)" (Ph.D. diss., Vanderbilt University, 1988).

23. George E. Simpson, "Religion and Social Justice: Some Reflections on the Rastafari Movement in Jamaica," *Phylon* 46, no. 4 (Dec. 1985): 286–91; Leonard Barrett, *The Rastafarians: Sounds of Cultural Dissonance*, rev. ed. (Boston: Beacon, 1988).

24. Ernest Cashmore, *Rastaman: The Rastafarian Movement in England* (Boston: Unwin, 1983), 128–44, 150–54.

25. Joseph Owens, *Dread: The Rastafarians of Jamaica* (Kingston, Jamaica: Sangster's, 1976).

26. Barry Chevannes, "Rastafari: Towards a New Approach," *New West Indian Guide* 64, nos. 3–4 (1990): 127–48; Barry Chevannes, "Era of the Dreadlocks," unpublished manuscript, n.d.; Barry Chevannes, *Rastafari: Roots and Ideology* (Syracuse, N.Y.: Syracuse University Press, 1994); and Barry Chevannes, ed., *Rastafari and Other African-Caribbean Worldviews* (New Brunswick, N.J.: Rutgers University Press, 1998).

27. *Yards* refer to the gathering places of the small groups of Rastas we have identified as houses. The designation comes from the fact that each venue is usually on the grounds surrounding the dwelling place of a leading Rasta. Jamaicans usually refer to the premises on which they live as their yards.

28. Carole D. Yawney, "Lions in Babylon"; Carole D. Yawney, "Dread Wasteland: Rastafarian Ritual in West Kingston, Jamaica," in *Ritual, Symbolism and Ceremonialism in the Americas: Studies in Symbolic Anthropology*, edited by N. Ross Crumrine (Greenley, Colo.: Museum of Anthropology, University of Northern Colorado, 1978), 154–78.

29. For Rastas, *Nyabinghi* originally meant "death to the white man" or "death to white and black oppressors." In Jamaica, it has come to refer to those Rastas who seek to maintain the strict ritual and ethical precepts that formed the original ethos of Rastafari.

30. John Paul Homiak, "The 'Ancient of Days' Seated Black: Eldership, Oral Tradition and Ritual in Rastafari Culture" (Ph.D. diss., Brandeis University, 1985).

31. Although families in Jamaica tend to be matrifocal, matrifocal is not the same as matriarchal. In spite of the fact that the stability of the families most often depends on mothers and grandmothers, Jamaican society is still rife with the ideology of male privilege and authority.

32. Maureen Rowe, "The Woman in Rastafari," *Rastafari* (Kingston, Jamaica: Caribbean Quarterly, University of the West Indies, 1985), 13–21; Maureen Rowe, "Gender and Family Relations in RastafarI: A Personal Perspective," in *Chanting Down Babylon: The Rastafari Reader*, edited by N. Samuel Murrell et al. (Philadelphia: Temple University Press, 1998), 73–88.

33. Imani M. Tafari-Ama, "Rastawoman as Rebel: Case Studies in Jamaica," in *Chanting Down Babylon: The Rastafari Reader*, edited by N. Samuel Murrell et al. (Philadephia: Temple University Press, 1998), 89–106.

34. Obiagele Lake, *Rastafari Women: Subordination in the Midst of Liberation Theology* (Durham, N.C.: Carolina Academic Press, 1998).

35. Carole Yawney, "Rastafarian Sistrin by the Rivers of Babylon," *Canadian Women Studies 5*, no. 2 (Winter 1983): 73–75, and "To Grow a Daughter: Cultural Liberation and the Dynamics of Oppression in Jamaica," in *Feminism in Canada*, edited by A. Miles and G. Ginn (Montreal: Black Rose, 1983), 119–44.

36. Diane J. Austin-Broos, "Pentecostals and Rastafarians: Cultural, Political and Gender Relations of Two Religious Movements," *Social and Economic Studies 36*, no. 4 (Dec. 1987): 1–39.

37. Barry Chevannes, "Case of Jah versus Society: Rastafari Exorcism of the Ideology of Racism in Jamaica," *Social Movement Seminar Paper 1* (1989): 1–27.

38. Dennis Forsythe, *Rastafari: For the Healing of the Nation* (Kingston, Jamaica: Zaika, 1983), 7.

39. Ibid., 10–35.

40. Ibid., chaps. 3, 4, and 8; Also see Dennis Forsythe, "West Indian Culture through the Prism of Rastafarianism," *Rastafari* (Kingston, Jamaica: Caribbean Quarterly, University of the West Indies, 1985): 62–85.

41. Forsythe, *Rastafari*, 113–34.

42. Douglas R. A. Mack, *From Babylon to Rastafari: Origin and History of the*

Rastafarian Movement (Chicago: Research Associates, School Times Publications, 1999).

43. Robert Athlyi Rogers, *The Holy Piby* (Chicago: Research Associates School Times Publications, 2000).

44. G. G. Maragh [Leonard P. Howell], *The Promised Key* (Brooklyn, N.Y.: A&B, 2001).

45. Alemu I Jahson Atiba, *The Rastafari Ible* (Chicago: Research Associates School Times Publications, 1994).

46. Gerald Hausman, ed., *The Kebra Negast: The Lost Bible of Rastafarian Wisdom and Faith from Ethiopia and Jamaica* (New York: Martin's, 1997).

47. Kalin Ray Salassi, *Haile Selassie and the Opening of the Seven Seals* (Chicago: Research Associates School Times Publications, 1997).

48. Rastafari Universal Zion, *The Important Utterances of H. I. M. Emperor Haile Selassie I Jah Rastafari* (London: Voice of Rasta, 1994).

49. Karl Phillpotts Naphtali, ed., *The Testimony of His Imperial Majesty Emperor Haile Selassie I, Defender of the Faith* (Washington, D.C: Zewd, 1999).

50. Jah Ahkell, *Rasta: Emperor Haile Selassie and the Rastafarians* (Chicago: Research Associates School Times Publications, 1999).

51. E. S. P. McPherson, *Rastafari and Politics: Sixty Years of a Developing Cultural Ideology: Sociology of Development Perspective* (Clarendon, Jamaica: Black International Iyahbinghi Press, 1991).

52. E. S. P. McPherson, *The Culture-History and Universal Spread of Rastafari* (Clarendon, Jamaica: Black International Iyahbinghi Press, 1993).

53. Ayotunde Amtac Babatunji, *Prophet on Reggae Mountain: Meditations of Ras Shabaka Maasai, Prophet of Jah Rastafari* (Rochester, N.Y.: Garvey-Tubman-Nanny-Nzinga Press, 1994).

54. Tekla Mekfet, *Christopher Columbus and Rastafari: Ironies of History and Other Reflections on the Symbol of Rastafari* (St. Ann, Jamaica: Jambasa, 1993).

55. Mihlawhdh Faristzaddi published three volumes of Itations: *Itations of Jamaica and I Rastafari*, 3 vols. (Miami, Fla.: Judah Ambesa Ihntanahshinahl, 1991–1997).

56. Leahcim Semaj is Michael James spelled backward. This is clearly an attempt to rid himself of the Europeanness that his original name suggests.

57. Leahcim Semaj, "Rastafari: From Religion to Social Theory," *Rastafari* (Kingston, Jamaica: Caribbean Quarterly, University of the West Indies, 1985), 22.

58. Ibid., 23.

59. Ibid.

60. Ibid., 26–30.

61. Lehkem (Leahcim) Semaj, "Revivalism, Mormonism and Rastafari," *Jamaica Record* (Jamaica), March 17, 1989, p. 9.

62. Semaj, "Rastafari: From Religion to Social Theory," 26.

63. N. Samuel Murrell, William D. Spencer, and Adrian A. McFarlane, eds., *Chanting Down Babylon: The Rastafari Reader* (Philadelphia: Temple University Press, 1998).

64. William D. Spencer, *Dread Jesus* (London: Society for Promoting Christian Knowledge, 1999).

65. Neil J. Savinshinsky, "Rastafari in the Promised Land: The Spread of a Jamaican Socio-religious Movement and Its Music and Culture among the Youth of Ghana and Senegambia" (Ph.D. diss., Columbia University, 1993).

66. Heidi Gjerset, "First Generation Rastafari in St. Eustatius: A Case Study in the Netherlands Antilles," *Caribbean Quarterly* 40, no. 1 (Mar. 1994): 64–77.

Selected Bibliography

Ahkell, Jah. *Rasta: Emperor Hailes Selassie and the Rastafarians*. Chicago: Research Associates School Times, 1999.

Atiba, Alemu I Jahson. *The Rastafari Ible*. Chicago: Research Associates School Times, 1994.

Austin-Broos, Diane J. "Pentecostals and Rastafarians: Cultural, Political and Gender Relations of Two Religious Movements." *Social and Economic Studies* 36, no. 4 (Dec. 1987): 1–39.

Babatunji, Ayotunde Amtac. *Prophet on Reggae Mountain: Meditations of Ras Shabaka Maasai, Prophet of Jah Rastafari*. Rochester, N.Y.: Garvey-Tubman-Nanny-Nzinga, 1994.

Banton, Michael. "Black and White: Male and Female," *New Society* 48, no. 872 (June 20, 1979): 704–6.

Barkun, Michael. *Disaster and the Millennium*. New Haven, Conn.: Yale University Press, 1974.

Barrett, Leonard E. "African Roots in Jamaican Indigenous Religion." *Journal of Religious Thought* 35 (Spring-Summer 1978): 7–26.

———. *The Rastafarians: Sounds of Cultural Dissonance*, rev. ed. Boston: Beacon, 1988.

———. *The Rastafarians: A Study of Messianic Cultism in Jamaica*. Puerto Rico: Institute of Caribbean Studies, University of Puerto Rico, 1969.

———. *Soul-force: African Heritage in Afro-American Religion*. Garden City, N.Y.: Anchor, 1974.

Bastide, Roger. *Les Ameriques noires*. Paris: Payot, 1967.

Beckford, George, and Michael Witter. *Small Garden . . . Bitter Weed: The Political Economy of Struggle and Change in Jamaica*. Morant Bay, Jamaica: Maroon, 1980.

Bender, Wolfgang. "Liberation from Babylon: Rasta Painters in Jamaica." In *Missile and Capsule*, edited by Jurgen Martini, 129-35. Bremen, Germany: Druckerei der Universität Bremen, 1983.

Bendix, Reinhard. *Max Weber: An Intellectual Portrait*. Garden City, N.Y.: Doubleday, 1960.

Berger, Peter L. "Charisma and Religious Innovation: The Social Location of Israelite Prophecy." *American Sociological Review* 28, no. 6 (1963): 940–50.

Bilby, Kenneth. "The Holy Herb: Notes on the Background of Cannabis in Jamaica." In *Rastafari*, 82–95. Kingston, Jamaica: Caribbean Quarterly, University of the West Indies, 1985.

Bilby, Kenneth, and Elliot Leib. "Kumina, the Howellite Church and the Emergence of Rastafarian Traditional Music in Jamaica." *Jamaica Journal* 19, no. 3 (Oct. 1986): 22–28.

Birhan, Iyata Farika. *Jah Is I Shepherd*. San Jose, Calif.: Rastas/Roots/Redemption/Repatriation Unlimited, 1981.

Bishton, Derek. *Black Heart Man*. London: Chatto and Windus, 1986.

Bisnauth, Dale. *A History of Religions in the Caribbean*. Kingston, Jamaica: Kingston Publishing, 1989.

Blacka, Razac [Garth White]. "Master Drummer." *Jamaica Journal* 11, nos. 1–2 (1977): 17.

Boot, Adrian. *Bob Marley: Soul Rebel, Natural Mystic*. New York: St. Martin's, 1982.

————. *Jamaica: Babylon on a Thin Wire*. London: Thames and Hudson, 1976.

Bowen, W. Errol. "Rastafarism and the New Society." *Savacou* 5 (June 1975): 41–50.

Boyne, Ian. "Jamaica: Breaking Barriers between Churches and Rastafarians." *One World* 86 (May 1983): 33–34.

Brake, Mike. "Under Heavy Manners: A Consideration of Racism, Black Youth Culture, and Crime in Britain." *Crime and Social Justice* 20 (1983): 1–15.

Breiner, Laurence A. "The English Bible in Jamaican Rastafarianism." *Journal of Religious Thought* 42, no. 2 (Fall-Winter 1985-86): 30–43.

Brown, Aggrey. *Color, Class, and Politics in Jamaica*. New Brunswick, N.J.: Transaction, 1979.

Brown, Calvin A. "Reggae Sunsplash: A Boom for MoBay." In *Reggae Sunsplash 1990: A Special Report*. Kingston, Jamaica: Daily Gleaner, 1990.

Bryan, Maurice. *Roots, Resistance and Redemption: The Rise of Rastafari*. Africansstory, 1997.

Burnett, Michael. *Jamaican Music*. Oxford: Oxford University Press, 1982.

Burnett, Paula, ed. *The Penguin Book of Caribbean Verse in English*. London: Penguin, 1986.

Bush, Diane Mitsch. "The Routinization of Social Movements Organizations: China as a Deviant Case." *Sociological Quarterly* 19, no. 2 (Spring 1978): 203–19.

Byfield, Bevis B. "Rastafarianism and Its Influence on Politics." Paper presented at a seminar on "Religion and Democracy." Sponsored by the Bustamante Institute of Public and International Affairs, Trinidad, Nov. 12–18, 1987.

————. "Transformation of the Jamaican Society." *Caribbean Journal of Religious Studies* 55 (Apr. 1983): 28–38.

Byfield, Hazel G. "Women in the Struggle for True Community: A Caribbean Perspective." *Mid-stream* 25, no. 1 (Jan. 1986): 49–56.

Callam, Neville. "Invitation to Docility: Defusing the Rastafarian Challenge." *Caribbean Journal of Religious Studies* 3 (Sept. 1980): 28-48.

Campbell, Horace. *Rasta and Resistance: From Marcus Garvey to Walter Rodney.* Trenton, N.J.: African World, 1987.

———. "Rastafari: A Culture of Resistance." *Race and Class* 22, no. 1 (Summer 1980): 1–22.

———. "The Rastafarians in the Eastern Caribbean." *Caribbean Quarterly* 26 (1980): 42–61.

Case, Charles G. "Rastafari and the Religion of Anthropology: An Epistemological Study." *Religious Education* 78 (Summer 1983): 420.

Cashmore, Ernest. "More Than a Version: A Study of Reality Creation." *British Journal of Sociology* 30, no. 3 (Sept. 1979): 307–21.

———. *Rastaman: The Rastafarian Movement in England.* Boston: Unwin, 1983.

———. "The Rastaman Cometh." *New Society* 41, no. 777 (Aug. 25, 1977): 382–84.

Cassidy, Frederic G. *Jamaica Talk.* London: Macmillan, 1961.

Chalfant, H. Paul, Robert E. Beckley, and E. Eddie Palmer. *Religion in Contemporary Society.* Sherman Oaks, Calif.: Alfred, 1981.

Chevannes, Barry. "Case of Jah versus Society: Rastafari Exorcism of the Ideology of Racism in Jamaica." *Social Movement Seminar Paper* 1 (1989): 1–27.

———. "Era of the Dreadlocks." Unpublished manuscript, n.d.

———. "The Literature of Rastafari." *Social and Economic Studies* 26 (1977): 239–62.

———. *Rastafari: Roots and Ideology.* Syracuse, N.Y.: Syracuse University Press, 1994.

———. "Rastafari: Towards a New Approach." *New West Indian Guide* 64, nos. 3–4 (1990): 127–48.

———. "The Rastafari of Jamaica." In *When Prophets Die,* edited by Timothy Miller, 335–37. Albany: State University of New York Press, 1991.

———. "Rastafarianism and the Class Struggle: The Search for a Method ology." In *Methodology and Change: Problems of Applied Social Science Research Techniques in the Commonwealth Caribbean,* edited by L. Lindsay, 244–51. Mona, Jamaica: Institute of Social and Economic Research, University of the West Indies, 1978.

———. "The Repairer of the Breach: Reverend Claudius Henry and Jamaican Society." In *Ethnicity in the Americas,* edited by Francis Henry, 263–69. The Hague: Mouton, 1976.

———. Review of *Dread: The Rastafarians of Jamaica,* by Joseph Owens. In *Caribbean Quarterly* 24, nos. 3–4 (Sept.–Dec. 1978): 61–69.

———. *The Social Origin of the Rastafari Movement.* Mona, Jamaica: Institute of Social and Economic Research, University of the West Indies, 1978.

Chevannes, Barry, ed. *Rastafari and Other African-Caribbean Worldviews.* New Brunswick, N.J.: Rutgers University Press, 1998.

Clarke, Peter B. *Black Paradise: The Rastafarian Movement*. Wellingborough, Northamptonshire, England: Aquarian, 1986.

Clarke, Sebastian. *Jah Music: The Evolution of the Popular Jamaican Song*. London: Heinemann, 1980.

Cohen, Abner. *Two-Dimensional Man*. London: Routledge and Kegan Paul, 1974.

Collum, Danny. "Jubilee, Rastafarian Style: A Vibrant Human Film on Reggae and Justice." *Sojourners* 9 (Nov. 1980): 35–36.

Cooper, Carolyn. "Chanting Down Babylon: Bob Marley's Song as Literary Text." *Jamaica Journal* 19, no. 4 (Nov. 1986–Jan. 1987): 2–8.

Coser, Lewis A. *Masters of Sociological Thought: Ideas in Historical and Social Context*, 2d ed. New York: Harcourt Brace Jovanovich, 1977.

Cushman, Thomas, "Rich Rasta and Communist Rockers: A Comparative Study of the Origin, Diffusion and Defusion of Revolutionary Musical Codes." *Journal of Popular Culture* 25 (Winter 1991): 17–61.

Dalrymple, Henderson. *Bob Marley: Music, Myth and the Rastas*. London: Cari-Arawak, 1976.

Dance, Daryl C. *Folklore from Contemporary Jamaicans*. Knoxville: University of Tennessee Press, 1985.

Davis, Stephen. *Bob Marley*. New York: Doubleday, 1985.

Davis, Stephen, and Peter Simon. *Reggae Bloodlines: In Search of the Music and Culture of Jamaica*. Garden City, N.Y.: Anchor, 1977.

———. *Reggae International*. New York: Rodner and Bernhard, 1982.

de Albuquerque, Klaus. "The Future of the Rastafarian Movement." *Caribbean Review* 8, no. 4 (1979): 22–25, 44–46.

Dekmejian, Richard H., and Margaret J. Wyszomirski. "Charismatic Leadership in Islam: The Mahdi of the Sudan." *Comparative Studies in Society and History* 14, no. 2 (Mar. 1972): 193–214.

Deschen, S. "On Religious Change: The Situational Analysis of Symbolic Action." *Comparative Studies in Society and History* 12 (1970): 260–74.

Dirk, Kaesler. *Max Weber: An Introduction to His Life and Work*. Translated by Philippa Hurd. Chicago: University of Chicago Press, 1988.

Dreher, M. C., and C. Rogers. "Getting High: Ganja Man and His Socio-Economic Milieu." *Caribbean Studies* 16, no. 2 (July 1976): 219–31.

Du Bois, W. E. B. *The Souls of Black Folk*. In *Writings*, edited by Nathan Huggins, 337–547. New York: Literary Classics of the United States, 1986.

Erskine, Noel Leo. *Decolonizing Theology: A Caribbean Perspective*. New York: Orbis, 1981.

Essien-Udom, E. U., and Amy Jacques-Garvey. *More Philosophy and Opinions of Marcus Garvey*, vol. 3. Totowa, N.J.: Cass, 1977.

Faristzaddi, Mihlawhdh. *Itations of Jamaica and I Rastafari*. 3 vols. Miami, Fla.: Judah Ambesa Ihntanahshinahl, 1991–1997.

Foner, Nancy. *Jamaica Farewell: Jamaican Migrants in London*. Berkeley: University of California Press, 1978.

Forsythe, Dennis. *Rastafari: For the Healing of the Nation*. Kingston, Jamaica: Zaika, 1983.

———. "West Indian Culture through the Prism of Rastafarianism." In *Rastafari*, 62–85. Kingston, Jamaica: Caribbean Quarterly, University of the West Indies, 1985.

Friday, Michael. "A Comparison of 'Dharma' and 'Dread' as the Determinants of Ethical Standards." *Caribbean Journal of Religious Studies* 5 (Sept. 1983): 29–37.

Gardner, William James. *A History of Jamaica from Its Discovery by Columbus to the Year 1872*. Totowa, N.J.: Cass, 1971.

Garrison, Ken. *Black Youth: Rastafarianism, and the Identity Crisis in Britain*. London: Afro-Caribbean Education Resource Project, 1979.

Gerth, Hans H., and C. Wright Mills, eds. *From Max Weber: Essays in Sociology*. London: Routledge and Kegan Paul, 1948.

Gjerset, Heidi. "First Generation Rastafari in St. Eustatius: A Case Study in the Netherlands Antilles." *Caribbean Quarterly* 40, no. 2 (March 1994): 64–77.

Glazier, Stephen D. *Marchin' the Pilgrims Home: Leadership and Decision in an Afro-Caribbean Faith*. Westport, Conn.: Greenwood, 1983.

———. "Religion and Contemporary Religious Movements in the Caribbean: A Report." *Sociological Analysis* 41, no. 2 (Summer 1980): 181–83.

———. "Syncretisim and Separation: Ritual Change in Afro-Caribbean Faith." *Journal of American Folklore* 98 (1985): 49–62.

Gonsalves, Ralph. "The Rodney Affair." *Caribbean Quarterly* 25 (Sept. 1979): 1–24.

Goulbourne, Erold. "Caribbean Paper on Rastafarianism: Cult or Religion?" Unpublished manuscript, 1980.

Graham, Margaret, and Franklin Knight, eds. *Africa and the Caribbean: The Legacies of a Link*. Baltimore, Md.: John Hopkins University Press, 1979.

Greenberg, Alan. "Reggae International: Spiritual Balm for a Trembling World: A Review of *Reggae International* by Stephen Davis and Peter Simon." *Caribbean Review* 12, no. 2 (1983): 32–33.

Griffin, Glenn A., Richard L. Gorsuch, and Andrea-Lee Davis. "A Cross-Cultural Investigation of Religious Orientations, Social Norms, and Prejudice." *Journal for the Scientific Study of Religion* 26, no. 3 (Sept. 1987): 358–65.

Hadden, Jeffrey K., and Anson Shupe, eds. *Prophetic Religions and Politics: Religion and the Political Order*. New York: Paragon, 1986.

Hausman, Gerald, ed. *The Kebra Negast: The Lost Bible of Rastafarian Wisdom and Faith from Ethiopia to Jamaica*. New York: Martin's, 1997.

Hayford, Casely. *Ethiopia Unbound: Studies in Race Emancipation*. 1911. Reprint, London: Cass, 1969.

Hebdige, Dick. *Subculture: The Meaning of Style*. London: Methuen, 1979.

Hellstrom, Jan A. "Jah Live: Selassie-I: En Studie Kring Reggae-Musik och Afrikansk Messiaskult pa Jamaica." *Svensk Teologisk Kvartalskrift* 53, no. 4 (1977): 145–55.

Henry, Paget. "Indigenous Religions and the Transformation of Peripheral Societies." In *Prophetic Religions and Politics: Religion and the Political Order,* edited by Jeffrey K. Hadden and Anson Shupe, 123–50. New York: Paragon, 1986.

Herskovits, Melville J. *The Myths of the Negro Past.* Boston: Beacon, 1965.

———. *The New World Negro.* Bloomington: Indiana University Press, 1966.

Hill, Robert A. "Leonard P. Howell and Millenarian Visions in Early Rastafari." *Jamaica Journal* 16, no. 1 (Feb. 1983): 24–39.

Hill, Robert, and Barbara Bair. *Marcus Garvey: Life and Lessons.* Berkeley: University of California Press, 1987.

Hiller, Harry H. "A Reconceptualization of the Dynamics of Social Movement Development." *Pacific Sociological Review* 18, no. 3 (July 1975): 243–60.

Hoenisch, Michael. "Symbolic Politics: Perceptions of the Early Rastafari Movement." *Massachusetts Review* 29 (Fall 1989): 432–49.

Hoetink, Harmannus. "National Identity, Culture, and Race in the Caribbean." In *Racial Tensions and National Identity,* edited by Ernest Q. Campbell, 17–44. Nashville, Tenn.: Vanderbilt University Press, 1972.

Hogg, Donald W. "Statement of a Ras Tafari Leader." *Caribbean Studies* 6, no. 1 (1981–1982): 37–38.

Homiak, John Paul. "The 'Ancient of Days' Seated Black: Eldership, Oral Tradition and Ritual in Rastafari Culture." Ph.D. diss., Brandeis University, 1985.

Hurbon, Laennec. "New Religious Movements in the Caribbean." In *New Religious Movements and Rapid Social Change,* edited by James A. Beckford, 146–76. Beverly Hills, Calif.: Sage/UNESCO, 1986.

Hurwitz, Samuel J., and Edith Hurwitz. *Jamaica: A Historical Portrait.* New York: Praeger, 1971.

Jackson, Michael. "Rastafarianism." *Theology* 83 (Jan. 1980): 26–34.

Jacobs, Virginia Lee. *Roots of Rastafari.* San Diego, Calif.: Avant, 1985.

Jacques-Garvey, Amy, ed. *Philosophy and Opinions of Marcus Garvey.* New York: Atheneum, 1974.

Jagessar, Michael N. "JPIC and Rastafarians." *One World,* Feb. 1991, pp. 15–17.

Johnson, Linton Kwesi. "Arts in Society: The Reggae Rebellion." *New Society* 36, no. 714 (June 10, 1976): 589.

———. *Dread Beat and Blood.* London: Bogle L'Ouverture, 1975.

———. "Jamaica Rebel Music." *Race and Class* 17, no. 4 (Spring 1976): 397–412.

———. "Roots and Rock: The Marley Enigma." *Race Today* 7, no. 10 (Oct. 1975): 237–38.

Johnson-Hill, Jack Anthony. "Elements of an Afro-Caribbean Social Ethic: A Disclosure of the World of Rastafari as a Liminal Process (Jamaica)." Ph.D. diss., Vanderbilt University, 1988.

———. *I-Sight: The World of Rastafari.* Latham, Md.: Scarecrow, 1995.

Jones, Robert Alun, and Robert M. Anservitz. "Saint-Simon and Saint-

Simonism: A Weberian View." *American Journal of Sociology* 10, no. 5 (Mar. 1975): 1095–1123.

Kallynder, Rolston, and Henderson Dalrymple. *Reggae: A People's Music*. London: Carib-Arawak, n.d.

Kerr, Madeline. *Personality and Conflict in Jamaica*. London: Collins, 1963.

Kettle, Martin. "The Racial Numbers Game in Our Prisons." *New Society* 61, no. 1037 (Sept. 30, 1982): 535–37.

Kilgore, John. "Rastafarianism: A Theology of the African Church." Doctor of Ministries thesis, School of Theology at Claremont, 1984.

Kitzinger, Sheila. "Protest and Mysticism: The Rastafarian Cult in Jamaica." *Journal for the Scientific Study of Religion* 8, no. 2 (Fall 1969): 240–62.

Kuper, Adam. *Changing Jamaica*. London: Routledge and Kegan Paul, 1976.

Lacey, Terry. *Violence and Politics in Jamaica, 1960–70: Internal Security in a Developing Country*. Totowa, N.J.: Cass, 1977.

Lake, Obiagele. *Rastafari Women: Subordination in the Midst of Liberation Theology*. Durham, N.C.: Carolina Academic, 1998.

Landman-Bogues. "Rastafarian Food Habits." *Cajanus* 9, no. 4 (1976): 228–33.

Lanternari, Vittorio. *The Religions of the Oppressed: A Study of Modern Messianic Cults*. Translated by Lisa Sergio. New York: Knopf, 1963.

Lewis, Linden F. "Living in the Heart of Babylon: Rastafari in the USA." *Bulletin of Eastern Caribbean Affairs* 15, no. 1 (Mar./Apr. 1989): 20–30.

Lewis, Rupert. "Black Nationalism in Jamaica in Recent Years." In *Perspectives on Jamaica in the Seventies*, edited by Carl Stone and Aggrey Brown, 65–71. Kingston, Jamaica: Jamaica Publishing, 1981.

Lewis, William F. "The Rastafari: Millennial Cultists or Unregenerated Peasants?" *Peasant Studies* 14 (Fall 1986): 5–26.

———. *Soul Rebels: The Rastafari*. Prospect Heights, Ill.: Waveland, 1993.

Long, Theodore. "Prophecy, Charisma and Politics: Reinterpreting the Weberian Thesis." In *Prophetic Religions and Politics: Religion and the Political Order*, edited by Jeffrey K. Hadden and Anson Shupe, 3–17. New York: Paragon, 1986.

Lowenthal, David. *West Indian Societies*. London: Oxford University Press, 1976.

Macionis, John J. *Sociology*, 2d ed. Englewood Cliffs, N.J.: Prentice Hall, 1989.

Mack, Douglas R. A. *From Babylon to Rastafari: Origin and History of the Rastafarian Movement*. Chicago: Research Associates School Times Publications, 1999.

Mais, Roger. *Brother Man*. London: Heinemann, 1982.

Malloch, Theodore. "Rastafarianism: A Radical Caribbean Movement/Religion." *Center Journal* 4, no. 4 (Fall 1985): 67–87.

Manley, Michael. *Jamaica: Struggle in the Periphery*. London: Writers and Readers Publishing Cooperative Society, 1982.

———. *The Politics of Change: A Jamaican Testament*. London: Deutsch, 1974.

Mansingh, Ajai, and Laxmi Mansingh. "Hindu Influences on Rastafarianism."

In *Rastafari*, 96–115. Kingston, Jamaica: Caribbean Quarterly, University of the West Indies, 1985.

Maragh, G. G. [Leonard P. Howell]. *The Promised Key*. Brooklyn, N.Y.: A & B, 2001.

Mau, James A. *Social Change and the Images of the Future: A Study of the Pursuit of Progress in Jamaica*. Cambridge: Mass.: Schenkman, 1968.

Mazrui, Ali A. "Religious Alternatives in the Black Diaspora: From Malcolm X to Rastafari." *Caribbean Affairs* 3, no. 1 (1990): 157–60.

McAdam, Doug, John D. McCarthy, and Mayer N. Zald. "Social Movements." In *Handbook of Sociology*, edited by Neil J. Smelser, 695–737. Newbury Park, Calif.: Sage, 1988.

McCormack, Ed. "Bob Marley with a Bullet." *Rolling Stone*, Aug. 12, 1976, pp. 37–41.

McPherson, E. S. P. *The Culture-History and Universal Spread of Rastafari*. Clarendon, Jamaica: Black International Iyahbinghi, 1993.

———. *Rastafari and Politics: Sixty Years of a Developing Cultural Ideology: Sociology of Development Perspective*. Clarendon, Jamaica: Black International Iyahbinghi, 1991.

Mekfet, Tekla. *Christopher Columbus and Rastafari: Ironies of History and Other Reflections on the Symbol of Rastafari*. St. Ann, Jamaica: Jambasa, 1993.

Miles, Leslie. "Reggae Sunsplash: A Brief History." In *Reggae Sunsplash 1990: A Special Report*. Kingston, Jamaica: Daily Gleaner, 1990.

Mintz, Sidney. "The Caribbean as a Socio-Cultural Area." In *Peoples and Cultures of the Caribbean*, edited by Michael M. Horowitz, 18–46. Garden City, N.Y.: Natural History Press, 1971.

Morris, Mervyn. *On Holy Week*. Kingston, Jamaica: Sangster's, 1977.

Morrish, Ivor. *Obeah, Christ and Rastaman: Jamaica and Its Religions*. Cambridge: Clarke, 1982.

Mulvaney, Becky Michele. *Rastafari and Reggae*. Westport, Conn.: Greenwood, 1990.

———. "Rhythms of Resistance: On Rhetoric and Reggae Music (Jamaica, Rastafari)." Ph.D. diss., University of Iowa, 1985.

Murrell, N. Samuel, William D. Spencer, and Adrian A. McFarlane, eds. *Chanting Down Babylon: The Rastafari Reader*. Philadelphia: Temple University Press, 1998.

Myers, Trevor C. *The Essence of Rastafari Nationalism and Black Economic Development*. New York: Vantage, 1989.

Nagashima, Yoshiko S. *Rastafarian Music in Contemporary Jamaica: A Study of the Socioreligious Music of the Rastafarian Movement in Jamaica*. Tokyo: Institute for the Study of Languages and Cultures of Asia and Africa, 1984.

Naphtali, Karl Phillpotts, ed. *The Testimony of His Imperial Majesty, Emperor Haile Selassie I, Defender of the Faith*. Washington, D.C.: Zewd, 1999.

Nettleford, Rex. "The Caribbean: The Cultural Imperative." *Caribbean Quarterly* 34, no. 3 (1989): 4–14.

———. *Caribbean Cultural Identity: The Case of Jamaica*. Kingston, Jamaica: Institute of Jamaica, 1978.

———. "Caribbean Perspectives: The Creative Potential and the Quality of Life." In *Caribbean Rhythms: The Emerging English Literature of the West Indies*, edited by James T. Livingstonm, 298–318. New York: Washington Square Press, 1974.

———. *Manley and the New Jamaica*. New York: African Publishing, 1979.

———. *Mirror, Mirror: Identity, Race and Protest in Jamaica*. Kingston, Jamaica: Collins and Sangster, 1970.

Nicholas, Tracy. *Rastafari: A Way of Life*. Garden City, N.Y.: Anchor, 1978.

Norris, Katrin. *Jamaica: The Search for Identity*. London: Oxford University Press, 1962.

Noyce, John L. *The Rastafarians in Britain and Jamaica*. Brighton, England: University of Sussex Press, 1978.

O'Gorman, Pamela. "An Approach to the Study of Jamaican Popular Music." *Jamaica Journal* 6, no. 7 (Dec. 1972): 50.

Orum, Anthony. *Introduction to Political Sociology: The Social Anatomy of the Body Politic*, 3d ed. Englewood Cliffs, N.J.: Prentice Hall, 1989.

Owens, Joseph. *Dread: The Rastafarians of Jamaica*. Kingston, Jamaica: Sangster's, 1976.

———. "Literature on the Rastafari Movement, 1955–1974: A Review." *Savacou* 11–12 (Sept. 1975): 86–105, 113–14.

———. "The Rastafarians of Jamaica." In *Troubling of the Waters*, edited by Idris Hamid, 165–70. San Fernando, Trinidad: Rahaman, 1973.

Patterson, Orlando. *The Children of Sisyphus*. Boston: Houghton Mifflin, 1965.

———. "Ras Tafari: Cult of Outcasts." *New Society* 4, no. 111 (Nov. 12, 1964): 15–17.

Phillips, Peter. "Race, Class, Nationalism: A Perspective on Twentieth Century Social Movements in Jamaica." *Social and Economic Studies* 37, no. 3 (1988): 97–123.

Pollard, Velma. "Dread Talk: The Speech of the Rastafarian in Jamaica." In *Rastafari*, 32–41. Kingston, Jamaica: Caribbean Quarterly, University of the West Indies, 1985.

———. "The Social History of Dread Talk." *Caribbean Quarterly* 28, no. 2 (Dec. 1982): 17–40.

———. "Word Sounds: The Language of Rastafari in Barbados and St. Lucia." *Jamaica Journal* 17, no. 1 (Feb. 1984): 57-62.

Post, Ken. "The Bible as Ideology: Ethiopianism in Jamaica, 1930–38." In *African Perspectives*, edited by Christopher Allen and R. W. Johnson, 185–207. Cambridge: Cambridge University Press, 1970.

Prescod, Colin. "The People's Cause in the Caribbean." *Race and Class* 17 (1975): 71–85.

Price, Raymond. "The Rastafari of Jamaica: A Study of Group Beliefs and Social Stress." Paper presented at the first meeting of the Caribbean Psychiatric Association, Ocho Rios, Jamaica, 1969.

Rastafari Universal Zion. *The Important Utterances of H. I. M. Emperor Haile Selassie I Jah Rastafari*. London: Voice of Rasta, 1994.

Reckford, Verena. "Rastafarian Music: An Introductory Study." *Jamaica Journal* 11, nos. 1–2 (1977): 2–13.

———. "Reggae, Rastafarianism and Cultural Identity." *Jamaica Journal* 16 (1982): 70–79.

Ringenberg, Roger. "Rastafarianism: An Expanding Jamaican Cult." Unpublished manuscript, n.d.

Robertson, Roland, ed. *Sociology of Religion: Selected Readings*. Bungay, Suffolk, England: Penguin, 1969.

Rodney, Walter. *Groundings with My Brothers*. London: Bogle L'Ouverture, 1969.

Rogers, Claudia. "Social Transformation in Jamaica: The Internal Dynamic of the Rastafarian Movement." Paper presented at the annual meeting of the Caribbean Studies Association, Fort–de–France, Martinique, 1978.

———. "What's a Rasta?" *Caribbean Review* 7, no. 1 (Jan.–Mar. 1977): 9–12.

Rogers, Robert Athlyi. *The Holy Piby*. Woodbridge, N.J.: 1924; reprint, Chicago: Research Associates School Times, 2000.

Rose, Terrence. "Emerging Problems in Jamaica and Their Pastoral Implications." *Caribbean Journal of Religious Studies* 6 (April 1985): 29–45.

Rowe, Maureen. "Gender and Family Relations in Rastafari: A Personal Perspective." In *Chanting Down Babylon: The Rastafari Reader*, edited by N. Samuel Murrell et al., 73–88. Philadelphia: Temple University Press, 1998.

———. "The Woman in Rastafari." In *Rastafari*, 13–21. Kingston, Jamaica: Caribbean Quarterly, University of the West Indies, 1985.

Rubin, Vera, and Lambros Comitas. *Ganga in Jamaica*. The Hague: Mouton, 1975.

Rycenssa, Seretha. "The Rastafarian Legacy: A Rich Cultural Gift." *Economic Report on Jamaica: Paul Cheng Young and Associates* 4, no. 1 (Aug. 1978): 22–24.

Saakana, Amon Saba. "Garvey and Rastafari." *Capital Issues Supplement*, Aug. 1987, p. 15.

Salassi, Ray Kalin. *Haile Selassie and the Opening of the Seven Seals*. Chicago: Research Associates School Times, 1997.

Savinshinsky, Neil J. "Rastafari in the Promised Land: The Spread of a Jamaican Socio–religious Movement and Its Music and Culture among the Youth of Ghana and Senegambia." Ph.D. diss., Columbia University, 1993.

Scavilla, Norma. "The Persistence of Charisma: A Re-interpretation of Routinization." *Review of Social Theory* 2, no. 2 (May 1974): 91–108.

Schmidt, Roger. *Exploring Religion*, 2d ed. Belmont, Calif.: Wadsworth, 1988.

Schuler, Monica. "Myalism and the African Religious Tradition in Jamaica." In *Africa and the Caribbean: The Legacies of a Link*, edited by Margaret Grahan and Franklin Knight, 65–79. Baltimore, Md.: Johns Hopkins University Press, 1979.

Schultz, Alfred, and Thomas Luckmann. *The Structures of the Life–World.* Translated by Richard M. Zanier and H. Tristram Engelhardt, Jr. Evanston, Ill.: Northwestern University Press, 1973.

Seaga, Edward. "Revival Cults in Jamaica." *Jamaica Journal* 3, no. 2 (June 1969): 3–13.

Sealey, John, and Krister Malm. *Music in the Caribbean.* London: Hodder and Stoughton, 1982.

Segal, Aaron. "The Land of Look Behind: A Film about Reggae and Rastafarianism: A Review Article." *Caribbean Review* 12, no. 2 (1973): 36–37.

Semaj, Leahcim. "Race and Identity and Children of the African Diaspora: Contributions of Rastafari." *Caribe* 4, no. 4 (1980): 14–18.

———. "Rastafari: From Religion to Social Theory." In *Rastafari,* 22–31. Kingston, Jamaica: Caribbean Quarterly, University of the West Indies, 1985.

Semaj, Lehkem [Leahcim]. "Rastafari and Jamaican Music." *Jamaica Record* (Jamaica), Nov. 3, 1989, p. 7b.

———. "Revivalism, Mormonism and Rastafari." *Jamaica Record* (Jamaica), Mar. 17, 1989, p. 9.

Sewell, Tony. *Garvey's Children: The Legacy of Marcus Garvey.* London and Basingstoke: Macmillan Caribbean/The Voice, 1990.

Signorile, Vito. "The Routinization of Hybris." *Qualitative Sociology* 6, no. 3 (Fall 1983): 266–77.

Simpson, George Eaton. *Black Religions in the New World.* New York: Columbia University Press, 1978.

———. "Political Cultism in Western Kingston." *Social and Economic Studies* 5 (1955): 133–49.

———. "The Ras Tafari Movement in Jamaica: A Study in Race and Class Conflict." *Social Forces* 34, no. 2 (Dec. 1955): 168–70.

———. "The Ras Tafari Movement in Jamaica in Its Millennial Aspect." In *Millennial Dreams in Action,* edited by Sylvia L. Thrupp, 160–65. The Hague: Mouton, 1970.

———. "Religion and Social Justice: Some Reflections of the Rastafari Movement." *Phylon* 46, no. 4 (Dec. 1985): 286–91.

———. *Religious Cults of the Caribbean: Trinidad, Jamaica and Haiti.* Rio Pedras, Puerto Rico: Institute of Caribbean Studies, University of Puerto Rico, 1970.

Singham, A. W., and N. L. Singham. "Cultural Domination and Political Subordination: Notes Towards a Theory of the Caribbean Political System." *Comparative Studies in Society and History* 15, no. 3 (1973): 258–88.

Smelser, Neil J., ed. *Handbook of Sociology.* Newbury Park, Calif.: Sage, 1988.

Smith, M. G., Roy Augier, and Rex Nettleford. *The Rastafari Movement in Kingston, Jamaica.* Mona, Jamaica: Institute of Social and Economic Research, University College of the West Indies, 1960.

Soukou, Ras. "Equality and Justice for All." In *Perceptions of the Environment: A Selection of Interpretative Essays,* edited by Yves Renard, 71–78. Bridgetown, Barbados: Caribbean Environmental Studies, 1979.

Spencer, William David. *Dread Jesus*. London: Society for Promoting Christian Knowledge, 1999.

Stephenson, Edward G. "Rastafari (Colonialism, Jamaica)." Ph.D. diss., University of California, Santa Cruz, 1987.

Stewart, Robert J. "Religion and Society in Jamaica, 1831–1880: Conflict, Compromise, and the Christian Churches in the Post-slave Colony." Ph.D. thesis, University of the West Indies, 1983.

Stone, Carl. *Class, Race, and Political Behaviours in Urban Jamaica*. Kingston, Jamaica: Institute of Social and Economic Research, University of the West Indies, 1973.

Stone, Carl, and Aggrey Brown, eds. *Essays on Power and Change in Jamaica*. Kingston, Jamaica: Jamaica Publishing, 1977.

———. *Perspectives on Jamaica in the 1970s*. Kingston, Jamaica: Jamaica Publishing, 1981.

Surlin, Stuart H. "Authoritarianism and Alienation among African-Oriented Jamaicans." *Journal of Black Studies* 19 (Dec. 1988): 232–49.

Tafari, I Jabulani. "The Rastafari: Successors of Marcus Garvey." In Rastafari, 1–12. Kingston, Jamaica: Caribbean Quarterly, University of the West Indies, 1985.

Tafari, Ikael. "Rastafari in Transition: Cultural Confrontation and Political Change in Ethiopia and the Caribbean." *Bulletin of Eastern Caribbean Affairs* 15, no. 1 (Mar./Apr. 1989): 1–13.

Tafari-Ama, Imani M. "Rastawoman as Rebel: Case Studies in Jamaica." In *Chanting Down Babylon: The Rastafari Reader*, edited by N. Samuel Murrell et al., 89–106. Philadelphia: Temple University Press, 1998.

Taylor, Patrick D. M. "Perspectives on History in Rastafari Thought." *Studies in Religion* 19 (Nov. 1990): 191–25.

———. "Rastafari, the Other and Exodus Politics: EATUP (Ethiopian-African Theocracy Union Policy)." *Journal of Religious Studies* 17, nos. 1–2 (1991): 95–107.

Theobald, Robin. "A Charisma Too Versatile?" *Archives Europeennes de Sociologie* 19, no. 1 (1978): 192–98.

Thomas, Curlew O., and Barbara Boston-Thomas. "Charisma and Charismatic Changes: A Study of a Black Sect." *Free Inquiry in Creative Sociology* 17, no. 1 (1989): 107–11.

Thomas, Michael. "The Rastas Are Coming, the Rastas Are Coming." *Rolling Stone*, Aug. 2, 1976, pp. 32–37.

Thompson, Winston A. "Reggae Music: The Affective Epistemology." *Union Seminary Quarterly Review* 36 (Summer 1981): 259–69.

Toch, Hans. *The Social Psychology of Social Movements*. Indianapolis, Ind.: Bobbs-Merrill, 1965.

Troeltsch, Ernst. *The Social Teaching of the Christian Churches*. Translated by Olive Wyon. New York: Macmillan, 1931.

Troyna, Barry A. "The Reggae War." *New Society* 39, no. 753 (Mar. 10, 1977): 491–92.

Turner, Jonathan H., Leonard Beeghley, and Charles Power. *The Emergence of Sociological Theory*, 2d ed. Belmont, Calif.: Dorsey, 1989.

van Dijk, Frank Jan. *Jahmaica: Rastafari and Jamaican Society, 1930–1990*. Utrecht, Netherlands: Intern Studenten Overlegorgaan Rotterdam (ISOR), 1993.

Vermaat, J. A. Emerson. "Church and State in Grenada during the Bishop Regime, 1979–1983." *Religion in Communist Lands* 14, no. 1 (Spring 1986): 43–58.

Walcott, Derek. *The Joker of Seville and O Babylon*. New York: Farrar, Straus and Giroux, 1978.

Wallace, Anthony. *Religion: An Anthropological View*. New York: Random House, 1966.

———. "Revitalization Movements." *American Anthropologist* 58 (1956): 264–81.

Wallis, Roy. "Processes in the Development of Social Movements." *Scottish Journal of Sociology* 1, no. 1 (Nov. 1976): 81–93.

Waters, Anita M. *Race, Class and Political Symbols: Rastafari and Reggae in Jamaican Politics*. New Brunswick, N.J.: Transactional, 1984.

Watson, Lewelyn. "Patterns of Black Protest in Jamaica: The Case of the Rastafarians." *Journal of Black Studies* 4 (Mar. 1974): 329–43.

Weber, Max. *Ancient Judaism*. Translated and edited by Hans Gerth and Don Martindale. Glencoe, Ill.: Free Press, 1952.

———. *Economy and Society: An Outline of Interpretive Sociology*, 3 vols. Edited by Guenther Roth and Claus Wittich. New York: Bedminster, 1968.

———. *The Protestant Ethic and the Spirit of Capitalism*. Translated by Talcott Parsons. New York: Scribner's, 1958.

———. *The Religion of China: Confucianism and Taoism*. Translated and edited by Hans Gerth and Don Martindale. New York: Collier and Macmillan, 1964.

———. *The Religion of India: The Sociology of Hinduism and Buddhism*. Translated and edited by Hans Gerth. New York: Free Press, 1967.

———. *The Sociology of Religion*. Translated by Ephraim Fischoff. Boston: Beacon, 1963.

———. *The Theory of Social and Economic Organization*. Translated by A. M. Henderson and Talcott Parsons. New York: Free Press, 1947.

Welcome, B. Patricia. "Prejudice, Discrimination, and the Rastafarian Experience." *Bulletin of Eastern Caribbean Affairs* 15, no. 1 (Mar./Apr. 1989): 14–19.

White, Garth. "The Development of Jamaican Popular Music. Part 2: The Urbanization of the Folk." *African-Caribbean Institute of Jamaica Research Review* 1 (1984): 47–80.

———. "Reggae: A Musical Weapon." *Caribe* 4, no. 4 (1980): 6–10.

———. "Ruddie, Oh Ruddie." *Caribbean Quarterly* 13 (Sept. 1967): 39–45.

White, Timothy. *Catch a Fire: Life of Bob Marley*. London: Corgi, 1983; rev. ed., New York: Holt, 1986.

Whitney, Malika Lee, and Dermott Hussey. *Bob Marley: Reggae King of the World*. Kingston, Jamaica: Kingston Publishers, 1984.

Williams, K. M. *The Rastafarians*. London: Ward Lock, 1981.

Willner, Ann Ruth. *Charismatic Political Leadership: A Theory*. Princeton, N.J.: Center of International Studies, Princeton University, 1968.

Willner, Ann Ruth, and Dorothy Willner. "The Rise of Charismatic Leaders." *Annals of the American Academy of Political and Social Science* 358 (1965): 77–89.

Wilson, Bryan R. *Magic and the Millennium*. London: Heinemann 1973.

Witvliet, Theo. *A Place in the Sun: Liberation Theology in the Third World*. New York: Orbis, 1985.

Worsley, Peter. *The Trumpet Shall Sound*. London: MacGibbon and Kee, 1957.

Wright, Christopher. "Cultural Continuity and the Growth of West Indian Religion in Britain." *Religion* 14 (Oct. 1984): 337–56.

Yawney, Carole D. "Don' Vex Then Pray: The Methodology of Initiation Fifteen Years Later." Paper presented at the Qualitative Research Conference, University of Waterloo, Canada, May 15–17, 1985.

———. "Dread Wasteland: Rastafarian Ritual in West Kingston, Jamaica." In *Ritual, Symbolism and Ceremonialism in the Americas: Studies in Symbolic Anthropology*, edited by N. Ross Crumrine, 154–74. Greenley, Colo.: Museum of Anthropology, University of Northern Colorado, 1978.

———. "The Global Status of Rastafari." *Caribbean Times*, July 10, 1990, pp. 24–25.

———. "To Grow a Daughter: Cultural Liberation and the Dynamics of Oppression in Jamaica." In *Feminism in Canada*, edited by A. Miles and G. Finn, 119–44. Montreal: Black Rose, 1983.

———. "Herb and the Chalice: The Symbolic Life of the Children of Slaves in Jamaica." Project G 218, Substudy no. 522. Toronto: Addiction Research Foundation, 1972.

———. "Lions in Babylon: The Rastafarians of Jamaica as Visionary Movement." Ph.D. diss., McGill University, 1978.

———. "Rastafarian Sistrin by the Rivers of Babylon." *Canadian Women Studies* 5, no. 2 (Winter 1983): 73–75.

———. "Remnant of All Nations: Rastafarian Attitudes to Race and Nationality." In *Ethnicity in the Americas*, edited by Francis Henry, 231–62. The Hague: Mouton, 1976.

Yawney, Carole D., and Clemanada Yawney. "As Smoke Drive Them Out: Rastafarians and the Sacred Herb." Paper presented at the Bucke Memorial Society Conference on the Transformation of Consciousness, Montreal, Oct. 24, 1973.

Zald, Mayer N., and Roberta Ash. "Social Movement Organizations: Growth, Decay and Change." *Social Forces* 44, no. 3 (March 1966): 27–42.

Index